DATE			
NOV 1 '79			
JUN 1 4 1990			
APR 1 1 1995			
APR 1 1 1997			
MAR 18 2002			

THE REMEMBERED GATE: ORIGINS of AMERICAN FEMINISM

THE URBAN LIFE IN AMERICA SERIES
RICHARD C. WADE, GENERAL EDITOR

GUNTHER BARTH
INSTANT CITIES: Urbanization and the Rise of San Francisco and Denver

BARBARA J. BERG
THE REMEMBERED GATE: ORIGINS OF AMERICAN FEMINISM: The Woman and the City, 1800–1860

LETITIA WOODS BROWN
FREE NEGROES IN THE DISTRICT OF COLUMBIA, 1790–1846

STANLEY BUDER
PULLMAN: An Experiment in Industrial Order and Community Planning, 1880–1930

HOWARD P. CHUDACOFF
MOBILE AMERICANS: Residential and Social Mobility in Omaha, 1880–1920

ALLEN F. DAVIS
SPEARHEADS FOR REFORM: The Social Settlements, and the Progressive Movement, 1890–1914

LYLE W. DORSETT
THE PENDERGAST MACHINE

MARK I. GELFAND
A NATION OF CITIES: The Federal Government and Urban America, 1933–1965

JOSEPH M. HAWES
CHILDREN IN URBAN SOCIETY: Juvenile Delinquency in Nineteenth-Century America

MELVIN G. HOLLI
REFORM IN DETROIT: Hazen S. Pingree and Urban Politics

KENNETH T. JACKSON
THE KU KLUX KLAN IN THE CITY, 1915–1930

THOMAS KESSNER
THE GOLDEN DOOR: Italian and Jewish Immigrant Mobility in New York City, 1880–1915

PETER R. KNIGHTS
THE PLAIN PEOPLE OF BOSTON, 1830–1860

ROGER W. LOTCHIN
SAN FRANCISCO, 1846–1856: From Hamlet to City

ZANE L. MILLER
BOSS COX'S CINCINNATI: Urban Politics in the Progressive Era

RAYMOND A. MOHL
POVERTY IN NEW YORK, 1783–1825

HUMBERT S. NELLI
ITALIANS IN CHICAGO, 1890–1930

THOMAS LEE PHILPOTT
THE SLUM AND THE GHETTO: Neighborhood Deterioration and Middle-Class Reform, Chicago, 1880–1930

HOWARD N. RABINOWITZ
RACE RELATIONS IN THE URBAN SOUTH, 1865–1890

JAMES F. RICHARDSON
THE NEW YORK POLICE: Colonial Times to 1901

JAMES W. SANDERS
THE EDUCATION OF AN URBAN MINORITY: Catholics in Chicago, 1833–1965

PETER SCHMITT
BACK TO NATURE: The Arcadian Myth in Urban America

STANLEY K. SCHULTZ
THE CULTURE FACTORY: Boston Public Schools, 1789–1860

CHARLES H. TROUT
BOSTON, THE GREAT DEPRESSION, and THE NEW DEAL

THE REMEMBERED GATE: ORIGINS of AMERICAN FEMINISM

The Woman and the City, 1800–1860

BARBARA J. BERG

New York
OXFORD UNIVERSITY PRESS
1978

Library of Congress Cataloging in Publication Data

Berg, Barbara J
The remembered gate.
(The Urban life in America series)
Bibliography: p.
Includes index.
1. Women—United States—History. 2. Women—United States—Social conditions. 3. Feminism—United States—History. 4. Urbanization—United States—History.
I. Title.
HQ1418.B5 301.41'2'0973 76-51709
ISBN 0-19-502280-7

Acknowledgment is made for permission to reprint the following materials:

Excerpts from the Beecher-Stowe Papers in The Schlesinger Library, Radcliffe College, used by permission of the Stowe-Day Foundation, Hartford, Connecticut.

Lyrics from "The Times They Are A-Changin' " by Bob Dylan. Copyright © 1963 Warner Bros. Inc. All rights reserved. Used by permission.

Excerpts from "Little Gidding" in *Four Quartets* by T. S. Eliot. Copyright © 1943 by T. S. Eliot; copyright © 1971 by Esme Valerie Eliot. Reprinted by permission of Harcourt Brace Jovanovich, Inc.

Excerpt from *Steppenwolf* by Hermann Hesse. Translated by Basil Creighton. Copyright © 1929 and renewed 1957 by Holt, Rinehart and Winston. Reprinted by permission of Holt, Rinehart and Winston, Publishers.

Excerpts from Pablo Neruda's Nobel Prize Lecture "Toward the Splendid City," published in the Nobel Prize Lecture Series and used by permission of the Elsevier Scientific Publishing Company and the Nobel Foundation.

Lines from the poem "Planetarium," reprinted from *The Will to Change, Poems, 1968–1970* by Adrienne Rich. By permission of W. W. Norton & Company, Inc. Copyright © 1971 by W. W. Norton & Company, Inc.

Excerpt from *Jean Christophe* by Romain Rolland, translated by Gilbert Cannan. Copyright © 1910, 1911 by Gilbert Cannan. Copyright © 1938, 1939 by Holt, Rinehart and Winston. Reprinted by permission of Holt, Rinehart and Winston, Publishers.

Printed in the United States of America

To my husband, Arnold G. Schlanger
—for every possible reason

Foreword

American scholars have arrived at the study of women in history by slow freight. It seems incredible, in retrospect, that half the population has been substantially lost in the writing about our national experience. Other groups, of course, have been neglected too, but, as in the case of the blacks, they were at least at the center of great national issues which provided their plight with continuous attention. Even the poor, which every generation has sought to hide, have generated a persistent interest by journalists and historians. Yet the amount of the literature on women is of the most touching modesty.

The development of a feminist dimension of American history necessarily began with women's participation in major movements in our national life. Since the Civil War constituted the central fact of the nineteenth century, historians quickly appreciated the role of female activists in the abolition movement and noted their equation of slavery with their own degradation. The suffragists comprised an equally visible group struggling for a very simple right. The rise of the International Ladies Garment Workers Union connected women with the emergence of organized labor. And their disproportionate influence in the development of settlement houses further identified female contributions to modern urban living.

Thus early scholarship established the historical credentials of those associated with high achievements. The present generation of historians confronts the more difficult problem of reconstructing the lives and attitudes of the less celebrated. Documents are scarce enough for men in this category, but frustratingly so for women. Excluded from public affairs, segregated in most associational activity, and largely confined to homemaking, they had little opportunity to leave behind more than a few traces of their lives.

Barbara Berg, however, has unearthed an extraordinary array of materials dealing with the condition, perceptions, and activity of urban women in the early nineteenth century. What emerges is a strikingly modern picture. Far from passively accepting their inferior role, they made an astute and penetrating analysis of their status, and organized, usually against fearful odds, to do something about it. From memoirs, diaries, newspapers, minutes of organizations, and the writings of female authors, Ms. Berg depicts a quiet crusade which laid the foundations of contemporary feminism one hundred and fifty years ago.

The author carefully distinguishes between feminism and women's rights. The former is "freedom to decide her own destiny; freedom from sex determined roles; freedom from society's oppressive restrictions; freedom to express her thoughts fully and convert them freely to actions." Women's rights, on the other hand, "implies a demand for particular privileges" that lay behind the drive for the suffrage, equal educational and employment opportunities, access to public facilities, and physicians of their own sex. The distinction is important because it provides the book with its organizing thesis and provides the framework for understanding the post-Civil War century as well as the early nineteenth century.

The rise of feminism was, ironically, a function of the declining role of women in post-revolutionary America. During the colonial period the status of women reflected the rough equality of a pioneer and farming world. To be sure, laws and ideology embodied separation and subordination, but the need for women's labor in a primitive economy recognized their worth if not their equality. But as the colonies grew into a republic and the forces of urbanization and industrialization insinuated their values into the young nation, the promise began to fade. As cities and factories developed, the female role was increasingly circumscribed, and the image of the colonial woman as an economic partner gave way to the woman-belle ideal—out of the fields and shops and onto the pedestal.

The woman-belle ideal saturated the literature by both male and female writers in the first half of the nineteenth century. Yet it was clearly contrived and artificial. No felicitous description of the female role could encompass the female experience. For poor women there was not much of a "home" to make as they set out to work in low paying jobs; for many upper- and middle-class women the ideal was confining and demeaning. This volume is the story of the response of the latter to the new position of women in the world's youngest democracy.

Resistance to the woman-belle ideal developed in the very center of its creation—the burgeoning cities. Between 1820 and 1860 the country witnessed its first urban explosion. The proportion of people living in cities jumped from five percent to twenty percent. With their size came all of the now familiar social problems—wretched housing, few and inadequate schools, irregular and poor paying jobs, primitive sanitation, high mortality, ubiquitous vagrancy, and persistent poverty. The smaller towns and rural areas had these same problems, but they were scattered and their presence diluted by space. In the cities, however, they were increasingly visible. As the numbers of the underclass mounted, so too did civic attention.

If the cities produced a growing underclass, they also developed the means to address the consequences. Local governments adopted at least palliative programs; but private societies comprised the major response. The new urban middle class, fearful of disorder and concerned for the welfare of the poor, created benevolent associations for the aid of the disadvantaged. Part of the impulse behind their formation was religious, and, accordingly, activities revolved around churches. Increasingly, however, secular and interdenominational groups joined in.

Men ran or dominated most of these societies, but not all of them. The author demonstrates that there was also a large female dimension to benevolent activity. They formed their own societies, conducted their own meetings, raised their own money, published their own journals, and devised their own programs. The number of participants, as in the case of men, was necessarily small. And like the men, they came from the newly successful urban middle class. Yet unlike the men, they had few other things to do. Discriminated against in economic, professional, and cultural affairs, they concentrated on the single area where men reluctantly sanctioned their work—benevolence.

In these societies they got to know one another. They were not only wives, mothers, and homemakers, but full individuals in their own right. Once out of the housekeeping closet they shared experiences, assuaged their loneliness, and discovered their worth as human beings. They also discovered the plight of destitute and poor women. Their activity carried them into the worst neighborhoods and brought them into contact with working women and the female castoffs of America's raw, young cities. In this way they identified themselves with women in much different circumstances.

In this identification lay the foundations of modern feminism. Male benevolence was always class-bound; a sense of noblesse oblige, indeed a subliminal fear, informed private charitable work and public poverty policy. It is Ms. Berg's arresting thesis that the women submerged their class bias in a genuine affection for their less fortunate sisters. This reaching out extended even to prostitutes, whom the woman-belle ideal had relegated to hell's lowest circle. Nor does this argument rest on sentimental speculation; it is based on a careful analysis of female writing and activity as well as on an examination of the skepticism, indeed often opposition, of the cities' most powerful benevolent societies.

In short, *The Remembered Gate: Origins of American Feminism* is a piece of original scholarship, written with clarity and verve, that challenges the prevailing interpretations of the historical roots of modern feminism. Indeed, it is fair to conclude from this volume that the concern of the women's movement with abolition and the franchise in the middle and later nineteenth century deflected a promising and deepening feminism which would not be recovered until our own time. At any rate no one will be able to write about women's history in America without consulting this fresh and compelling work. Like other volumes in the *Urban Life in America* series, it provides an historical perspective to an important contemporary problem.

New York
August 1977

RICHARD C. WADE
GENERAL EDITOR
URBAN LIFE IN AMERICA SERIES

Acknowledgments

I am fortunate to have received constant encouragement and assistance while writing this book. The invaluable counsel of Richard C. Wade enhanced my study, while his enthusiasm and unfailing sense of humor helped me through many discouraging moments. Throughout the entire process he was both a mentor and a friend. I have also benefited from the suggestions of Arthur M. Schlesinger, Jr. and Harold C. Syrett.

A grant from the Colonial Dames of America made it possible for me to concentrate fully on the study during 1973 and 1974. Additionally, the help of many librarians significantly facilitated the research. I am indebted to the staffs of the City University of New York Graduate Center Library, the New York State Library at Albany, the Library of Congress, and the Schlesinger Library at Radcliffe for their aid, and I am especially thankful to Jerry Stoker and Steven Conangelo of the 42nd Street Library.

My work has been enriched by countless discussions with Joel Blatt, Jane Brickman, Nina Cobb, and Terry Ruderman, as I have been by their friendships. Susan Maier and Rosalind Reisman not only read and criticized portions of the manuscript but have been a constant source of strength and joy throughout our many years as friends. Although I met my colleagues and students at Sarah Lawrence College after this book was written, they brought to life the reasons I wrote it—an experience both profound and enduring. I am grateful as well to Gerald Barrett for his skillful typing and to my editor at Oxford, Susan Rabiner, and to Mary Walker, who both have done a masterful job with my mangled prose.

I would also like to thank my parents, Professor Samuel and Matilda Goldberg, whose help and commitment to scholarship encouraged my own efforts. To Laura Schlanger, who cheerfully spent many of her weekends with us in libraries and bookstores, a note of appreciation is also due.

Finally, my husband, Arnie, has given me so much more than his enthusiastic participation in every phase of this endeavor that there are no words to thank him. Without him this book would have remained an idea.

Contents

THE REMEMBERED GATE: ORIGINS of AMERICAN FEMINISM

Introduction

We shall not cease from exploration
And the end of all our exploring
Will be to arrive where we started
And know the place for the first time.

T. S. Eliot
Little Gidding

In 1892, Elizabeth Cady Stanton demanded that women finally be given the vote. "[The] individuality of each human soul . . . , the right of individual conscience and judgment . . . , the rights of a woman . . . as arbiter of her own destiny, . . . [the rights she holds] to use all her faculties for her own safety and happiness," call out, she argued, for women's suffrage. The conviction that women were endowed with the same abilities and entitled to the same natural rights as men provided the initial ideology of the campaign.[1]

Less than seventy years earlier, Stanton would have met with strong resistance from women themselves had she tried to make this argument. Prior to the Civil War, most women perceived themselves quite differently. Their views were shaped largely by accepted theories of feminine inferiority, which rejected distinct identities for women apart from those they secured through the marital bonds and even went so far as to deny that women were individuals at all. Solely as an appendage of a particular male—as wife, mother, sister, or daughter—it was propounded, could women find value in their lives.

These confining custodial tenets received vigorous reinforcement in early nineteenth-century America. In time, they acquired not only the status and obligations of a rigid ethos but an identity as well: the woman-belle ideal. Those women who chafed under the bonds of this code had little choice but to accept their subordinate positions; yet during the antebellum era, tens of thousands of upper- and middle-class women began, first for themselves but later for the rest of the sex, to question and ultimately to defy the monolithic creed of the woman-belle ideal. What was responsible for this transformation in woman's sense of self? How did woman, so long thwarted in her efforts to find and fulfill herself, come to seek her common humanity? What mixture of events and circumstances led her to claim rights and prerogatives equal to those enjoyed by the other sex? In summary, how did American feminism begin?

These questions have been all but ignored by contemporary scholars. Historians, directing their attention principally to the drive for the vote, have not actually examined the origins of feminism in the United States. In trying to explain the genesis of suffrage agitation, they have looked back only as far as the female antislavery societies and have credited abolitionism with the creation of the nineteenth-century woman's movement. This prevailing interpretation limits the perspective of those seeking to understand the history of American women. And it provides a truncated analysis of the sources leading to the suffrage campaign.

Moreover, the tendency to confuse feminism with woman's rights has been endemic among those attempting to explore woman's past. One historian has written that "the most important involvement of American women in the years between the American Revolution and the outbreak of the Civil War was in the antislavery movement. The *woman's rights* movement was indeed an offshoot of the agitation against slavery, a campaign most of whose soldiers and many of whose officers were women." Another, asking "Why did the feminist movement appear in the United States in the second third of the nineteenth century?" replied: "The immediate cause was the experience of a few women in the abolition movement. . . . The *feminist movement* was founded by abolitionists and grew directly out of their experiences within the abolitionist movement." Yet feminism and woman's rights are not the same, and the distinction is of great significance.[2]

For purposes of this study, feminism is used to describe a broad movement embracing numerous phases of woman's emancipation. It is the freedom to decide her own destiny; freedom from sex-determined roles; freedom from society's oppressive restrictions; freedom to express her thoughts fully and to convert them freely to actions. Feminism demands the acceptance of woman's right to individual conscience and judgment. It postulates that woman's essential worth stems from her common humanity and does not depend on the other relationships of her life.[3]

Woman's rights, however, implies a demand for particular privileges. At different times in the history of this country, the rights for which women struggled have included the right to vote, the right to equal educational and employment opportunities, the right to be treated by physicians of their own sex, the right to be served at male clubs and restaurants. Each specific request is rooted in the basic ideology of woman as an autonomous being. But this collection of isolated rights does not add up to feminism. For feminism directs itself inward first—seeking to free the woman herself from society's pressures to conform to externally established social standards. As such, it transcends any changing set of demands.

Historians who have identified the advent of feminism with female abolitionist activity have recounted familiar tales—the Grimké sisters being denied the right to address mixed audiences; the World Anti-Slavery Convention's refusal to admit women in 1840; the subsequent friendship of Lucretia Mott and Elizabeth Cady Stanton. They have argued that "it was in the aboliton movement that women first learned to organize, to hold public meetings, to conduct petition campaigns. As abolitionists they . . . began to evolve a philosophy of their place in society and of their basic rights." Scholars have further argued that female abolitionists "began to ponder the parallels between woman's status and the Negro's status" and thus came to recognize their own oppression. This analysis has enjoyed a long and widespread acceptance. Yet it has distorted and obscured the rich history of American women. And in so doing, it has obliterated the origins of feminism.[4]

Female abolitionists did not represent a radical departure from antebellum tradition. The break was made decades before antislavery fervor caught the public imagination. It actually started when tens of thousands of women in cities throughout the nation insulted custom and authority by forming associations dedicated to helping members of their own sex, including such controversial females as prostitutes and criminals. In numerous and varied ways it was these women who took the first steps to expand woman's sphere by claiming for women unprecedented prerogatives.

Female voluntary associations flourished in urban America after 1800, and the pioneer efforts of the women who established them made it possible for other women, years later, to found their own antislavery societies. Many leading female abolitionists, including Lucretia Mott, Lydia Maria Child, Abby Hopper Gibbons, and Lucy Stone, were active in these benevolent organizations. Moreover, the records of female abolition societies acknowledge their debt to those before them and invoke the legitimacy of earlier associations in defense of their own endeavors. The Boston Female Anti-Slavery Society, for example, insisted upon its right to advertise in 1835 by declaring that it was merely doing what "other ladies' societies have always done." And it pointed to the annual meetings of women's urban associations in support of its assemblies.[5]

Yet its failure to acknowledge and deal with the relationship between antislavery and other female associations is only one of the defects in the abolition-feminist theory. Another important flaw is its assertion that women first became aware of their degradation in noticing similarities between their condition and that of the slave. To accept this thesis is to dismiss the compelling volume of writings produced by antebellum women years earlier revealing their distraught existences. It is to discount the thoughts and activities of innumerable females between 1800 and 1860. And, most significantly, it is to ignore the responses of both men and women to the complicated dynamics of change, including urbanization, which created profound alterations in perceptions and ideas and unwittingly fostered the development of American feminism.

Woman's sense of the oppression of her sex originated in American cities. It matured slowly as upper- and middle-class women began to assimilate the meaning of their intense involvement both with one another and with the destitute of their sex. Woman's recognition of the privations, responsibilities, and rights of her sex could only be gained through intimate association with women of every background. Abolition did not inaugurate nineteenth-century feminism, nor did it generate the suffrage campaign. To be sure, some women dedicated to freeing the slaves later agitated for woman's right to vote. But many early suffragists, including Antionette Blackwell, Isabella Beecher Hooker, Ernestine Rose, and Amelia Bloomer, had little or no direct involvement with abolitionist activities. Moreover, the drive for female enfranchisement, although invigorated by its leaders, did not actually commence with the activities of specific individuals. Rather it grew out of fundamental changes in woman's conceptions of herself, the rest of her sex, and her society. The philosophy behind the agitation for the vote shared a common etiology with the demand for expanded economic and social opportunities. It was one more facet of woman's ongoing quest for total emancipation, a quest that originated and developed in American cities between 1800 and 1860.

TOWARDS THE WOMAN-BELLE IDEAL

Now there are times when a whole generation is caught . . . between two ages, two modes of life, with the consequence that it loses all power to understand itself and has no standards, no security, no simple acquiescence.

—*Steppenwolf*
Herman Hesse

1

American Women in the Eighteenth Century

What tho' we read in days of yore
the woman's occupation,
Was to direct the wheel and loom
not to direct the Nation;
This narrow-minded policy
by us both met detection;
While woman's bound, men can't be free
nor have a *fair* Election.

—"A Woman"
in a New Jersey newspaper, 1796

Do you suppose the mind of woman the only work of God that was made in vain?

—Elizabeth Southgate

The status of American women deteriorated dramatically in the years between the end of the colonial period and the early decades of the nineteenth century. Beginning slowly, the decline accelerated as the youthful nation began to adapt more fully to the complex changes accompanying its transformation from a series of scattered and rural sovereignties to an increasingly urbanized and industrial national democracy. These changes profoundly altered the texture of American life and significantly worsened the position of the female population. Ironically, they ultimately made possible the development of American feminism.

Eighteenth-century colonial women had, surprisingly, made significant headway in establishing for themselves a place in the original settlements. In part they were able to do so because of the compelling needs of these early communities. Survival depended upon the contribution and cooperation of every member, man and woman. Fortitude and initiative were of great value and were therefore not easily rejected for questionable philosophic biases. Women's labor was essential. Thus, necessity diluted restrictions on the allegedly inferior sex, and early colonial women enjoyed access to most occupations.

The imperatives of colonial growth, however, were only one of several influences positively establishing women's place in society. The writings of eighteenth-century European and American philosophers were another. Their descriptions of women as educable, contributory community members made the necessary work of women also socially acceptable.

As far back as one hundred years before the American Revolution, British and French philosophers had begun to argue the obligation of society to allow women access to educational and job opportunities. Their ideas crossed the Atlantic in a variety of literary forms, among them periodical essays, novels, and pamphlets, all of which appeared abundantly in America. As the century progressed, colonial writings more often showed the influence of European rationalism. But the earlier writings contained frequent references to the Scriptures, as authors initially sought to buttress their arguments with Biblical authority.

Marie de Gournay, a scholar and protégée of the French essayist Michel de Montaigne, proposed opening all occupations, including the ministry, to women. Gournay's essay, published in 1622, cited Socrates, Plato, Plutarch, Saint Jerome, Saint Basil, and Saint John's epistle to the Elect Lady. From the Scriptures it took the argument that God created man both male and female. Hence, the author asserted that God did not place one sex above the other, and men and women, having identical natures, deserved the same treatment by their society.[1]

Although it is doubtful that Gournay's work found a large audience in America, Cotton Mather evidently knew of her. He referred to the French scholar in a letter to his sister-in-law: "I have thought that Mademoiselle de Gournay, the Lady, who a while since wrote an essay to demonstrate the *Equality of Women to Men* might victoriously enough defend her problem . . . while she had such as you, as friend, who help so notably to render your husbands useful and considerable."[2]

A work more widely read on both sides of the Atlantic, John Bunyan's *The Pilgrim's Progress,* portrayed Christiana as completing the identical pilgrimage that her husband completes. Bunyan, asked to defend this example of equality, drew on New Testament passages to argue that woman "shared with [man] in the grace of life."[3]

Similarly, the theoretical position of women in Puritan culture was based on a literal interpretation of the Scriptures. Eve's actions had brought the curse of subjection, but Mary had redeemed her sex, thereby making all women again worthy of respect. The Puritans clearly assumed that both sexes could attain salvation. Additionally, Cotton Mather, in his widely read *Ornaments for the Daughters of Zion,* gave another reason for honoring women: "The Sex may be esteemed [for] the Share which it has had in writing those Oracles, which make us wise unto Salvation. As one woman is the Mother of Him who is the essential word of God so diverse women have been the writers of his Declarative word."[4]

Mather referred to the songs of Deborah, Hannah, and Mary; the prophecy of Huldah; and the instructions of Bathsheba. But he also praised more modern women authors, "for even the Books Published by that sex were enough to make a Library far from contemptible; nor has even New England part of the American Strand been without authoresses that would challenge a Room in Such a Library." The inclusion of a list of distinguished women in the preface to his own book provided further proof of Mather's awareness of feminine capability.[5]

There is sufficient evidence to indicate that many of Mather's Puritan colleagues shared his high opinion of women. Puritan sermons, journals, and letters reveal many positive views of females. In a sermon delivered at the funeral of his mother, Thomas Foxcraft thanked the Lord "who has given such Grace, and so many Excellences to a Frail woman." And Samuel Sewall, who rigorously defended feminine religious equality, expressed his thoughts in a letter to John Winthrop:

> Besides Hannah in the Old Testament and Blessed Mary in the New, there is a numerous company of Holy Women listed in Christ's Army which *renders that sex* honourable. And if your sons should be taken away which God forbid, yet, as your worthy ancestours were the builders of the walls of our Jerusalem so you and your daughters will engage in the pleasant and profitable employment of repairing them.[6]

Others in the community also encouraged varied feminine activity and praised special achievement. Deborah Prince's father proudly claimed that Deborah had enjoyed history, divinity, and especially "Experimental Writing." Jane Colman, the daughter of another Boston minister, also earned commendation for her prose. At her death in 1735, Jane's husband wrote: "I find that she was sometimes fir'd with a laudable ambition of raising the honor of her Sex, who are therefore under obligations to her; and all will be ready to own she had a fine *Genius* and is to be placed among those who have excell'd."[7]

New England women from enlightened and successful families—Jane Colman, Deborah Prince, and the talented poet, Anne Bradstreet—achieved distinction. Most of their sisters occupied a position more obscure but shaped, nonetheless, by theological tenets. Puritan men expected their wives to heed Saint Paul's order that they be in subjection to their husbands. But the religion also communicated a sense of importance to women that mitigated the harshness of the Biblical decree. Numerous clergymen rigorously defended woman's right to sainthood and, indeed, Cotton Mather asserted that more females than males had attained salvation.[8]

The theologians who bestowed lavish praise on feminine accomplishments may have sought to cultivate the spirit, but their words had a compelling effect on the mind also. They extolled females of intellectual excellence and often acknowledged that differences in achievement between the sexes related to training. Moreover, by describing efforts to elevate female status as "laudable" and by publicly recognizing creative, effective women, clerical leaders demonstrated their respect for the sex. To be sure, New England women experienced subjugation and deprivation. But our Puritan forefathers found cause to believe that men could "safely account the Female sex . . . more than a little Dignify'd."[9]

Religious precepts defined only part of the eighteenth-century inquiry into the nature of woman. Authors of varied backgrounds and persuasions articulated other facets of the debate, emphasizing the social and intellectual aspects of feminine life. Approaching the topic from different perspectives, writers revealed their general attitudes about women through specific suggestions on feminine education and behavior. Joseph Addison and Richard Steele expressed their views casually through periodical essays in the *Spectator* and the *Tatler*. These magazines, immensely popular in America, probably exerted greater influence than the more formal treatises of Mary Astell and Daniel Defoe; yet the latter, also read in the colonies, are of interest for their progressive views.

Mary Astell, pamphleteer and friend of the intellectually prominent in British society, believed that men kept women in submission in order to assure masculine ascendancy. She maintained, in *An Essay in Defense of the Female Sex,* that there would be no intellectual differences between the sexes if both received similar educations. In keeping with her view, Astell proposed a lay nunnery where women, divorced from the burdens of the world, could indulge their academic interests. Defoe agreed: feminine education desperately required improvement. Men kept women in ignorance and then ridiculed the sex for follies a proper education would have prevented. In *An Essay on Projects,* he called such behavior "barbarious."[10]

Contributors to the *Tatler* and the *Spectator* often treated their subjects with good-natured humor. But they also demonstrated their sensitivity to woman's psychological needs. These periodicals, heralded by American booksellers, devoted considerable space to feminine activity. Both attempted to bolster woman's self-image and strongly condemned anything that degraded her. The *Tatler* criticized the educational system, which fostered "an indolent state of body and mind" and made women feel "they were so insignificant as to be wholly provided for when they are fed and clothed." Steele, in the *Spectator,* hazarded the opinion that women's faults and weaknesses were due to the false standards set for them by men rather than to any difference in their natures: "I have often thought that there has not been sufficient pains taken in taking out proper employment and diversions for the fair ones. Their amusements seem contrived for them, rather as they are women, than as they are reasonable creatures."[11]

Steele's defense of women was compatible with the eighteenth century's commitment to rationalism and humanitarianism in that it emphasized the female as a reasonable being. Enlightenment thinkers frequently argued that women and men shared a rational nature. William Wollaston articulated this view clearly and forcibly in *The Religion of Nature Delineated,* a popular deistical work that appeared in 1726. He believed marriage to be a reciprocal arrangement, requiring mutual help and love. Unlike Puritan authors, Wollaston's view of matrimony did not necessarily imply female subordination:

> I have designedly forborne to mention that *authority* of a husband over his wife, which is usually given to him, not only by private writers but even by laws; because I think it has been *carried much too high.* I would have them live so far upon the level (according to my constant lesson) to be governed *both* by reason.[12]

Wollaston's influence on Benjamin Franklin is evident in the latter's *Reflections on Courtship and Marriage:* "Whatever tyrannick and arbitrary Power the Laws of a Country may give a Man over his Wife, or should they do the reverse, there is no such kind of Dominion derived from the Reason of Nature." Franklin admitted that man's faculties for governing seemed superior. But a faulty education truncated feminine development and prevented true comparisons. In a tirade against men who contrived to keep women inferior, Franklin echoed Defoe and Steele: "Do we not in general flatter them with a heap of bombast Stuff, and then laugh at them for seeming pleased with it?" The author expressed amazement at "how ingeniously we thus labor to make her a positive and empty, a conceited and fanatical Simpleton." He added: "Thus modelled, we soon come to despise her and curse our marriage."[13]

Whereas Wollaston and Franklin presented general views on the relationship between the sexes, Dr. John Gregory offered practical advice. In *A Father's Legacy to his Daughter,* the Scottish physician articulated his awareness of the prejudice against intellectual women: "Women with knowledge should keep it a profound secret, especially from men, who generally look with a jealous and malignant eye on a woman of . . . cultivated understanding." Gregory suggested that women accept their fate. Yet, as a perspicacious observer, he saw through the superficial embroidery and grasped the underlying threads holding woman in misery. "Your whole life is often a life of suffering. You cannot plunge into business or dissipate yourselves in pleasure and riot as men too often do, when under the pressures of misfortunes you must bear your sorrows in silence, unknown and unpitied."[14]

The compassionate spirit with which Gregory wrote was not ubiquitous; a winnowing of Enlightenment thought reveals theories totally unsympathetic to woman as well. Jean Jacques Rousseau's well-known book *Emile* argued for woman's subordination. Feminine education should impress upon women the aim of their existence: "To please, to be useful to [men]." Rousseau argued that having neither the genius nor the power to study abstract truths, girls should be conditioned for a life of subjugation at an early age. "This daily constraint will produce the docility that women need all their lives. . . . She must learn to submit uncomplainingly."[15]

Rousseau's harsh judgments did not go unnoticed. Numerous contemporaries refuted the French philosopher's theories and offered alternatives. Benjamin Rush, the famous physician, member of the American Philosophical Society, and one of Philadelphia's prominent citizens, urged that women be given a practical and varied education. Enos Hitchcock, a Rhode Island minister and an associate of Rush, also challenged Rousseau's depiction of woman as an inferior species with no natural rights. Yet, he concluded that as there must be a head in society it should be man.[16]

In the highly provocative *Vindication of the Rights of Woman*, published in 1792, Mary Wollstonecraft vigorously condemned Rousseau's theories as rendering women "artificial, weak characters." Further, she vehemently attacked, as "mistaken notions which enslave my sex," beliefs that the stability of civilization depended upon the mastery of one sex over the other:

> Would men but generously snap our chains, and be content with rational fellowship instead of slavish obedience, they would find us more observant daughters, more faithful wives, more reasonable mothers—in a word, better citizens.

Because both sexes enjoyed the "gift of reason," Wollstonecraft argued, woman deserved full participation in the natural rights of mankind. Her exclusion from these rights jeopardized the functioning of society: "Take away natural rights, and duties become null."[17]

A Vindication of the Rights of Woman stimulated controversy both on the Continent and in the States. Most of the American press responded negatively, attacking the book as an argument for deism and as an indictment of marriage. But Charles Brockden Brown, America's first serious novelist, incorporated Wollstonecraft's theories in his book *Alcuin: A Dialogue,* which appeared in 1798.

Taking the form of a conversation between a gentleman and a lady, *Alcuin* presented a powerful plea for the extension of women's rights. The lady argued that the present system, by requiring a woman's dependence upon a man, reduced her to the level of "a beast or an insect." Wollstonecraft's impact on the author is apparent in his female character's determination to believe in herself despite the deleterious effects of society's degradations:

> While I am conscious of being an intelligent and moral being; . . . when I see myself . . . passed over in the distribution of public duties, by those who disdain to assign the least apology for their injustice—what though politicians say I am nothing, it is impossible that I should assent to their opinion as long as I am conscious of willing and moving.[18]

Judith Sargent Murray shared Brown's indebtedness to Mary Wollstonecraft and similarly espoused liberal views on women. Publishing under the name Constantia, Murray wrote several essays on women in avowed imitation of the *Spectator*. Murray's articles, popularized first in the *Massachusetts Magazine,* were later reprinted in three volumes under the title *The Gleaner*. The book, published in 1798, contained two plays, a novel, and several essays.

In one of the longer articles, Murray put forth the opinion that any woman given a proper education could enjoy Mary Wollstonecraft's freedom. Woman was inherently as capable as any man and had, in fact, achieved astonishing success throughout history in various fields of endeavor. The author described many occupations in which women had distinguished themselves and praised those females whose independent business ventures had brought their families prosperity. Murray wrote with glowing optimism. She congratulated her countrywomen on the revolution of thought in recent years that had ushered in a "new and enlightened era in female history." In the new age, "The Rights of Women," just beginning to be understood, would make the idea of woman's incapacity in any area inadmissible.[19]

Thus by 1800 Americans had shared and absorbed the lessons of an intensive inquiry, for over a century, into the different facets of feminine existence. In their efforts to evaluate woman's role in society, these theorists had combined history, religion, and rationalism as they searched for fundamental precepts of human behavior. Predictably, this admixture of intellectual sources and methods produced conflicts and tensions. Yet even these disagreements, when channeled creatively, envigorated the dialogue, which assumed an increasingly liberal tone as the 1700s drew to a close.

Certainly, conservative opinion existed. Rousseau accurately represented the numerous philosophers who would make woman's entire personal development relative to man's wishes. Liberal views of women did not dominate eighteenth-century philosophy. But theories of feminine competence and value continued to gain impressive adherents and to make important inroads.

Espoused by able and prominent men and women with diverse political, religious, and social views, this agglomeration of theory thwarts facile generalizations. Marie de Gournay and Judith Sargent Murray wished to remove the limitations on feminine occupations. Benjamin Franklin, who also criticized female oppression, still shared with Cotton Mather the belief in woman's essential domesticity, although the source of his ideas differed from that of the clergyman. Dr. Benjamin Rush advocated a more comprehensive system of education, but his plans had little in common with the methods described by either Mary Astell or Daniel Defoe.

Some authors wrote with audacity: Richard Steele, Marie de Gournay, Daniel Defoe, and Benjamin Franklin asserted that men reinforced women's feelings of inferiority. Charles Brockden Brown attacked the existing legal system. And Mary Wollstonecraft, insisting that women were rational beings entitled to natural rights, argued that they be granted full equality with men. Other writers tempered sympathy with caution. Dr. John Gregory, though compassionate, advised his readers to accommodate themselves to their plight. And Enos Hitchcock, who argued from the same premises as Wollstonecraft, ultimately accepted man as the ruler of society.

However eclectic and disparate these elements of thought appear, there is an essential unity to them. Each work expresses, either implicitly or explicitly, the belief that woman was an individual with a mind capable and worthy of cultivation. She possessed a nature similar to man's, had the potential to make important contributions to her community, and deserved to be respected and valued as an autonomous being. Though the philosophers drew differing conclusions from these assumptions, their basically positive view of woman posed a formidable challenge to traditionalist thinking.

This collision of ideas—subtle distinctions as well as blatant disagreements—stimulated and diffused the controversy. At the Yale commencement of 1773, two graduates debated "Whether the Education of Daughters be not without reason more neglected than that of sons." Ezra Stiles, elected president of Yale in 1777, frequently asked his students to explore the benefits of female academies. One of his favorite themes for senior essays, "Whether women ought to be admitted to partake in Civil Government, Dominion and Sovereignty," surely encouraged speculation about the female position in America.[20]

But the issue of woman's political activity was just one aspect of the more encompassing decision facing Stiles and all colonial Americans: what form shall the new government assume? The colonists looked to history and to the Scriptures. Yet in the end, Enlightenment ideology seemed the most relevant to their decision.

As early as 1768 many believed that "never was there a People whom it more immediately concerned to search into the Nature and Extent of their Rights and Privileges than it does the People of America at this Day." Drawing heavily on Whig theorists—John Locke, Algernon Sidney, and particularly John Trenchard and Thomas Gorden—colonial publicists perceived their struggle as a quest for liberty, defined as that which "exempts one Man from Subjection to another."[21]

Natural law and natural rights, Whig constitutionalism, and virtue formed then the three supports crucial to liberty's endurance. The pervasive belief in natural law—a scheme of moral absolutes to be discovered and understood principally through the use of reason—

carried important corollaries. The preservation of natural rights as the chief end of government, the doctrine that magistrates are servants rather than rulers of the people, the right of rebellion against leaders violating the laws of nature, and the belief in a natural equality of man—all emerged from the revolutionary ideology. These principles constituted the staples of American political theory and produced a fertile ground for liberal thought and egalitarian practices.[22]

Ironically, however, the soil of the young republic provided little nourishment for progressive ideas about women. The arguments that came to be used to justify replacing a monarchy with a republic could just as well have furnished a persuasive justification for extending women's rights. Instead, the excoriating literature of the pre-Civil War period made a mockery of Mrs. Murray's confident predictions of a "new and enlightened era in female history." The women who appeared in antebellum depictions would hardly be considered the natural heirs of eighteenth-century struggles and advances. For the wan, dependent creature of antebellum writings bore little semblance to the majority of her contemporaries and surely would have been unrecognizable to her colonial ancestors.

Women in colonial America never attained equality with men. But they enjoyed more rights than those granted them by English law. Under common law, females had many duties and few privileges. Married women in particular suffered civil death, having no rights to property and no legal standing or existence apart from their husbands: "Man and wife are one person, but understand in what manner. . . . A Woman as soon as she is married, is called *cover*, in Latin *Nupta*, that is veiled, as it were, clouded and overshadowed, she hath lost her streame. . . . To a married woman her new self is her superior, her companion, her master." This concept, known as "femme covert," continued into the nineteenth century. Nevertheless, in many colonies, the exigencies of life and the scarcity of females proved advantageous to the sex, both elevating the status of women. These two factors specifically expanded the occupational opportunities of women and enlarged their legal rights in property, conveyance of land, marriage and divorce, inheritance, contracts, torts, and testimony well beyond the reactionary confines of the law.[23]

Also, theology sided with necessity rather than English common law. Believing industry a virtue and idleness a sin, Puritan authorities punished those who did not work. The town of Salem sent Margarett Page "to Boston Gaole as a lazy, idle, loytering person," and in 1640 the community charged Mary Boutwell with "exorbitancy not working but liveinge idly."[24]

The attitude toward the employment of women is evident in the Bay Colony's laws for 1692–93. Every unmarried person under twenty-one years of age had to live "under some orderly family government." But an additional provision stipulated that "this act shall not be construed to extend to hinder any single woman of good repute from the exercise of any lawful trade of employment for a livelihood, whereunto she shall have the allowance and approbation of the selectmen . . . *any law, usage or custom to the contrary notwithstanding.*"[25]

Town officials expected working women to help defray community expenses. In 1695 a law required "all single women that live at their own hand [to pay a poll tax] at two shillings each, except such as through age or extreame poverty . . . are unable to contribute towards the public charge." But females contributed far more than wages to the development of their colonies. In the growing towns and in the isolated countryside, they performed innumerable essential tasks. The women who helped their men carve homes out of the wilderness toiled incessantly and courageously. Working alongside their husbands, women built log cabins and farmed the fields. They also assumed responsibility for all domestic chores, including the production of food, clothing, and medicines. Abigail Foote, a young girl living in Connecticut, recorded the activities of one day in her diary:

> Fix'd gown for Prude, Mend Mother's Riding-Hood—spun short thread—Fix'd two gowns for Welsh's girls—carded tow—spun

> linen—worked on cheese basket,—Hatchel'd flax with Hannah we did 51 pounds apiece,—pleated and ironed—Read a Sermon of Doddridge's,—spooled a piece—milked the cows—spun linen, did 50 knots—made a broom of Guinea wheat straw spun thread to whiten,—Set a Red Dye,—Had two scholars from Mrs. Taylor's—I carded two pounds of whole wool and felt nationally—spun harness twine—scoured the pewter.[26]

The physical strength required of pioneer women corresponded to the emotional fortitude made necessary by life on the frontier. Often without assistance, women bore, raised, and educated children. They lived in constant fear of Indian attack and of the wilderness itself. Remote from the codes of civilization, wives and husbands participated equally in the struggles for survival. Reciprocity in the marriage relationship frequently emerged as the natural consequence of their shared adversities.

Women also made significant contributions to their families and to society in the emerging colonial cities. The New England town, of course, encouraged those members of the community without financial support to work. But even colonies untouched by Puritan theology permitted women to support themselves and their relatives. Social mores throughout populated colonial settlements allowed married women who wished to supplement their husbands' income the freedom to do so. Trade did not negate gentility. The woman merchant, innkeeper, teacher, or printer did her work without apology or sense of restriction, knowing she would be judged on her achievements.[27]

The occupations engaged in by colonial women demanded energy, business acumen, and executive ability. As tavernkeepers, they gave their skills to operating these important urban institutions that furnished recreational facilities and provided a focus to town life. No one objected to women selling liquor. Indeed, the tradition seems to have been established early in the colonial period. In 1654, Henry Dunster, president of Harvard College, wrote on behalf of Sister Bradish "that she might be encouraged and countenanced in her present calling for the baking of bread and brewing and the selling of penny beer."[28]

More women than men received permits to run taverns, and they did not think it unladylike to publicize their activities in colonial newspapers. Mary Ballard advertised her inn, "for the Entertainment of Gentlemen, Benefit of Commerce and the Dispatch of Business," in the *Boston Evening Post.* Anne Jones, who ran the Plume of Feathers on Philadelphia's Second Street, utilized the newspaper to notify her debtors to settle their accounts. Female merchants also relied upon newspaper circulation to conduct their businesses. Hannah Cazneau of Boston announced that her latest shipment from London included "a variety of ivory and Bone Stock Fans, the best Pins and Needles, and fine bohea and Green tea." And Cornelia Blau described her interesting assortment of wines and brandies in the *New York Gazette* of 28 August 1766.[29]

The commercial spirit energized colonial cities and led to social and cultural ties of utmost importance. It infused women with confidence in their abilities and verified Jean de Crèvecoeur's observation that mercantile experience "ripens their judgment and justly entitles them to a rank superior to that of other wives." Mrs. Sueton Grant, a young widow with several small children, acted with self-assurance when commercial dealings involved her in litigation. Upon learning of her counsel's dishonesty, Mrs. Grant went to court and argued her own case with dignity and clarity. After a short deliberation the jury decided in her favor.[30]

In New York City, the "She Merchants" who wrote to John Peter Zenger in 1733 vigorously proclaimed their attributes:

> We, the widdows of this city, have had a Meeting, and as our case is something Deplorable, we beg you will give it Place in your Weekly Journal, that we may be Relieved, it is as follows. We are House keepers, Pay our Taxes, carry on Trade, and most of us are she Merchants, and as we in some measure contribute to the Support of Government, we ought to be Intitled to some of the Sweets of it; but we find ourselves entirely neglected, while the Husbands that live in our Neighborhood are daily invited to Dine at Court; we have the vanity to think we can be fully as Entertaining, and make as brave a Defense in Case of an Invasion and perhaps not turn Taile so soon as some of them.

Trade flourished, and the expanding cities created a market for the goods of retail shops. This petty trade which reached the highest degree of specialization in Boston often provided the chief means of support to widows, enabling women like Mrs. Hannah Boydell, who sold "Grocery Ware" near the Bunch of Grapes Tavern, to be self-sufficient.[31]

Women tried various ways to make their trades successful. They frequently attended night school to learn to keep merchant's accounts and displayed imagination and determination in efforts to make their enterprises thrive. Mary Spratt, widowed at nineteen, attracted attention and business to her deceased husband's counting-house by laying flat stones along the property, thereby creating New York's first sidewalk. And John Peter Zenger's widow did not hesitate to deny publicly the reports of "Some evil minded Persons . . . [that] the Widow Zenger, Publisher of this Paper, had entirely dropped the printing business."[32]

Other women equalled Widow Zenger's commitment to running family businesses upon the demise of their spouses. Cornelia Bradford conducted her late husband's business of printing, bookselling, and publishing the *American Weekly Mercury* for eight years without any assistance. Jonas Green's *Annapolis Gazette* prospered under the auspices of his efficient widow, who also did government printing. The assembly, evidencing their satisfaction with the work, agreed to pay her the annual sum of "nine hundred forty-eight and one-half dollars" for her services. When Anne Green died in March 1775, the *Maryland Gazette* called her "an Example to her Sex."[33]

Female energy provided a multitude of useful services. Women real estate agents, cutlers, coachmakers, and ropemakers strengthened the colonial economy. With the granting of a legal monopoly, midwifery became recognized as an exclusively feminine occupation in the eighteenth century. The midwife performed her tasks often under the most adverse circumstances. Mrs. Whitman of Vermont, who officiated at more than two thousand births and never lost a patient, "travelled through the woods on snowshoes . . . both by night and day to relieve the distressed."[34]

Teaching offered another occupational opportunity to those women who had some specialized training. The profession included females with a wide range of knowledge, sophistication, and skill. The New England goodwife who taught reading on a regular basis in her kitchen and charged a modest fee thus established a "dame school." She differed considerably from a Mistress Rogers whose Young Ladies School in Trenton, New Jersey, emphasized needlework and painting.[35]

The amount and type of education colonial children received were largely a function of their parents' economic and cultural background. Instruction varied markedly and determined the demand for teachers in any particular area. City boys and girls, until the age of seven, learned elementary reading together, tutored at home by their parents or by a schoolmistress, often the wife of a craftsman. Daughters of wealthy families might then attend a school where the "female embellishments"—drawing, waxwork, and embroidery—were mixed with doses of spelling, arithmetic, history, and writing, while ambitious daughters of artisans prepared to support themselves by learning cooking or weaving from women dedicated to teaching these skills.[36]

In its early years, then, the nation needed female labor. And many derived personal benefits from their employment. They developed and utilized diverse skills, while gaining confidence in their abilities to provide vital services. As printers, midwives, tavernkeepers, pioneer-settlers, and merchants, women became an integal part of the community while supporting themselves and their families.

Of course, not all colonial women pursued careers. Many, no doubt, found professional aspirations stifled by domineering husbands. Others, enjoying financial security, chose to remain at home and give all their attention to domestic concerns. Yet women who confined their activities, either by desire or necessity, knew that this limited sphere evolved from specific personal situations. It neither reflected inherent inferiorities in the sex nor implied that females had to remain at home because they could be effective only within its secure boundaries. Moreover, before industrialization separated the work place from the home, woman's labors in the household were highly valued, producing goods for sale as well as for the family.

The appreciation and respect that society showed to those women who made special talents and abilities evident through varied enterprises, both in and outside the home, positively affected the status of all women. These talented and industrious women furnished models of feminine capability and enabled women to feel proud of their sex, regardless of individual circumstances. Through their daily activities, American women achieved far greater recognition than did their sisters in Europe and England. But the essential importance of the colonial period in the history of feminism transcends the routines of female life. Although modified by legal, economic, and personal restrictions, many women had the freedom to determine their duties and responsibilities to themselves, to their families, and to society. And in that sense they exercised some measure of control over their lives.[37]

Yet the rights and responsibilities enjoyed by colonial women diminished markedly as the last decades of the seventeenth century passed. This deterioration in position, actual and perceived, received strong endorsement from nineteenth-century writers. Indeed, a phenomenal outpouring of writings appeared at this time, stipulating universal standards of behavior for American females. These writings represent a startling development in American social history and in anti-feminist thinking, but historians have not really explained the origins of this body of literature. Some have tried to account for this interest in rigidly defining women's "sphere" as a consequence of the "mania for codifying laws" after the revolution. Others have noted that the institutionalization of education and the professionalization of occupations took away from women the opportunities they had had to rise to respected positions.[38]

These explanations are tantalizing: they seem to provide answers but, in reality, only raise more questions. Why did codification make the laws more stringent instead of reflecting existing liberal practices? Why did the institutionalization of education automatically exclude females, especially if that education led to a professional life in which women had historically participated or had displayed the inclination or talent to pursue?

The answers to these questions are intertwined with other, more basic questions that must be answered before the evolution of feminism in the nineteenth century can be fully understood. If women had been valuable participants in society, usefully contributing their labor and skill, why did their society deny their effectiveness and denigrate their abilities? If they had worked, and would continue to work, long hours in fields and factories, why epitomize the sex as frail and delicate? If females had found fulfillment in a broad range of occupations, why tell them they should be happy only at home? If women had displayed the same talents and abilities as men, why insist that the sexes had entirely different natures?

A response to these fundamental inquiries requires an understanding of the transformations in society. It involves an awareness of how men and women perceived these changes: the fears they evoked, the hopes they raised and often crushed, and the insecurities and tensions they engendered.

2

The Fading Order: Cities in Collision

Is the Nineteenth Century to be
a contrast to the Eighteenth. . . .
Is it to extinguish all the
lights of its Predecessor

—John Adams to Thomas Jefferson, 1815

I consider you going to such a city as New York for the purpose of going into mercantile business like a young physician going into the midst of pestilence to become proficient in the art of healing.

—Jeremiah Day, president of Yale
University, to his son, 1826

Cities give us collision. . . .

—Ralph Waldo Emerson

The slow one now will later be fast,
As the present now, will later be past,
The order is rapidly fading
The first one now will later be last
For the times they are a-changin'

—Bob Dylan

For we cannot tarry here,
We must march . . . we must bear the brunt of danger
We the youthful sinewy races, all the rest on us depend[1]

Walt Whitman, celebrating a rhapsodic faith in democracy, articulated for his countrymen the sprit of crusading optimism that shaped the perceptions and responses of the emerging nation. From the beginning, Americans shared a sense of mission that imbued their actions with a special significance. The Puritans sought to establish a "city on the hill" and the revolutionary generations struggled to vindicate the natural rights of mankind before the eyes of the world. But those living during the early nineteenth century seemed to be charged with a special responsibility. As the inheritors and interpreters of a precious past, Americans reaching maturity in the early 1800s had the difficult task of preserving the traditional national goals and character from the ravaging effects of material prosperity and physical expansion.

Jeffersonian thought gave clear expression to the American ideal. It depicted a society of democratic farmers who, becoming prosperous through their industry, eschewed all special privilege and unfair practice. One statesman exalted the "native, substantial, independent yeomanry [who] constitute our pride, efficiency and strength." He proclaimed that "no population is more distinguished for an elevated love of freedom—for morality, virtue, frugality and independence." The vision of the United States as an abundant garden inhabited by yeoman farmers never accurately reflected American society. Yet the yearning for an uncomplicated life, which gave content to the myth of a pastoral, noncompetitive social order, assumed a special urgency as the strains of growth and change challenged the philosophic dreams of a better world that accompanied the emergence of the nation.[2]

Americans, deeply conscious of their trust to keep the nation a model for democracy, examined the first two decades of the nineteenth century with apprehension. The events of those years—a war, an inflation, and a sectional dispute—had given real cause for concern. Yet their unease went back to fears more deeply rooted. John Adams, in a letter to Thomas Jefferson, touched upon the more subtle aspects of the problem:

> Let me ask you, very seriously my Friend, Where are now in 1813, the Perfection and perfectability of human Nature? Where is now the progress of the human Mind? Where is the Amelioration of Society? Where the Augmentations of human Comforts? Where the diminutions of human Pains and Miseries . . . When? Where? and how? is the present Chaos to be arranged into Order?[3]

In ensuing decades, the nation would feel even more strongly the impact of political, economic, and social changes that would not only increase mobility and transform the traditional symbols of status and prestige but would also make the old ways of life seem obsolete. These rapid and often incomprehensible alterations appeared to destroy the cherished ideal of a simple agrarian republic. They generated anxiety and insecurity while heightening the quest for stability and unifying beliefs.

By 1820 the trend toward universal white male suffrage became apparent, and by 1850 all states except North Carolina had abandoned the property qualifications for voting. A low tax restriction lingered in only six states. This extension, as it brought in new votes, carried new men into politics also. Since they lacked prior experience in public affairs, these newcomers developed their own tactics and ethics in the vote-getting arena. Pragmatic, opportunistic, and often ruthless, these novices accomplished significant changes in the nature of American politics. First and most apparent, the well-bred elites who had previously been dominant were slowly pushed from the scene. Visiting the country in 1831, the astute social observer Alexis de Tocqueville remarked: "The most affluent classes of society are . . . entirely removed from the direction of political affairs in the United States. . . . The wealthy members of the community abandon the lists through unwillingness to contend, and frequently to contend in vain against the poorest classes of their fellow-citizens."[4]

As traditional party leaders retired from public life, they took with them their conventional methods of conducting elections. The innovative modes of campaigning continued to appeal most to the recently enfranchised electorate that had put new men into office. The election of Andrew Jackson in 1828 is historically credited with having inaugurated the era of the professional politician. Old Hickory owed his success in part to the skillful maneuvers of his campaign manager, Martin Van Buren. A consummate politician and an adroit tactician, Van Buren commanded the important Bucktail faction of the New York Republican Party. And his control of the effective political machine, the Albany Regency, enabled Van Buren to reestablish the old Jeffersonian coalition between New York and Virginia. Within a period of two years he and his political cohorts, John Eaton, Thomas Ritchie, and Thomas Hart Benton, created a new, vigorous Democratic Party, demonstrating the worth of these novel campaign methods.[5]

Predictably, Jackson's victory, aided substantially by the support of the lower classes, aroused anxiety among those who had formerly determined the outcome of elections. Members of the traditional elite expressed alarm at what they perceived as the surging power of the poorer ranks of society. Justice Joseph Story, attending Jackson's inaugural reception, noted that the guests included "the most vulgar and gross [people] in the nation." As the judge watched the reception turn into a destructive melee, he concluded sorrowfully that "the reign of 'King Mob' " had arrived. The venerable Philip Hone, mayor of New York City from 1825 to 1826, worried that Jackson and Van Buren had raised up forces greater than they could control. Hone's diary records his fear of mass violence, of class hatred, and of the "poor and ignorant" intent upon "pulling down the well-to-do and enlightened." The extension of suffrage, the advent of the professional politician with his new techniques and aggressive approach, the election of a president whose rhetoric clearly identified the class enemy of the people as "the money power"—all diluted the effectiveness of those upper- and middle-class men who attempted to fight the tide of greater democratization of American politics and life. And they reinforced the deep concern these former elites felt over their diminished status in the new nation.[6]

As the customary roots of political power eroded in the early nineteenth century, so, too, did the traditional sources of holy authority. Swells of religious zeal, known as the Second Great Awakening, swept members from the two leading churches of the colonial period: the Congregational and the Episcopal. Religious excitement waxed and waned in the early 1800s, reaching a crescendo between 1825 and 1837. Within those years, the flames of strenuous evangelicalism ignited New England and crisscrossed western New York with such intensity that the region received the label "The Burned-over District." Revivalism had a powerful appeal: theology became subordinate to faith; Christian behavior and conduct all but assured salvation; camp meetings imparted a sense of urgency to their participants.[7]

The revivalist preachers' hell-fire tactics excited their listeners with fear of eternal damnation, while the orthodox clergy cringed with disgust at the "millions of wretches biting and gnawing" their way to salvation. But the searing currents of evangelicalism could not be ignored. The Methodists and Baptists, the most aggressive revivalist sects, grew rampantly, becoming the two largest denominations in the country before the Civil War. Clearly, the suggestion that all could be saved had greater compatibility with the democratic tendencies of the antebellum era than did the doctrines of predestination and election.[8]

The enthusiasm with which men embraced this new and personal religion portended the end of the all-powerful ministry of colonial Protestantism. As the acknowledged interpreters of God's word, the Protestant clergy had dictated morals and defined appropriate behavior. But evangelism divested these symbols of their authority, thereby lessening the disciplining, integrative role of the clergy in the community. Charles Finney, the most intellectually inclined of the revivalists, thought it "all a farce to suppose that a literary ministry . . . [could] convert the world." Generally, the participants in the meetings "accepted the leadership of itinerant evangelists, men of their own class and order of talents, without superior intellect or learning."[9]

The deterioration of community cohesion, signified by the diminishing prestige of the learned clergy, seemed all the more certain as the seeds of revivalism sprouted into an unruly garden of sects, utopian schemes, and spiritual movements. The more eccentric of these included the Millerists, who preached that the Second Advent would occur in 1843, and those who believed that the Fox sisters could communicate with the spirits. These religious radicals, or ultraists, always remained in the minority. But their unusual activities attracted widespread attention, magnifying their dislocating impact on society, particularly as innovations in communication and transportation spread the news of the Second Great Awakening throughout the nation.

Rushed on by furious and persistent technological changes, the decline of political and religious deference all but destroyed the existence of an orderly country ruled by recognizable elites and organized around clearly identifiable national goals. Revolutionary improvements in transportation accelerated all movement, further eroding the nation's stability and accentuating egalitarianism.

With the advent of steamboats, steam engines, canals, turnpikes, and railroads, average Americans could afford to travel. The lack of first-class accommodations in the majority of vehicles caused one gentleman to complain that "the rich and the poor, the educated and the ignorant, the polite and the vulgar, all herd on the cabin floor of the steamer, feed at the same table, sit on each others laps, as it were, in the cars. . . . Steam, so useful in many respects, interferes with the comfort of travelling, [and] destroys every salutary distinction in society." The popular song "The Railroad Chorus," written in 1837, also took note of the disparate sorts of men brought together within the public transportation facilities:

> Men of different 'stations'
> In the eye of fame
> Here are very quickly

Coming to the same
High and lowly people
Birds of every feather
On a common levelling
Traveling together.[10]

Steamboats, canals, and railroads laced the country together in the forty years before the Civil War. Restructuring the economy with a rapidity both startling and incomprehensible, they promoted regional specialization and created national markets. This dramatic change in the means and methods of transport also drastically lowered the cost of moving goods, which, coupled with a widening market for specialized products, stimulated the development of industry.

Manufacturing generated multiple tensions in American society. The growth of industry lured increasing numbers away from the farm, foretelling the end of a dominantly rural America. But the pastoral myth remained strong. And the widening gap between the reality of life and the national ideal passed on by America's founders made many feel that they had betrayed the ancestral heritage. Those who still clung to the agrarian legends argued that democracy, presumed to be based on an independent yeomanry, could not survive the mercurial changes of an industrializing and urbanizing country.

Moreover, the velocity of mechanization itself played havoc with the traditional social structure, deepening status insecurities. Investment in industry quickly rewarded those with ready capital, an enterprising spirit, and an ample supply of good fortune. During the Jacksonian period, this emerging industrialist class challenged the hegemony of the old landed and commercial aristocracy. The latter showed no inclination to admit these "interlopers"—formerly thrifty farmers, skilled craftsmen, retired sea captains, men of modest means—into their ranks and struggled to maintain their ascendancy. But with their recently acquired fortunes and political power, these rising entrepreneurs posed a formidable threat to the continuing leadership of the old elites.

Jacksonian society, however, did not divide men only into two groups—the ones making their fortune versus the ones guarding it. The changes in industry and transportation that enabled some to accumulate vast wealth seriously weakened the position of a substantial part of the population. Western farmers prospered from the innovations in travel, but shipments of western wheat "demoralized farmers in the older communities, who were already struggling with declining fertility, low yields, parasitic infestations, increasing costs, and declining prices." Those farmers who were victimized, rather than helped, by change generally resided in the older regions of the Middle Atlantic States, in New England, and in parts of the South.[11]

Along with that of eastern farmers, the status of other members of society seemed to be plummeting uncontrollably. During the Jacksonian period the appearance of the merchant-capitalist injured both the master mechanic and the journeyman. This new group "began to invade the mechanical trades and to establish small scale factories which produced goods cheaply and in large quantities." The shifting wealth of this era, little understood and little accepted in a nation supposedly committed to an equal and noncompetitive society, heightened anxieties, particularly in the growing cities.[12]

Throughout the antebellum era, farm dwellers outnumbered city residents; however, a definite trend of movement to urban areas became observable. In 1800 farmers outnumbered those living in the towns and cities of the United States by a ratio of 15 to 1. By 1830 the ratio had deteriorated to slightly less than 10.5 to 1; in 1850 it was only 5.5 to 1. The years between 1820 and 1860 witnessed the most rapid proportional growth of cities in American history.

This incredible rate of urban expansion exacerbated tensions associated with the national political, economic, and social changes in the years after 1820. As the centers of commerce, business, industry, intellectual life, and fashion, cities exercised a dominant influence over the rest of the country. An analysis of the urban response to the alterations of the pre–Civil War era, therefore, is crucial to an understanding of Jacksonian society. Study of the antebellum city provides valuable insights into the ways in which men and women perceived their mutable environment and discloses how they attempted to compensate and adjust to the bewildering transformations.[13]

Nineteenth-century American cities tended to resemble one another. All stemming from commercial necessity, they developed parallel institutions and related patterns of response. Their local officials regularly shared methods of handling problems common to urban growth. Pockets of homology within the larger nation, cities transcended regional differences and fostered a strikingly similar texture of life. The experiences of New York City, therefore, are in many ways a reliable indicator of the response of other urban centers to the antebellum years.[14]

Between 1800 and 1820 New York City stood poised at the threshold of an age of cataclysmic development. Still relatively small and stable, the city showed but a few of the characteristics that would so deeply trouble inhabitants and visitors in the ensuing decades. It retained much of the flavor of its early days: a well-regulated society with a strong sense of community.

Throughout the colonial period the city fathers took responsibility for dealing with such critical matters as fire protection, public safety, morality, poverty, and public health. The continuing provision of adequate services gave the city an atmosphere of order and cohesiveness. Other stabilizing influences benefited the port city in the beginning of the nineteenth century. Physically compact, New York extended northward only to the triangular park formed by the intersection of Broadway, Chambers Street, and Chatham Street (chosen as the site for the new City Hall building in 1803). And within these limited confines, a fairly homogeneous population, still accepting the wisdom of the traditional elites, fostered internal order. Bolstered by commercial prosperity, New York's first families displayed a paternalistic concern for their neighbors. Authority flowed downward from the expected sources—the clergy, the men of wealth, and the civic leaders—and knit the city into a tight social cloth.[15]

Before the sweeping political innovations of the 1820s, the conservative state constitution of 1777 restricted New Yorkers' participation in local government. The administration of New York State, headed by the aristocratic Governor De Witt Clinton, who spoke "the purest brand of Hamiltonianism," aroused the enmity of Martin Van Buren and the Bucktails. Appearing as champion of the populace, the Bucktail faction gained support and forced the convening of a convention in 1821 to amend the anachronistic constitution. But the question of removing property qualifications for voting provoked "one of the great suffrage debates in American history." Led by the eloquent James Kent, chancellor of the state, an eminent group of old-style Federalists vehemently opposed an increase in voting rights. They feared that extension of male suffrage would enable the cities, with their large lower-class population, to rule the state. Democratic sentiment, however, overrode conservative objections. A new document was ratified in 1822. Every white male citizen who was more than twenty-one years of age, who had resided one year within the state and six months within his district, and who paid taxes or worked on the public roads or served in the militia became qualified to vote.[16]

Men of wealth and power residing in cities recognized the threat to their position inherent in political reforms. Fears of distinguished New Yorkers, vivified by the proximity of lower-class urban life, often found expression in private diaries and letters. The civic-minded John Pintard wrote to his daughter that at election time "we have the Working people and Fanny right men [*sic*] arrayed to level all distinctions to equalize property, abrogate marriage, release children from parental restraint." These subversive doctrines, he added, "loosen the bonds of society and government." Philip Hone also worried that the masses would be attracted to the ideas of the radical Miss Wright: "Her doctrines are similar to those of Paine and Godwin, and . . . [would] unsettle the foundations of civil society and subvert our fundamental principles of morality."[17]

Frightened by the absence of order, the upper segments of urban society also suffered from the rapidity with which the economic milieu changed. New York City's wealth had always been in commerce.

The Grinnells, the Griswolds, the Lows, the Phelps, the Tappans, the Pecks—this merchant nobility had enjoyed an unrivalled position in the years before the opening of the Erie Canal. A song written by Samuel Woodworth for the dedication of the canal joyfully proclaimed, "Let the day be forever remembered with pride, That beheld the proud Hudson to Erie allied." But to New York's merchant elite, the completion of this remarkable man-made river signalled the end of their aristocratic hegemony. Levi Beardsley noted that the "canal enlarged the views and removed many prejudices against internal improvements, so that men began to believe things possible which they did not fully comprehend."[18]

Thus spurred, men began to experiment aggressively in industry. Clothing, shoe, and boot factories, as well as printing and publishing establishments, proliferated after 1825. The new wealth created by these and other industries challenged the traditional elites. A different kind of threat was posed by the flood of newspapers and publications that resulted from the mechanization of printing. Cities across the nation were inundated with new types of journals, appealing to those groups in society just gaining recognition. Philadelphia produced the first labor paper in the United States, the *Mechanic Free Press* (1828), followed by New York's *Working Man's Advocate* (1829) and *Man* (1834). *Irishman* (1832), the *Irishman and Foreigner's Advocate* (1835), and the *Staats-Zeitung* (1834) spoke to immigrant groups in New York, while the German population of Cincinnati read the *Volksblatt* (1836). And the New York *Evangelist* (1830) became popular with those devoted to revivalism.[19]

With the development of the penny press, the production of published material increased at a phenomenal pace. By 1835, Benjamin Day's New York *Sun* could sell fifty-five thousand papers a day at one penny each, and its rival, the sensational New York *Morning Herald*, fared as well. This explosion in the publishing industry fostered the diffusion of information throughout the community. Traditionally, knowledge had been the exclusive property of the established gentry. Respected, educated civic and religious leaders, interpreting and filtering information, effectively controlled the flow of news to the masses. But the printing revolution changed this limited, vertical method of communication. The broad, horizontal dissemination of newspapers, pamphlets, and handbills throughout the cities made recent events the topic of daily conversation, publicized meetings, and organized dissent.[20]

Speaking directly to the masses—immigrants, laborers, women, and even children—these publications not only made possible public access to a wide variety of information but also encouraged the common American to form independent opinions of events. In so doing, they destroyed an important source of authority and aroused deep fears of mob activities among established residents of cities with large, uncontrollable poor populations. As Tocqueville observed, "In cities men cannot be prevented from concerting together and awakening a mutual excitement that prompts sudden and passionate resolutions." Indeed, the French reformer believed that the "lower ranks which inhabit these cities constitute a rabble even more formidable than the populace of European towns."[21]

The dual impact of antebellum immigration and industrialization greatly increased the size of the "lower ranks" of urban America, while also substantially degrading their position. Between the mid-1820s and the mid-1840s, the circumstances and the prestige of the wage-worker deteriorated dramatically. Inevitably, the mixture of declining wages and waning social status impelled laborers, many newly enfranchised, into direct political action.

The first city-wide combination of unions, the Mechanics Union of Trade Associations, evolved from a strike of building trade workers in Philadelphia for a ten-hour day. A year later, in 1828, this group formed the Working Men's Labor Party. Yet despite labor's impressive early gains, work hours actually increased steadily throughout the 1830s. Labor's worsening status heightened frustrations and added to class consciousness. Rampant inflation and speculation, culminating in the Panic of 1837, increased the militancy of labor's demands and, in turn, spread the fear of class warfare throughout urban areas. The leaders of the New York Typographical Association declared in 1833: "The time has now arrived for the mechanics of our city to arise in their strength and determine that they will no longer submit to the thraldom which they have patiently borne for many years, nor suffer employers to appropriate an undue share of the avails of the labourer to his disadvantage."[22]

Philip Hone was among the many who worried that hostility to the upper classes would excite the crowds and lead to anarchy. In February 1837, when mass demonstrations against unemployment and inflated prices of foodstuffs and fuel led the protesters to sack the city flour warehouse, Hone copied into his journal a leaflet that announced the demonstration. The notice, calling upon all those "determined to resist Monopoly and Extortioners" to attend, predicted that "the People . . . Will Prevail."[23]

During one of the periods of economic hardship in the city, diarist George Templeton Strong wrote that "people talk ominously about rebellions and revolutions on this side of the Atlantic." British novelist Fredrick Marryat related that New York City's unemployed mechanics had "an air of famished wolves." The menacing demands of the workers became intensified as the steady influx of immigrants further distended the labor force and multiplied the suspicions and insecurities of native residents.[24]

Of the 5.5 million aliens who arrived in America between 1815 and 1860, more than two-thirds entered through the port of New York, swelling the city's transient population. Some went to western regions, but many settled in the Empire City. By 1850 foreign-born persons constituted as much as 48 percent of the city's population. The increasing numbers of immigrants arriving from Europe in the 1830s and 1840s glutted the labor market, lowering wages and causing greater unemployment. Workers resented the foreign competition. "Our labouring men, native and naturalized, are met at every turn and every avenue of employment with recently imported workmen from the low wage countries of the world," protested a newspaper reporter in 1844.[25]

The availability of massive numbers of immigrants undermined the status of the native laborer and exacerbated his antagonism towards the rest of society. But the American worker shared with his fellow wealthy New Yorker both a sense of superiority to the "foreigner" and a conviction that the alien customs of these immigrants posed a dangerous threat to the future of the city. Once overwhelmingly English and Protestant, American cities became home to thousands of Irish and German Catholics whose mores seemed to clash dangerously with those of the native population. The disquieting presence of immigrant groups became inescapable in the small "walking city" of the early nineteenth century. Before mass transportation revolutionized urban life by allowing the affluent to reside away from bustling business areas and dismal immigrant neighborhoods, all levels of the social strata lived and worked near each other.

Visitors to New York often expressed amazement at the strange juxtaposition of elegant mansions and broken-down shanties. These crude dwellings, clustered close to one another for security, formed frightening pockets of destitution within the city's wealthier communities. Located in the Sixth Ward, bounded by the fashionable Broadway to the west, Chatham Street to the south, the Bowery to the east, and Canal Street to the north, stood the "Five Points," one of the country's most notorious slums. In this dark, dank, and unhealthy area, on the former site of the Collect Swamp, lived the poorer Irish immigrants. The Old Brewery, erected in 1792 and transformed into a dwelling in 1837, housed several hundred men, women, and children. Living several families in each room and usually lacking means of support, the Irish, Black, and, later, Italian inhabitants of this quarter experienced the severest deprivation.

The filth, poverty, and misery of the neighborhood bred murderers, thieves, pickpockets, beggars, and degenerates of every type. After visiting New York in 1842, Charles Dickens wrote that "poverty, wretchedness, and vice" characterized the Five Points. The buildings, "reeking everywhere with dirt and filth," house "all that is loathsome, drooping, and decayed."[26]

For many New Yorkers, the Five Points epitomized the devastating effects of immigration on their city. The Old Brewery became the symbol of a degenerating metropolis of the future, dominated by foreigners with their strange and "abhorrent habits." John Pintard wrote: "The vice of drunkenness among the lower labouring classes is growing to a frightful excess, . . . and the multitudes of low Irish Catholics, . . . restricted by poverty in their own country, run riot in this." He saw little hope for improvement: "As long as we are overwhelmed with Irish emigrants, so long will the evil abound. . . . Theft, incendiaries and murders which prevail, all rise from this source."[27]

Native New Yorkers, struggling to minimize the impact of immigration, recoiled in horror at the efforts of Tammany politicians to court the foreign vote. George Templeton Strong expressed his disdain: "It was enough to turn a man's stomach—to make him abjure republicanism forever—to see the way they were naturalizing this morning at the hall. . . . Wretched filthy bestial-looking Italians and Irish, . . . in short the very scum and dregs of human nature filled the Clerk of C[ommon] P[leas] office so completely that I was almost afraid of being poisoned by going in." Viewed with hostility and distrust, the immigrants seemed to form unruly enclaves within a tempestuous society. They adhered to strange traditions, attended their own churches, often spoke an indecipherable language, read their own newspapers, and sometimes became the innocent dupes of unscrupulous politicians' attempts to gain power.[28]

The desperate condition of the foreign born compelled them to work for paltry sums. They unwittingly took jobs away from native laborers and unknowingly kept nineteenth-century cities in "a great scramble, in which all are troubled and none are satisfied," where "everyone [was] tugging, trying, scheming to advance—to get ahead." Tocqueville, writing of the "innumerable multitude of those who seek to throw off their original condition," believed that "no Americans are devoid of a yearning to rise." The last lines of a popular song of the era lyrically conveyed the same thought: "There is success in the future for me, Only an emigrant tho' I may be."[29]

The myth of America as the land of plenty and the verified success of more than a few in accumulating wealth infused Jacksonians with an insatiable craving to try to reach the top. This drive rendered them acutely competitive as they carefully guarded any miniscule advance, any small symbol of prosperity, from the covetous designs of those beneath them. Francis Grund, noted that the high society in the United States "think themselves beset by dogs and are continually kicking for fear of being bitten." Particularly in the cities, with their large numbers of transient and resident poor and their increasing populations of parvenus, the perpetual striving for advancement assumed a special urgency.[30]

Yet despite an individual's frenzied struggles to move to the top, his success was often fleeting, as unpredictable economic whirlwinds made it very difficult for most to stabilize their positions. Visitors frequently remarked on the erratic social structure. Tocqueville found it "not uncommon for the same man in the course of his life to rise and sink again through all the grades that lead from opulence to poverty." Thomas Hamilton, visiting New York in 1831 and 1832, also remarked on the fluctuating society: "Rich men spring up like mushrooms. . . . Fortunes are made and lost by a single speculation. . . . There is comparatively no settled and permanent body of leading capitalists." "In New York," declared Francis Grund, "every new quotation of the exchange excludes a dozen families from the pale of fashion and creates a dozen new candidates for its imaginary honours."[31]

But even the knowledge that all effort might be in vain did not deter urban citizens from their frenetic quest for wealth. They still sought the perquisites of status, which, as Tocqueville observed, "perpetually retires from them, yet without hiding itself from their sight, and in retiring draws them on." Comparatively few Americans realized their dreams, but the tantalizing vision of success endured. The disparity between men's hopes and the true conditions of their lives generated extreme tension. And this stress was heightened by the knowledge that their fierce aspirations for wealth hastened the demise of the idyllic, simple, noncompetitive agrarian republic they philosophically still espoused.[32]

Relentlessly vying with one another for money and position, nineteenth-century Americans unwittingly accelerated the deterioration of community cohesion. Jacksonians everywhere attempted to adjust to their chaotic society. But those living in the burgeoning cities had a particularly difficult task. The many transformations of society became magnified in American cities. And, additionally, the monumental urban growth in the years after 1820 complicated the city dweller's ability to deal positively with change.

Unplanned expansion brought a new set of problems and psychic demands. The lack of adequate public services, the pervasiveness of poverty and crime, the increasingly heterogeneous population, and the atomization of the family were all tangentially related to the broader alterations in American society. But they quickly developed an independent momentum and came to be intimately associated with the nation's image of urban life.

By the second decade of the nineteenth century, American cities entered an epoch of frenzied growth, which disregarded all boundaries and limitations and introduced a host of seemingly insurmountable problems. Public services were unable to keep pace with the increase in physical size and population. The cluttered streets of New York, with their squalid smells and ever-present menagerie of animals, became the first indication of urban malaise. Travelers complained of "the inequalities and gaps in the sidewalk" and of "the numberless moveable and immoveable incumbrances." With a population swelling from less than 100,000 in 1815 to more than 371,000 in 1845, the restless city quickened its northward march. In that thirty-year period Twentieth Street replaced Houston Street and Greenwich Village as the northern boundary. Residents responded with amazement. "The city is spreading north . . . out of all reason and measure," wrote George Templeton Strong. Within a few years the "Jack the Giant-killer's beanstalk of a city" surpassed the ability of local government to provide for the safety and comfort of its citizens.[33]

Without sufficient water supplies or sanitation facilities, city dwellers experienced constant discomfort and fear. New York developed a reputation for dirt, with pigs serving as scavengers for garbage well into the nineteenth century. Contemporaries attributed the "terrible havoc" of yellow fever and cholera to the lack of water and inadequate sanitation.[34]

Fires became another blight on urban existence. As Hone wrote, "Scarcely a night passes without citizens being awakened by the cry of 'Fire.' " Volunteer firemen, sometimes contentious, served "more for the love of excitement than from any praiseworthy desire for the preservation of property." The blazes often proved too great a match for their amateur opponents, causing destruction, human misery, and uncertainty.[35]

Urban residents also had to endure continued threats of violence by rowdy gangs. Bands of youthful criminals roamed the streets, fighting with one another and terrorizing neighborhoods. Philadelphia had its Buffaloes, Blood Tubs, Rugs, and Copper Heads, while the Stringers looted Baltimore. New Yorkers feared the Bowery Boys, Plug-Uglies, Highbinders, Swipers, and Dead Rabbits; the Crawfish Boys of Cincinnati proved that even western cities had no immunity. Strong wrote of an "epidemic of crime" that induced most of his friends to carry revolvers with them at night. In 1840 Philip Hone recorded that "riot, disorder, and violence increase in our city; every night is marked by some outrage committed by the gangs of young ruffians."[36]

The method of police protection used in the colonial period obviously could not accommodate the needs of growing cities. Until 1844, however, when New York became the first city to abolish its antiquated system, every urban area relied on the eighteenth-century combination of day policemen and night watchmen to patrol the streets. Yet, the innovations provided little relief. As late as 1853 New Yorkers called their police "the worst in the world" and thought them to be "partly awed by the blackguards . . . and partly intimate with them."[37]

The prevalence of crime generated apprehension among urban residents. It seemed that those responsible for the welfare of the city could not or would not protect it. Fearing attack on their person and property, residents loathed the criminal and the tensions he produced. At the same time, the intimacy of the antebellum city forced wealthier citizens into daily contact with devastating poverty and brought to some the recognition of its responsibility for so much of the vice.

Inescapable scenes of human anguish left a deep imprint on the urban mind. A small town might have its poor folk, a local drunkard, and perhaps a few beggars, but they could be ignored, helped, and ultimately absorbed within the social structure of a small, well-regulated community. In the frantic nineteenth-century cities, the magnitude of these problems appeared to mock corrective measures. The sheer numbers condemned to hopeless destitution, who would steal, beg, prostitute themselves, or turn to the bottle out of desperation, presented an alarming dilemma. A potentially explosive population emerged, trapped in a situation beyond the reach of individual comprehension or alleviation.

The more fortunate city resident might feel guilt at his own untrammeled pursuit of wealth. At the same time, the enormity of urban poverty seemingly defied his ability to give meaningful relief and rendered him virtually impotent to effect social change. A visitor to New York City in 1842 recorded the "beseeching looks, begging the comfort and hope [she had] no power to give." She ardently wished to walk the streets "without having misery forced on [her] notice, which [she had] no power to relieve."[38]

A diverse population, with heterogeneous values, also emphasized individual isolation and further thwarted attempts to control or ameliorate urban conditions. The ever enlarging numbers admitted a wide range of personality traits, cultural styles, and occupational interests. Exhibiting a plurality of social standards and relative values not found in rural areas, urban life made consensus difficult and produced a disquieting loneliness. "It is sad walking in the city," remarked author and reformer Lydia Maria Child. "The busy throng passing and repassing . . . offer no sympathy. The loneliness of the soul is deeper and far more restless than in the solitude of the mighty forest."[39]

With few norms common to the entire city, the imperatives of life and livelihood in the urban context required interaction with a greater number of people on an impersonal basis than in a rural environment. In a farming district, families relied on specific and intimate associates to satisfy their wants. In the industrializing cities, however, an individual required the services of numerous, but unknown, persons for his necessities and comforts. This division of labor demanded from the individual an ever more one-sided accomplishment and made the particular person less important than the task he or she performed. Frequent close contact, coupled with great social distance, produced a "population of strangers." As Rev. John Todd noted, city dwellers did not "form [the] deep attachments . . . which we do in country life." This lack of intimacy aggravated the loneliness and isolation of the urban milieu.[40]

The anonymous masses of the city accentuated man's sense of his insignificance, especially as the dynamics of urbanization weakened the ancient citadel of masculine authority: the patriarchal family. In rural or village families, fathers had little difficulty asserting their will. They felt confident that their wisdom and experience qualified them to educate their offspring for the future and to command their respect. Expecting obedience, fathers usually worked near enough to their families to supervise activities and to see that wives and children followed given directives.

In the cities, however, the diversity of life rendered men virtually incapable of finding meaning and coherence in their own lives and thus unable to instruct their children adequately. With fortunes and friends constantly changing, with every kind of social habit in obvious display, who could foretell the future? Who knew what knowledge and which ideas would help children to understand an incomprehensible and unpredictable society?

Ironically, children had less difficulty adjusting to the tumultuous environment than their parents did. Visitors generally agreed that the American youth was "too early his own master." Without preconceived notions or prejudices to restrict their responses, juveniles in the nation's cities were infinitely more malleable than their parents. Better able to cope with urban life, they developed a source of independent strength, difficult to accommodate within the family structure. Moreover, the father's absences from home and the assumption of traditional family responsibilities by outside agencies intensified the difficulty of disciplining assertive children.[41]

In the expanding urban areas, a man's occupation took him away from the home, sometimes for weeks at a time. The *Monthly Religious Magazine* found that the "necessity . . . of going long distances to . . . [men's] places of duty," combining with the lure of a variety of city recreational facilities, produced "little short of an absolute separation from their families." The transfer of industrial and recreational pursuits to institutions outside the home deprived the family of some of its most important historic functions and substituted secondary contacts for the closer kinship ties.[42]

With less time, confidence, and energy for personal supervision of his wife and children, the paternal position in the household became unclear. The ambiguity of the father's role heightened his insecurity and seemed to be fragmenting the family. In a nation deeply committed to the belief that "a family is society in miniature . . . and [that] whatever destroys . . . [it] must . . . affect the whole community," the attentuation of familial ties became particularly disquieting. This anxiety was aggravated in the unstable city.[43]

New York City derived its dynamism from the vitality of its effervescent society as well as from the quickening vigor of its commercial life. Timothy Dwight, president of Yale University, visited the city in 1833 and found "everything . . . in movement, and not a nook or corner but what is brim-full of business." Few failed to note the fevered tempo of New York, which exasperated and exhausted both visitors and residents. "The hurry-scurry of Broadway and Wall-Street with their driving, jostling, and elbowing" annoyed Andrew Bell, an English traveler of 1835. And the Swedish social critic, Fredrika Bremer, wrote: "On Broadway again there is an endless tumult and stir, crowd and bustle, and in the city . . . people crowd as if for dear life."[44]

Desperate for equanimity, but impelled by the unquenchable thirst for status, urban Americans went from house to house, from job to job, and from city to city at a hectic pace. Lydia Maria Child was amazed that "people should move so *often*. . . . Aspirations after the infinite lead them to perpetual change, in the restless hope of finding something better still." When urban residents depleted one city's ability to provide them with a livelihood, they moved their families and possessions to another. A recent study of Boston by Stephen Thernstrom and Peter Knights reveals an extensive outpouring of population from that city between the years 1830 and 1860. It suggests that migration from other nineteenth-century cities equaled or surpassed Boston's example. If masses of humanity flowed out of as well as into antebellum cities, then the urban areas had populations even more fluid and volatile than has been previously thought.[45]

Thus, the city dweller had little opportunity to form deep or lasting ties to neighbors and associates, many of whom he viewed with jealousy or suspicion. As he watched his influence in the family diminish, his economic condition fluctuate uncontrollably, and his ability to effect social change erode dramatically, the unstable and plural environment also rendered his ideals and aspirations unattainable. Basic assumptions around which he had organized his life began to collapse. Urban residents became increasingly insecure and isolated in a land where children's schoolbooks taught that "the principle of free government adheres to the American soil . . . [and] is bedded in it." The nation clung to the belief that ruralism had a special moral significance in a democracy; the city seemed to have no place in the "home of the free."[46]

Bucolic imagery saturated American culture. The pastoral ideal, articulated by statesmen, philosophers, poets, and novelists, had been used throughout the nation's history to sanction activities, explain attitudes, and articulate hope. The agrarian vision of the eighteenth century lent itself to encouraging and justifying the conquest of the wilderness. But in the nineteenth century it seemed to define the promise of American life as an ever expanding, harmonious agricultural paradise inhabited by virtuous farmers. Jacksonians embraced this myth with a growing enthusiasm, especially as the transfigurations of the era created a world so distant from their idyllic fantasy. Through the repeated sentimentalizing of a rural existence they had not known and would never experience, Americans expressed their yearning for a simpler society. Unable to understand or even acknowledge their present way of life, they held fast to the symbol of a fecund garden.

Underlying the apotheosis of the country, with its small villages and lovely landscapes, was the longing for an orderly, noncompetitive community. In this ideal setting all shared fully in nature's bounties. James Kirk Paulding's poem *The Backwoodsman* reveals much of the appeal of agrarianism for nineteenth-century Americans:

> To cultivated fields, the forest chang'd,
> Where golden harvests wav'd, and cattle rang'd,
> The curling smoke amid the wilds was seen,
> The village church now whiten'd on the green,
> And by its side arose the little school,
> Where rod and reason, lusty urchins rule,
> Whose loud repeated lessons might be heard,
> Whene'er along the road a wight appear'd.

In Paulding's imaginary rustic scene, the church and the school, two important institutions of stability, are conspicuous. Reason and discipline prevail, curtailing mischievous behavior and proclaiming their ascendancy.[47]

Other benefits of a rural society also received commendation. Timothy Flint, a Massachusetts clergyman, emphasized the munificence of the county's western lands. "Thousands of independent and happy yeomen . . . have emigrated . . . with their numerous, healthy and happy families." A lush nature provided "ample abundance that fills their granaries, with their young orchards, whose branches must be propped to sustain the weight of their fruit." The unspoiled environment, so rank and luxurious, nourished a special kind of humanity. "Farmers and their children," Flint wrote, "are strong, and innocent and moral almost of necessity." Enriched by their plenteous surroundings, "farmers [could] rear their families in peace . . . and privacy, under the guardian genius of our laws."[48]

The nostalgic pastoral image nurtured the myth of an opulent land dotted with towns peacefully resting under "a lovely sky" and "a cloudless sun." It declared the superiority of agrarianism to other ways of life. Authors urged their readers to reside in the country "where no noisy crowd will jostle you in the chase of wealth." Timothy Flint could not believe that his fellow countrymen would "be willing to exchange . . . their fee simple empire . . . and the ability to employ the leisure of half their time as they choose, for the interior of square stones or brick walls, to breathe floccules of cotton and to contemplate the whirl of innumerable wheels for fourteen hours of six days of every week in the year."[49]

Yet as increasing numbers traded country homes for those in the metropolis, the scattered voices of warning against the nation's cities harmonized into a strong chorus loudly chanting a fear and distrust of urban life. Literature hostile to the city poured forth. Sensationalized descriptions of urban life fed the farmer's already active imagination with more dread and subjected the city dweller to greater stress. By magnifying the difficulties inherent in urbanization and by conveying the impression of a pervasive national aversion to the city way of life, these writings intensified the urban resident's sense of alienation.

Throughout the nineteenth century, Americans wrote about cities with varying degrees of skill, creativity, and aversion. Nathaniel Hawthorne described Rome, the scene of his story *The Marble Faun,* as a "heap of broken rubbish" and a "long decaying corpse." The hero of Hawthorne's tale, Donatello, the ideal man of nature, tries to escape from the "evil smells," "uneasy streets," and the "wicked," "corrupt," and "blood-stained" pavements of the eternal city by living in a tower. In *My Kinsman, Major Molineaux,* Hawthorne uses the character of Robin, a "country-bred youth," to demonstrate urban indifference. At age eighteen Robin makes his first sojourn to Boston. He is searching for a wealthy relative to launch him in a career. As he wanders through a "succession of crooked and narrow streets," he encounters the alleged evils of the city: a tavern, a seductive housekeeper, and an unsympathetic watchman who threatens to put him in the stocks. With no one willing to help him, Robin experiences a "sensation of loneliness stronger than he had ever felt in the remotest depths of his native woods." The young man finally asks the ferryman to take him home, saying, "I begin to grow weary of a town life." Hawthorne undoubtedly hoped that Robin's experiences would teach all country folk who yearned for excitement that only peril and isolation awaited them in the big cities.[50]

In *The Celestial Railroad,* a modern *Pilgrim's Progress,* Hawthorne used satire most effectively to criticize the inhabitants of the "populous and flourishing City of Destruction." These unthinking city dwellers built a railroad to reach the Celestial City, willingly sacrificing culture for technology and happiness for material gain. At the end of the tale those on the train realize they have been tricked; the Celestial Railroad has actually led them to a hideous land. Fortunately the hero escapes a dire fate by awakening in time to realize that the entire trip was a bad dream. But the characters of other antiurban tales are not as fortunate.[51]

Pierre, in Herman Melville's story of the same name, is ruined by the commercialism and cruelty of New York City. "Born and nurtured in the country, surrounded by scenery whose common loveliness was the perfect mould of a delicate and poetc mind," Pierre is ill-suited for urban life. As a struggling writer he tries to support three young women, but Pierre is ultimately destroyed by what Melville portrays as the greedy, inhuman city.[52]

In one of Edgar Allan Poe's poems, *The City of the Sea* (1845), published earlier under the titles *The Doomed City* and *The City of Sin,* the metropolis itself is vanquished by water. For in this "Strange city lying alone, Death has reared himself a throne."

> No rays from the holy heavens come down
> On the long night-time of that town;

Suddenly "that wilderness of glass" is shattered by a huge wave, burying the entire city:

And when, amid no earthly moans
Down, down, that town shall settle hence,
Hell, rising from a thousand thrones,
Shall do it reverence.[53]

Just as the unsavory qualities of the city could be concealed by immersing the town in water, so too the waves of humanity enveloping urban areas camouflaged the sinister individuals lurking among the "tumultuous sea of heads." Poe uses the motif of the anonymous city where "men are little known" and "imperfectly restrained" in *The Man of the Crowd.* Set in London, this tale relates the narrator's attempts to follow one desperate man through the streets of the city. The narrator passes "tall, antique, worm-eaten wooden tenements" and "horrible filth festered in dammed-up gutters." He pursues his subject far into the night where darkness "[brings] forth every species of infamy from its den." The storyteller finally concludes that the man he followed "is the type and genius of deep crime. He refuses to be alone. *He is the man of the crowd.*"[54]

Urban criminality provided the material for another of Poe's stories, *The Mystery of Marie Rogêt.* Based upon the 1841 murder of Mary Roger, a New York tobacco store worker, this tale disputed the official version of Mary's death. The autopsy performed on Mary's body indicated that she had been mistreated and murdered by a group of ruffians. The case aroused great excitement in the city and called forth demands that citizens be protected against the water front gangs. In Poe's fictionalized account, which takes place in Paris, Marie is murdered by one of her many former lovers. The author's descriptions of Paris as "odious" and a "sink of pollution" clearly link the crime to the moral turpitude of the city.[55]

In the late 1830s and 1840s, fictionalized portrayals of city crime increased markedly. Steeped in lurid detail, these exaggerated stories confirmed the country's worst fears of urban decay and added to the pressure on the city dweller to improve his society. Like Edgar Allan Poe, the prolific Joseph Holt Ingraham, who wrote more than seventy "novels" between 1840 and 1849, also departed from the facts in his version of Mary Roger's death. In *The Beautiful Cigar Girl,* Mary escapes death. But Ingraham's vivid depictions of criminal bands and other "evils of the city" contributed to the growing body of sensational literature that revealed the "true nature" of urban life to the American people.[56]

"Anyone who is at all acquainted with the mysteries of this city, knows that New York cannot be itself by day," wrote Ned Buntline in *The Mysteries and Miseries of New York* (1848). Under the cloak of darkness the "villains," the "miserable courtesans," and the "gamblers" emerge to do their dastardly deeds. These evil doings also formed the subject matter for George Lippard's *New York: Its Upper Ten and Lower Million.* Published in 1853, this book contained graphic accounts of six rapes, seven adulteries, and twelve murders.[57]

A trilogy by Newton Mallory Curtis, which bore the subtitle "A Tale of Life in the Great Metropolis," uses the plot of family conflict to alert its readers to the dangers of the city. Curtis details none of the traditional catalogue of urban evils. Rather, his perception of the real threat of urbanization to the nation is presented in the allegorical form of a feud between two brothers in their wealthy Dutch home during the year 1834. The house, standing "at the upper end of Broadway," "large and old fashioned," "seem[s] to have been preserved as a memorial of the revolution." Located in "a beautiful yard of native flowers," surrounded by "a garden studded with arbors and fruit trees," the Sydenham mansion seems to have been *in* the city but not *of* it.[58]

This fine old house represents the promise of America. The democratic principle, embodied by Floyd, the good brother, must be on constant guard against the rapacity of those in the nation who by their greed would destroy the goals of the founding fathers. These grasping citizens are represented in the book by the bad brother, Seymour, who has "given himself up to dissipation and vice." The Sydenham home, a repository of the revolutionary ideals, is destroyed by the evil son's brutal murder of his mother in an attempt to secure her fortune. This dreadful act is of central importance: "The citizens in the street came rushing up the stairs and into the room. Omnibuses and cabs stopped in the street. . . . The ordinary business of the day was suspended, and men came hurrying to the scene of blood and death, looked at each other and asked: 'What has caused this heinous crime?' "[59]

The author gives an allegorical answer to the cause of Mrs. Sydenham's slaying. While New York City plays a minimal part in this "Tale of Life in the Great Metropolis," the urban influence is represented through the avarice and ruthlessness of the scoundrelly son. The rich mother, of fine Dutch ancestry, symbolizes America's bountiful and precious heritage. Her murder denotes the ultimate betrayal of the ideals and aspirations of an earlier, more virtuous, and rural nation by the acquisitive residents of the "Great Metropolis," who would sacrifice America's democratic mission at the altar of material gain.

The profusion of literature dealing with city life both reflected and intensified the growing awareness—of a people reluctant to awaken from their agricultural dreams—that inevitably urbanization would prevail. Vividly demonstrating that the urban experience could not be eradicated from the national consciousness, the writings hyperbolizing city problems affected citizens regardless of residence. The antiurban fiction reinforced rural America's fears of the metropolis while heightening the insecurities and anxieties of those living in the cities. Exaggerated presentations of urban poverty, crimes, and greed gave a special urgency to the resolution of these problems. The stories magnified the individual's feeling of impotence to accomplish the desired social change and yet burdened him with the heavy responsibility of remedying urban ills that supposedly threatened the nation's health.

The literary depiction of the city as the serpent in the garden added to the city dweller's already numerous woes. His authority and effectiveness, both at home and in society, had diminished markedly. A highly competitive, unstable social structure and a heterogeneous, often volatile population resulted in the loss of a cohesive community and shared values. As the assumptions around which they had organized and integrated their lives collapsed, urban residents experienced, more acutely perhaps than other Americans, a crisis in the meaning of their existences.

The belief in an agrarian utopia could no longer help the increasing numbers of city dwellers to perceive or adapt to their environment. In the early decades of the nineteenth century, bucolic imagery had provided the nation with an outlet for its aspirations and fantasies. Even as the growth of cities, industrialization, and immigration altered the texture of society, the literary portrayal of idyllic, rustic villages had permitted Americans to escape temporarily from the harsh realities of confusing transition. Yet as relentless urban expansion exacerbated the tensions and produced a body of literature that vivified and diffused the worst aspects of urban life throughout the country, the traditional versions of the pastoral myths lost their soothing effect. For how could images of a rural, harmonious society be reconciled with the burgeoning cities and their perpetual struggle for wealth, their filth, their disorder, their devastating poverty? How could tales of simple yeomen farmers struggling to actualize America's glorious mission mitigate the anxieties of those made to feel that their way of life was shattering the vision of the founding fathers? Thus, rather than easing the accommodation of Americans to their increasingly urban and industrial society, the agrarian images became an additional source of stress, a constant reminder of a paradise lost by the sins of the cities.

As the old beliefs became less relevant to a large segment of the population, Americans—particularly those in the cities—fervently sought a way to assimilate their existences within the framework of a coherent philosophy. They yearned for a system of thought that would allow them to cling to the cherished qualities of an exalted past, while enabling them to welcome the future wholeheartedly. Old ideas needed to be adjusted; new theories and values had to be developed to help Americans comprehend and compensate for their chaotic society. Within the context of nineteenth-century urbanization, the complicated search for shared ideals, identity, and security significantly transformed the shape and direction of American thoughts and customs and dramatically affected the position of women in the United States.

3

Homeward Bound

Where lieth woman's sphere?—Not there
Where strife and fierce contentions are, . . .
Not in the wild and angry crowd,
Mid threat'nings high and clamors loud;
Nor in the halls of rude debate
And legislation, is *her* seat; . . .

What then *is* woman's sphere? The sweet
And quiet precincts of her home;
Home!—where the blest affections meet,
Where strife and hatred may not come!
Home!—sweetest word in mother-tongue,
Long since in verse undying sung!

—*Ladies' Repository,* 1845

Nineteenth-century urban Americans viewed their tumultuous environment with foreboding. "We . . . live in the very midst of change and fluctuation," noted the author John Neal, and "are never the same for two minutes together." City dwellers worried whether society, "despising all forms and distinctions, all boundaries and rules, . . . [would] break up and become a chaos of disjointed and unsightly elements." The commotion of the cities gave impetus to the quest for an organized body of ideas through which to understand and direct society.[1]

Urban instability was further abetted when traditional class distinctions began to lose their restraining influence within the urban collage. "As each class gradually approaches others and mingles with them, its members become undifferentiated and lose their class identity for each other," remarked Tocqueville. Francis Grund also commented on the peculiarity of American society where "gradations[,] not being regulated according to rank and titles," became difficult to discern and impossible to enforce. The German aristocrat believed that the wealthier groups had "nothing which could mark them as a distinct class" and thus developed "incessant cravings after artificial distinctions."[2]

Wealth and leisure, conspicuously displayed, became a part of the urban industrial American's quest for identity and emerged as important symbols of status. "In all commercial cities," wrote novelist Mrs. A. J. Graves, "the class . . . whose distinction is solely gained by profuse expenditure and gorgeous display must always be a large one." As a contemporary New Yorker remarked, "In this city there is no higher rank in society than that of a rich man." The ostentatiousness of the middle and upper classes in nineteenth-century cities also reflected a troubled and ambiguous search for identity. For men tried to gain internal dignity, equanimity, and purpose through their ability to purchase exterior finery.[3]

Few failed to note the prodigious luxury of New York City. Lydia Maria Child recorded that "there will soon be more houses in New York furnished according to the fortune and taste of noblemen, than there are either in Paris or London." The homes of the affluent did indeed radiate a palatial splendor with their "rosewood and satin, mirrors, cabinets and vetu." Scottish geologist Sir Charles Lyell, visiting New York in 1841, "saw many houses gorgeously fitted up with satin and velvet draperies, rich Axminster carpets, marble and inlaid tables, and large looking-glasses, the style in general being Parisian."[4]

Feminine fashions, which truly enthralled New York's visitors, became another badge of masculine status. Sumptuous female attire turned the city's avenues into a rainbow of colors and fabrics, evoking the praise and amazement of observers. Mrs. Anne Royall, a southern visitor to the city, thought it "impossible to give even an idea of the beauty and fashion displayed in Broadway." And, William Thackeray described "New York damsels" who wore "embroidered muslin, of the finest and costliest kind," paid exorbitant amounts "for a single pocket handkerchief," and carried "extravagantly expensive fans, with ruby or emerald pins."[5]

Conspicuous leisure of women provided many urban men with another effective vehicle for displaying their financial and social success. A woman's dress that had features testifying to the wearer's exemption from or incapacity for any "vulgarly" productive employment demonstrated to all that her husband or father provided well for his family. The fashions worn by city women, as pictured in the ladies' magazines of the era, prohibited strenuous exercise and probably made even walking difficult. The high heels and long, full, flowing skirts, heavily trimmed with flouncing and fringes, obviously prevented the exhibitor of these garments from all forms of labor. Hoops and stays, tight corsets, and weighty crinolines further restricted activity. The custom of carrying fans, gloves, and purses indicated that the woman's hands did not have to be free for utilitarian purposes. Indeed, the entire costume, properly exhibited in slow strolls down Broadway, proclaimed the idleness of woman's existence and the achievements of her husband.

The exhibition of wealth and leisure gave man a feeling of accomplishment by providing a tangible expression of his successful struggles with a precarious economy. Sensing that his inner feelings of worth related directly to his accumulation of wealth and ability to bestow luxuries upon his family, the urban male became consumed by the desire to make money. "The great object" of New Yorkers, complained a visiting southerner, was "the *penny;* upon *it* turns every action of their lives as well as motive of their natures." Adam de Gurowski, a Polish revolutionary, observed the fevered race to start the day's business activities: "Even if Sebastopol had been in their way, those men would have run over it at one rush."[6]

Predictably, the emphasis upon observable wealth intensified competition for better jobs and higher salaries. Vying with one another for more lucrative positions, men of different classes jealously guarded their occupations from unwelcome rivals. Unlike colonial towns where the scarcity of workers encouraged entry into the labor market, in the industrializing cities swarms of able men hunted for employment. Anxious over the transformation in their own situation brought on by the change to factory production, men became increasingly hostile to female contenders for jobs.

Discrimination against training and employing females affected all occupations and levels of society. Even desperately impoverished women, compelled to take the lowest-paying jobs, found themselves the objects of bitter resentment. As early as 1820 an "Emigrant's Directory" advised tailors not to come to New York because in that city their trade had been "much injured by the employment of women . . . who work from 25 to 50 percent cheaper than men."[7]

Union policies also proved vehemently opposed to the employment of women. Any attempt to give work to women evoked vigorous protest among union members in the eastern cities. Working wives and daughters encroached upon man's prerogative, complained a writer in the *Boston Courier* of 25 August 1831. And a New York man, urging low salaries for women, wrote an article describing a town where women received good pay: "[The] town was filled with the most lazy, drunken, worthless set of men I ever saw."[8]

The opposition to feminine participation in the labor force emanated from the intermingling demands of status, security, and often subsistence. By effectively relegating women to the lowest echelon of available jobs, urban men could devote all their time and energy to the struggle for higher income with its enticing promises. But the glittering appeal of prosperity proved to be only fool's gold. "The young, the ardent, the keen, and the gifted [who] rushed into [the] great marts" soon discovered that despite all their efforts and hopes only "a few can do it. . . . [A]n amazing proportion fall in the race!"[9]

Conspicuous wealth and leisure may have satisfied the cravings of some for a readily observable set of standards, but they could not palliate the uneasiness of most men who longed for a sense of identity and security more substantial than filigreed fans or silk gowns. Indeed, the all-consuming quest for money tended to intensify frustration and anxiety. Absorption with business meant more time away from home and, therefore, less direct authority over one's family. A fluctuating economy rendered man impotent to control his financial position and often caused humiliation before relatives and friends. And the constant battle for jobs and success kept him alienated from his neighbors and increasingly isolated from his fellow countrymen, who distrusted his motives and disapproved of his actions.

Urban males faced a complex dilemma. Both anticipating and exaggerating the plight of other Americans, they were forced to reconcile the impulses of stability and security, intimately associated with an illusory agrarian past, with the compelling imperatives of the present. The pastoral ideal, too deeply embedded in the nation's imagination and folklore to be obliterated, had to be adapted to accommodate an increasingly industrial and urban society.

Characterizations of Americans as "a people of cultivators, scattered over an immense territory" and boasts that "we are all animated with the spirit of an industry which is unfettered and unrestrained because each person works for himself" had little relevance to life in the nation's cities and could provide no relief to its residents. Authors warned of urban "disorganization." They depicted "a military despotism, into whose arms all will be driven by the intolerable evils of anarchy and rapine," which surely would occur "when millions shall be crowded into our manufactories and commercial cities." Each admonition emphasized the need for a body of literature that could assimilate the comforting qualities of pastoral imagery into the urban milieu.[10]

During the 1820s and 1830s, gift books, periodicals, and novels exhibited a special form of writing, expressive of an attempt to harmonize the agricultural tradition with the urban experience. Avoiding tales of peaceful village life with its traditional churches, orderly schoolrooms, and virtuous farmers, a new agrarianism, an *urban-agrarianism,* developed. It focused exclusively on descriptions of the home and its immediate environs. Invariably nested snugly amidst "a fine range of green, softly swelling hills," overlooking a "lovely valley through which a stream was gliding," the simple cottage home presented its quaint charms to urban readers. Poems, stories, and pictures entitled "Home," "Coming Home," "My Father's Home," "We Ne'er Forget Our Childhood Home" dotted the pages of antebellum literature. They reminded readers of "the flowery haunts we used to tread" and of the days spent "chasing the painted butterfly" or roaming "around [the] mountain-cinctured home," plucking "the sweetest flowers."[11]

Repeated images of the "cottage-home," where "nature's hand had spread her choicest gifts around," conveyed the blissful serenity of youth. In "The Cottage Girl's Return Home," the author recalled: "I loved its shrubbery, and its vines—I loved its murmuring brooks, I loved its groves and its forest pines." The poem "Home of Youth," appearing in the *Ladies' Magazine* of 1829, reminisced about "the clear rippling brook with curls so white" which "went laughing on in sunniest light." One poet confessed:

My heart is in my childhood's home,
And by the far-off sunny brae,
Where musing once I loved to roam,
In early youth's romantic days.

The American Literary Emporium memorialized the "home in the beautiful country, amid tree-crested hills, where the streams, gushing from their mountain sources, leaped and danced." "Nor shall I ever forget," vowed another contributor to the *Literary Emporium,* "the happy days that followed while I made my home there."[12]

Nostalgic visions of home, clothed in rural imagery, served a significant function for urban Americans. The "happy homes of the deep valley . . . the symbols of youth and a happy liberty," encapsulated the precious qualities of an earlier time. These images became the literary device through which Americans made the transition from an exalted bygone age to a tumultuous present. The panegyrizing of childhood homes in poems and stories simultaneously represented an individual's longing for youth and a people's yearning for the glorious days of America's infancy. Yet, implicit in this urban-agrarianism, which returned to "My Father's Home" and to the "Home of My Youth," was the realization that adulthood had come. The mature man would never be a child again and the nation could not regress to its original state.[13]

Youth could not be relived. Yet by visiting one's place of birth, by savoring and paying homage to early beliefs, it became possible to exist in the present without losing yesterday's ideals. The past receded from them, but city dwellers managed in subtle and complex ways to preserve the qualities they valued most. By perceiving the home as the embodiment of all the worthy characteristics of a former era, they could leave the agricultural society behind, assured that stability and security would have a domicile in urban America.

The endowment of home with transcendent attributes was part of an intricate web of ideas which enveloped American women. It reflected the yearning for order in a chaotic society and enabled accommodation to the present without completely relinquishing the past. The apotheosis of the household acknowledged that Americans, no longer idealized yeomen farmers, endured the perplexities of city life. The exemplary home was a paradigm of serenity and harmony, a dramatic contrast to its tempestuous surroundings. Envisioning their dwelling as a refuge from a bruising world, urban men insisted that home be an enclave securely sheltered from strife and asperity. The nineteenth-century home called forth gushing praise and provided an important antipode to the urban environment.

"Let us have a place of quiet, . . . which the din of our public war never embroils," begged Horace Bushnell. The abodes of men should be "a realm into which the poor . . . fighters, with their passions galled, and their minds scarred with wrong—their hates, disappointments, grudges, and hard-worn ambitions—may come in, to be quieted and civilized." "It is this that gives repose to the anxieties of the statesman and soothes his troubled breast amid the bustles and turmoil of political strife," wrote William B. Taylor in his essay, "Home." And Donald Grant Mitchell, in *Reveries of a Bachelor,* told men that at home "your errors will meet ever with gentlest forgiveness; . . . there your troubles will be smiled away."[14]

This inordinate craving for home dictated the specific sublime qualities required to heal man's lacerated feelings. To enable him "to recover his equanimity and composure, home must be a place of repose, of peace, [and] of comfort." Seeking an antidote to the confusion of "our streets and caucuses and courts," men urged that their domestic shrines be models of tranquility. Timothy Shay Arthur, author and social critic, described his visit to an ideal home: "Everything was conducted with the utmost regularity. I was never sensible of any little inconveniences. All was system and perfect order."[15]

A paragon of harmony, organization, and quietude, the stereotyped home eased the psychological transition from an exalted agrarian society to a nation of industrial and urban growth. Yet, the vision of home, inspiring adulatory sentiments, did not conjure up images of bricks and logs. When Jacksonian Americans were asked, "What gives light and life to that home; what binds us by an indissoluble, sacred tie to that altar; what calls forth the full, warm gush of grateful affection; what imparts existence, name, worth to those domestic virtues?" they answered resoundingly, "Woman!"[16]

Emphasis upon woman's essential domesticity completed the transfer of the pastoral legend to the urban environment. The insistence that woman's sphere be limited to the home became a prevailing dogma of nineteenth-century faith. "To render *home* happy is woman's peculiar province, home is *her world,*" claimed a contributor to the *Ladies' Magazine* in 1830. James Fenimore Cooper wrote in *The Crater:* "It is seldom that [woman's] wishes cross the limits of the domestic circle which to her is earth itself." "Mother! Home! Heaven!" formed a "sacred trio of words linked together in the heart's vocabulary," according to Rev. J. W. Jackson. And Dr. Charles Meigs told a class of medical students that "the household altar is [woman's] place of service."[17]

The era abounded with assertions that in "every domestic circle woman is the centre," responsible for "the good government of families which leads to the . . . welfare of State." Constant declarations that the "strength of the country is found . . . in the quiet influence of the fireside" added a new dimension to the symbolic importance of the sex. Women became identified as the special guardians, not only of the home, but of democracy itself. Her unique role also made her arbiter of all morality. Rev. J. F. Stearns, speaking before the First Presbyterian Church in Newburyport on 30 July 1837, told women: "Yours it is to decide . . . whether we shall be a nation of refined and high minded Christians, or whether . . . we shall become a fierce race of semi-barbarians before whom neither order, nor honor . . . can stand."[18]

Similarly, children's schoolbooks emphasized woman's special role. "It is in the inculcation of high pure morals . . . that in a free republic woman performs her sacred duty and fulfills her destiny," wrote G. S. Hillard in *A First Class Reader. The Literary Reader for Academies and High Schools* carried an analogous message:

> Her effect
> Lies not in voting, warring, clerical
> oil
> But germinating grace, forth-putting
> virtue.[19]

Woman replaced nature as the sole repository of goodness and ethicality. Absolving males from guilt that their unbridled pursuit of wealth might be injurious to the fabric of the nation, she emerged as a substitute for the allegedly democratic proclivities of yeoman farmers. In her domestic role, idealized and fantasized, woman embodied all the attributes of bountiful nature. Untainted by the corrupt world, she soothed, purified, and nurtured. In a home atmosphere as serene as the rural landscape, woman became the succedaneum for "Mother Earth" as the nourisher of her family. Woman's sensitivity to the natural order enabled her to "discern that there can be no happiness . . . where there is a perpetual struggle for power." "No . . . force" existed strong enough "to . . . foster woman into an independent and rival power, man's jealous competitor." Shielding her home from strife, she shunned all competition with her husband. Woman's domain emulated the peaceful garden idyllically free from vying for power, money, and position that characterized American cities.[20]

The literary and psychological substitution of images and perceptions of woman for the sustenance of nature gave impetus to the argument that women remain at home. But the demand that "she must be a 'keeper at home,' " the decree that "she must be a 'mother at home,' " and the commandment that "her feet must abide within her own dwelling" also reflected other deeply rooted tensions of the era. Remanding the female's intellectual, emotional, and physical life to the limits of home, men sought to make woman a ballast on their unsteady journey into an urbanized America. In a world of motion, where fortunes, friends, homes, and beliefs changed perpetually, the delineation of a specific sphere of feminine activity provided a sense of comfort and a modicum of stability. As the imperatives of urbanization and industrialization compelled men to spend less time at home, the enjoiner that women stay within the domestic realm performing prescribed functions enabled fathers and husbands to exercise control over their families.[21]

Blithely overlooking the thousands of women forced to work for a livelihood, men frequently declared that "home is to her—a place of habitation, . . . [she] has no call to forsake it." Statements that woman is "encumbered with no avocations or business which force her away from [home]" satisfied the requirements of an emerging capitalist society. They enhanced man's image as an effective provider while assuring the longevity of the patriarchal family. Moreover, the consignment of woman to the domestic province, emanating also from the fear of economic competition, effectively restricted entry into the labor force of all but the most destitute females.[22]

The insistence that home comprise the essence of feminine existence at once obfuscated woman's history and distorted her present. It was reinforced by literature defining appropriate masculine and feminine behavior. Relentless recitation of social roles, always emphasizing the differences between proper actions for males and females, represented part of the quest for security and identity. Tocqueville believed that "[in] no country has such constant care been taken as in America to trace two clearly distinct lines of action for the two sexes."[23]

During the Jacksonian period the magazines, novels, and gift books describing the divergent spheres of man and woman proliferated. "Man profits by connection with the world; but woman never," claimed an article in the literary annual *Forget-me-not.* William B. Taylor, writing for the *Ladies' Garland* of 1839, believed that the "active scenes in which the attention of man is . . . engaged are unsuited to [woman's] gentle character" and that "her natural delicacy will shrink from the rude contact of such boisterous occupations."[24]

Totally unlike "the delicate and tender form of woman," man was made for "the rougher and more exacting labor . . . of mechanism, and of commerce," claimed the author of *The True Woman.* Man "may appear upon the stage of public and professional life. . . . But woman, timid, shrinking, retiring woman was formed for kindlier labor, where delicate sentiment . . . can soften the asperities of life."[25]

Rev. Hubbard Winslow of the Bowdoin Street Church of Boston told his parish: "The more severe manual labors, the toils of the field, the mechanics, the cares and burdens of mercantile business, the exposures and perils of absence from home, the duties of the learned professions devolve upon man; while the more delicate and retired cares and labors of the household devolve upon woman."[26]

This constant ingemination of sex-linked roles had great significance. Duties and responsibilities, inexorably tied to basic rights, were determined by one's nature. Woman was relegated to the home because the "characteristic endowments of women . . . are not of a commanding and imposing nature such as man may boast of and which enable him to contend with . . . difficulties and danger," wrote a contemporary author. "Her springs are infinitely delicate and differ from those of man," claimed "Sherlock" in the *Forget-me-not*, and the *Ladies' Garland* of 1837 printed the verse:

> Man is a rugged lofty pine
> That frowns on many a wave-beat shore;
> Woman's the slender, graceful vine
> Whose curling tendrils round it twine,
> And deck its rough bark sweetly o'er.[27]

The arguments of nineteenth-century theorists alternated between the decree that women remain at home because of their "feeble," "different and confiding" natures and the declaration that woman had fewer abilities because domestic life required only a small number of skills. Yet whether these writers described woman's limited sphere as cause or effect of her weaker nature, they completely agreed that "there is a natural *difference* in the mental as well as the physical constitution of the two [sexes]." "There is a decided inferiority of intellectual strength in women," wrote one author; others cited specific examples to impress females with their lack of acumen. "The great administrative facilities are not hers. The strength of Milton's poetic vision was far beyond her fine and delicate perceptions," asserted Dr. Charles Meigs, while the author of *Woman in her Social and Domestic Character* (1842) commented that the "female pencil has never yet limned the immortal forms of beauty. The mind of woman is . . . incapable of the originality and strength requisite for the sublime."[28]

The demarcation of the feminine sphere and the delineation of female responsibilities and abilities formed yet another important response to the insecurities of antebellum life. Imputing women with innately inferior qualities strengthened the male's self-esteem. Whether rich or poor, native American or immigrant, he automatically became superior to a large segment of the population whose presence served as a constant reminder of his more excellent attributes.

The repetitive stipulation of proper behavior and duties for women by men fostered the image of females as totally passive, dependent beings whose actions had to be determined by the other sex. Horace Bushnell believed that "[women] have never in any one case shown . . . authority and capacity of rule in themselves." George Templeton Strong admired feminine "talent for obedience and submission to . . . authority," and the leading characters in James Fenimore Cooper's *The Ways of the Hour* endorsed Strong's sentiments: "I declare, John Wilmeter," vowed Anna, "I should almost despise the man who could consent to live with me on any terms but those in which nature, the church and reason unite in telling us he ought to be the superior." "[Woman] was not formed for independence," wrote a contributor to the *Ladies' Magazine*, "but [she is] endowed with those peculiar properties which enable her firmly but steadfastly to adhere to her natural protector."[29]

The recitation of woman's natural submissiveness served a significant function for urban males. Thwarted in efforts to dominate the changing national economic, political, and social scene and overwhelmed in attempts to alleviate urban problems, men became desperate to exercise some measure of control over their existences and environments. They finally found an outlet for these emotions through their domination of women.

Conforming to the imperatives of the era, the prevailing views in antebellum America also decreed that woman's nature, like her sphere, remain rigid. It was impervious to time and circumstance. The *Christian Wreath* likened the "true character of woman" to "the beacon-tower, she is fast-anchored—immovably fixed upon the elements of her nature." "Woman needs fixedness—fixedness both in character and place," proclaimed a speaker before a maternal association in 1846; and Washington Irving in *The Broken Heart* wrote that "woman's is comparatively a fixed, a secluded life."[30]

The static definitions of woman arose from the troubled search for identity in a social context that prevented all but casual attachment to beliefs, institutions, places, and persons. In highly mobile urban America, different classes, particularly the middle and upper segments of society, had "no fixed standard by which to govern their actions, either with regard to themselves or their fellow beings." As Francis Grund observed, they had "no manners, customs, modes of thinking . . . of their own, no community of feelings, nothing which could mark them as a distinct class." For those living in the first few decades of the nineteenth century, the combined effects of political democratization, evangelicalism, urbanization, industrialization, and immigration radically altered the social structure and seemed to make class distinctions meaningless.[31]

In the Jacksonian era a laborer could vote, an uneducated itinerant preacher could save thousands of souls, and the enterprising son of an immigrant could become a wealthy man. Politics, religion, and even the economy seemed determined to prove essential equality within the masculine world. As it became increasingly difficult to claim *natural* differences among men, the male sense of personal identity crumbled. Men reached out for inner direction and self-awareness, which they ultimately realized through the creation of complicated theories about women. Confused and unsure of themselves, men found a foil for their own ambiguous identities through the specific and stagnant qualities they ascribed to women. The definitions of woman provided males with a fixed standard by which to evaluate their own behavior and attributes. Women in the antebellum era formed the negative imprint of the desirable male self-portrait. Men may not have known who they were or what characteristics they had, but by insisting that woman possessed all the weak and inferior traits, they at least knew what they were not.

Woman's nature, then, perceived as the opposite of man's, gave clear expression to the elusive male identity. Moreover, the alleged and exaggerated differences between the sexes substituted for the absence of rigid class distinctions in the first part of the nineteenth century. Because masculine security depended so heavily on the distance man set between himself and woman, every effort had to be made to indicate vast differences in the natures of the two sexes. Any area of similarity, any small degree of likeness in feeling, interest, or aptitude might be used to prove that men and women should have the same responsibilities, should enjoy the same activities, and did, indeed, possess the same qualities. Thus there developed an elaborate philosophy of womanhood that insisted upon woman's total dissimilarity to man. It defined her entirely through her feminine gender and dictated that the rights, duties, and responsibilities of woman were totally a function of her sex.

The ideas and attitudes about women merged into a rigid theory. This pattern of thought, propounded with relentless vigor, ineluctably molded custom and practice, as its scrutinizing, judgmental, and instructive tenets came to be widely accepted. For these views of feminine nature—perhaps more than any political ideology, religious creed, or interpretation of the nation's future—gave antebellum Americans searching for coherence and unifying values a systematic set of beliefs to share.

4
The Woman-Belle Ideal

Stone walls do not a prison make,
  Nor iron bars a cage;
Minds innocent and quiet take
  That for an heritage;

—Robert Lovelace,
To Althea from Prison

An intricate chain of myths imprisoned the nineteenth-century American woman, defining the boundaries of her existence and imparting content to her life. The implacable presentation of these views etched a static, monolithic image of womanhood deep into the nation's mind. Based upon insecurity, prejudice, and ignorance, writings on feminine nature flooded antebellum America. This torrent of polemical literature sought to give justification for the relegation of woman to the domestic sphere, substance to the doctrines of feminine weakness, inferiority, and submission, and support to the theory that males and females possessed totally different natures.

Those wishing to provide theological evidence for woman's subservient position frequently quoted from the Bible. Rev. J. F. Stearns devoted a substantial portion of his discourse in Newburyport to reminding women that the first Epistle to the Corinthians admonished them to "keep silence in the Churches. . . . If they will learn anything, let them ask their husbands at home; for it is a shame for women to speak in the churches." Stearns further noted that the Epistle to Titus advised teaching "young women to be sober, to love their husbands, to love their children, to be discreet, chaste, keepers at home, [and to be] good and obedient to their own husbands."[1]

The seemingly irrefutable scriptural arguments used with growing frequency and force in the antebellum period harmonized with the teachings of science. Dr. Chandler Gilman, in an introductory address to the medical students of the College of Physicians and Surgeons in 1840, taught that women had "an inferiority of the locomotive apparatus." The doctor carefully detailed the physiological roots of feminine character: "The great nervous center, the brain, is both absolutely and relatively smaller in woman than in man. But the nerves . . . pervade her structure to a much greater extent, and bear a much larger proportion to the rest of her body than they do that of man." This uniquely female nervous system "gives to every part a susceptibility so acute, that . . . the sensations excited . . . are always of the most vehement character; and these being less under the control of the brain, woman becomes from the very necessity of her nature, a creature rather . . . of passion than of reason."[2]

Emboldened by the prestigious support of religion and science, an assorted array of writers and theorists diffused the vitiated image of woman throughout the nation. George Burnap, articulating the "sphere" and "duties" of woman, believed that a "state of high intellectual culture and social refinement [was] unfavorable to physical health." An address before the Pittsford Young Ladies' Institute carried the message that "the impulses of woman are constitutionally quicker and her feelings more intense than those of man." And Charles Butler, in *The American Lady,* explained that woman's "gay vivacity, and the quickness of imagination, . . . have a tendency to lead to unsteadiness of mind . . . to trifling employment . . . [and] to repugnance to grave studies."[3]

"Women are by nature weak and defenseless," declared the author of a Boston schoolbook, as fragility came to epitomize females. Another children's textbook told of an aunt complaining to her niece's teacher that the child had once been "pale and delicate" but now, unhappily, was in "a rude state of health." Girls needed to be taught at an early age that their dainty bodies could not tolerate the rigorous activity of their brothers' world. The story of "Miss Sophie," included in the 1837 edition of *Rhymes for the Nursery,* told of Sophie's fate when she "tried to climb and scramble o'er a gate as high as any door":

Now little girls should never climb,
And Sophie won't another time
For when upon the highest rail
Her frock was caught upon a nail,
She lost her hold, and sad to tell,
Was hurt and bruis'd—for down she fell.[4]

The frail female form, praised and desired, had to be constantly guarded, for the pale and wan heroines of the antebellum era seemed to be perpetually "drifting off" or "fainting away." In "The Return," a short story by George Gordon, "the lovely Cordelia . . . pined away" because her "frame was too fragile to endure [a] long separation" from her lover; while a song commemorating the demise of a precious young lady lamented: "Like a rose we saw thee wither, Poor Mary-Anne!" In Lewis J. Cist's tearful tune, "Death of the Beautiful," which appeared in *Godey's Lady's Book,* a "fair and fragile" woman "faded, drooped and passed away." Melodies of the period abounded with descriptions of "meek" and "gentle" women, "half of earth—the rest of Heaven." These ethereal beings, celebrated in song and prose, had to avoid all energetic movement. Mr. Lee, in T. S. Arthur's *Maiden,* warns his wife: "Even the slight exertion of pouring out tea may disturb your nervous system."[5]

With minds too weak for serious scholarship, with bodies too delicate for strenuous endeavor, and with emotions too brittle to cope with reality, nineteenth-century American women seemed to require constant assistance from men. One of Francis Grund's associates noted: "London Women of the middle and even higher classes can walk alone, stand alone, and when taking tea or coffee do not require a gentleman to hold the saucer for them." But in the United States the "ladies must be helped . . . the ladies must be put into the carriage . . . the ladies must have their shoe strings tied . . . on every occasion they are treated as poor helpless creatures." The flower-like creations who languished through the pages of antebellum literature enhanced the male self-image; weakness in women bolstered men's feelings of strength. Horace Bushnell astutely commented: "The man will be manlier, that he has a true womanly wife [because] the power we . . . get on our masculine character is not so much from what women do to us, as from what we do to them." Man's security depended heavily on the conception of woman as fair and feeble: "Destroy [womanhood's] claim to concession and protection and courtesy . . . and manhood is gone too," warned George Templeton Strong.[6]

The prevailing image of woman as delicate and irrational provided a further reason to keep her tucked away in the domestic sphere, far from the harsh world of politics and business. But if feminine nature dictated that woman shun the outside world, theorists assured her: "Your influence is not less because it is obscure. . . . The broad river takes its waters from the little rills that supply it." "No! by no means," exclaimed the author of *The World Enlightened, Improved and Harmonized by Woman,* "the influence of the female character is not confined to their homes; it is felt through society; felt where they are never seen." Woman's impact on society supposedly flowed from the instruction she gave to her children. Rev. Winslow asserted that "upon woman depends the destiny of the nation! for she is rearing up senators and statesmen." Though secluded, dependent, and emotional, woman received the persistent guarantee that she, nonetheless, played an important role in society by remaining within the confines of her dwelling.[7]

Charged with the responsibility of making her household "the scene of all pure and holy thoughts, the first discoverable source of . . . the happiness of religion," woman had to be pure and pious in every aspect of her life. Nineteenth-century authors agreed that "there is no gem which so much adorns the female character, and which adds so brilliant a lustre to her charm, as unaffected and deep-toned piety." And their writings illuminated different aspects of woman's relationship to religion. Some emphasized an inherent inclination for holiness. "The female is naturally prone to be religious. Hers is a pious mind," wrote Dr. Charles Meigs. Rev. Stearns thought that "religion seem[ed] almost to have been entrusted by its author to her particular custody." Other authors stressed the compensatory quality in woman's devoutness. "Females need the comforts . . . of religion, more . . . than the other sex. Subjected to the . . . weakness of a feeble constitution, their state, when raised by improvement, and propped with Christian consolations, is still a state of . . . pain," believed a contributor to the *Ladies' Literary Cabinet.* And another writer stressed: "She needs solace and occupation, and religion affords her both."[8]

Not only to assuage grief did woman need religion, but her role as the "arbitress of taste and of manners" demanded the cleansing influence of her personal piety. "It is her province to *adorn* social life, to throw a *charm* over the intercourse of the world," declared Rev. Stearns, and his colleague Rev. Spring agreed: "Public taste and manners, public virtues and vices are under the control of woman." Writing for the *Ladies' Garland* in 1837, the latter stated that only "pious mothers" could raise children of a "moral and religious character" who would develop into virtuous citizens capable of governing the nation.[9]

By their insistence upon feminine piety, writers wove another thread in the web of myths which entangled women. Religiosity, like delicacy, submission, and intellectual inferiority, came to be associated with female nature and provided males with a clearer image from which to distinguish themselves. Pious feelings and behavior, though, could not suffice to make woman an "image of love and truth." Above all else the antebellum female had to be *pure.* Women were perpetually assailed by directives instructing them on the importance of untainted thought and conduct. Schoolchildren learned that women's only strength lay "in their modest charms and chaste deportment," for the female sex had "no shield but unsullied purity." The heroine of a popular song, "Charming Nancy," had many worthy qualities—"Her beauty delights me, her kindness invites me"—but most important of all: "Her pleasant behavior is free from all stain." Literary and artistic alembics permeated nineteenth-century society. They monitored women by dictating inflexible tenets of behavior.[10]

"Frequent not the busy parts of the city, nor sit in the high places of the theatre," warned a book on feminine decorum, which also cautioned women to "move not thy foot too often to the sprightly sound of music, lest thy reputation should also dance away." Thomas Branagan cautioned that "the fashionable female, who exposes publicly what prudence should conceal, not only entices the male of ardent passions to perpetuate, but also commits the crime of sentimental fornication herself." Because the Jacksonians believed "a passionate woman is a disgrace to her sex," all phases of feminine life had to be regulated and moderated. John Pintard thought that although men did not have to be too concerned with their speech, "a Female's conversation should be the index of her mind, pure, chaste and unaffected." Conforming to the directives on modest speech, American women even refrained from saying the word "leg." Captain Marryat noted that females referred to the "limb" of a table rather than risk being thought indelicate.[11]

There could be no halfway point between purity and pollution for nineteenth-century American women. "Chastity alone" would make a woman "honoured of God . . . happy in [herself] . . . [and] lovely in the view of the world"; without it "the consequences are vain remorse, and certain misery." At the commencement address of Columbia College in 1837, Nathaniel W. Chittenden asserted that "woman's influence is either of the most exalted or of the most debasing tendency. For, in the female character there is no mid-region; it must exist in spotless innocence, or else in hopeless vice."[12]

Numerous paintings illustrated the dire fate awaiting the

misguided or defiant woman who challenged the precepts of seraphic behavior. In Richard Redgrave's picture *The Outcast,* an unyielding father turns his daughter out into the cold, dark night. A letter crumbled on the floor apparently has exposed the illegitimacy of the babe whom the defiled young woman clasps to her breast. The pleas of a younger sister and the anguish of a brother cannot deter the strict parent in his determination to banish the offending member of the family.[13]

Augustus Egg's *Past and Present, Number 1,* also depicts the misery caused by a woman's fall from morality. As in *The Outcast,* a letter has revealed the female's sinful actions. Her husband sits with the note clutched in his hand, so stunned by the odious revelation that he simply gazes into space. The wife, ashamed and remorseful

Plate I. "The Outcast," by Richard Redgrave. The Royal Academy of Arts, London.

Plate II. "Past and Present," by Augustus Egg. The Tate Gallery, London.

beyond words, lies prostrate at his feet, her hands clasped in supplication. The ensuing breakup of the family is symbolically represented by a worm in the half-eaten apple on the table and by the collapse of the house of cards that the children were constructing at the time of their mother's exposure.[14]

Found by Dante Gabriel Rossetti could well have been sketched as the logical sequel to the paintings described above, for it portrays the eventual destiny of many women who took one step outside the path of virtue. Once blemished, no matter what her previous position in life, a woman could never again be accepted by decent society. She generally had no choice but to support herself by prostitu-

Plate III. "Found," by Dante Gabriel Rossetti. The Samuel and Mary R. Bancroft Collection, The Delaware Art Museum, Wilmington, Delaware.

tion. In *Found* a young man on his way to market with a calf meets his former lover slumped against a brick wall. As he tries to raise her up, she pulls away from him, turning her face toward the hard brick, demonstrating the depth of her shame. The woman's clothing—the gaudy silks and feathers of a harlot—forms a dramatic contrast to the simple, practical garments of her onetime beloved.

The tension in their hands underlines the incompatibility of their two ways of life. So absorbed is the youth with this woman that he leaves his calf unattended. But there is nothing to fear: the young white animal, a symbol of innocence, has been carefully bound by a web-like rope and cannot stray from his master. The artist seems to be communicating the prevalent belief that female virtue could be preserved only if a woman's activities, thoughts, and behavior were strictly confined.[15]

The decree that women be chaste intensified the image of a passive, porcelain being whose immaculate delicacy made her willing to submit to the superior wisdom of her worldly, knowledgeable husband or father. Furthermore, a man who could count among his "properties" a modest and unseducible wife would surely consider himself the superior to one without such a possession. The cult of purity denied that women had natural sex drives. Dr. William Acton, author of *The Functions and Disorders of the Reproductive Organs,* one of the most widely quoted books on sexuality in the English-speaking world during the mid-nineteenth century, wrote: "The majority of women (happily for them) are not very much troubled with sexual feelings of any kind. What men are habitually, women are only exceptionally." Lurid tales or passionate encounters with profligate men could, of course, arouse some sexual yearning. This desire, however, created social misfits who threatened the harmony of society, for Acton shared the dominant view that "the best mothers, wives and managers of households know little or nothing of sexual indulgence. Love of home, children and domestic duties are the only passions they feel."[16]

Deliberate refutations of ardent feminine sexual feelings had significant implications. Passion connoted an intensity of feeling that defied control and jeopardized social tranquility. By refusing to recognize that any except the most debased female could have sexual desires, antebellum males made certain that their women remained at home, malleable and immobile. Moreover, although doctors, clergymen, artists, and theorists obdurately insisted upon a single norm of behavior, thought, and feeling for all women, men enjoyed a wide range of freedom in their social and sexual conduct.

Americans believed that a "man may tarnish his name and brighten it again," but woman, once fallen, could never be reclaimed. The espousal of a double standard gave further support to the assumption that men and women possessed completely different natures. As the era increasingly defined females totally through gender, a new image emerged. Abilities, actions, conduct, and worth—all became functions of an undivided particular female nature that either adhered to the tight pattern of perfection or forfeited the name of "Woman."[17]

Pious and pure, fragile and weak, submissive and domestic, passive and unintellectual, this imaginary woman was a composite of myths that fettered energy and activity. She comprised the nineteenth-century conception of the quintessential female: the *woman-belle ideal.* Careful to exhibit all the requisite qualities, this paragon of excellence had to relinquish willingly her own comforts and interests for the pleasures of others. "A pure true heart, a self-forgetful spirit . . . a wish and an effort to please," and a readiness to minister "to the wants of others" characterized the image of feminine faultlessness. For the ethos of the woman-belle ideal expected women to "lay aside all considerations of themselves" and to make their "joys . . . the results of the gratification of others."[18]

Tocqueville observed that Americans "require much abnegation on the part of woman and a constant sacrifice of her pleasures to her duties, when it is seldom demanded of her in Europe." "If you would live happy—endeavor to promote the happiness of others," preached the *Ladies' Companion* in 1836. The following year Washington Irving wrote an essay, "The Wife," for the *Ladies' Garland* containing this advice: "Woman, who is the mere dependent and ornament of man in his happier hours, should be his stay and solace when smitten with sudden calamity." In "Confessions of a Platonic Lover," T. S. Arthur asserted that the perfect woman was "always ready to concede her own pain lest others should suffer."[19]

Throughout this period, women received rigorous instruction in self-renunciation. In the story "Bear and Forbear," Margaret asks her Aunt Hannah, "Would you have a wife never think of herself?" The older woman replies that "the less she thinks of herself . . . the better." "Man lives for himself," proclaimed an essay in *Christian Wreath*, but "woman lives . . . for all. . . . She cannot be said to live—even for herself. She is forgotten in the unfoldings of her duty." And *The American Instructor*, a schoolbook, taught little girls that their sole aim in life should be "to recompense [man's] care with soft endearments."[20]

In addition to the selfless, "beautiful devotion" and the "angelic ministration" demanded of her, the female striving to fulfill the requirements of the woman-belle ideal also learned that "it is the part of woman to adapt herself to her husband" and to "endeavor to assimilate all . . . views and customs to [his]." Primary school texts preached that "girls should be taught to give up their opinions betimes, and not pertinaciously to carry on a dispute, even should they know themselves to be in the right."[21]

Thus, throughout their lives, nineteenth-century women received an education that denied them any worth as autonomous beings. They were deprived a sense of personal identity by a creed that perpetually admonished them to sacrifice all independent activities and interests for the happiness of others. Consistently urged to blend separate opinions and ideas into those of the "superior sex," the female became a mere appendage of her male relations. Feminine individuality dissolved within the monolithic ethos of the woman-belle ideal. The word "woman," which during the eighteenth century commanded respect and evoked a serious and important philosophical discussion, practically disappeared. In its place the fragmenting, identity-negating terms "wife," "mother," "sister," and "daughter" furnished the dominant modes of reference to members of the female sex. These terms cast women into set molds and gave clear expression to the antebellum era's conception of feminine value and place in society.

Each of the rigid roles stipulated for woman dictated specific behavior. A contemporary author wrote that "a good daughter is the steady light of her parent's house. She is the pride and ornament of his hospitality, and the gentle nurse of his sickness." "Misconduct of daughters is . . . fatal to family peace," warned Noah Webster in his reader. And *The New Pleasing Instructure: Or, Young Lady's Guide to Virtue and Happiness* taught the schoolgirl that even ill-treatment by her father "by no means releases [her] from . . . duty to him." A popular song dramatically illustrated the importance of daughters' yielding to paternal wishes. When Dinah's father wants her to marry, she replies,

> Oh papa, oh papa, I've not made up my mind
> And to marry just yet, why I don't feel inclined.

But Dinah pays for her disobedience and ultimately poisons herself. The sorrowful ballad concludes with the moral:

> Now all you young maidens take warning by her,
> Never not by no means disobey your governor.[22]

Rev. Spring considered a submissive sister equally as important as an obedient daughter and William Henry Fry lyrically extolled sisterly affection:

> No love is like a sister's love, unselfish,
> free and pure;
> A flame that lighted from above,
> May guide but ne'er allure.

Charles Butler, in *The American Lady,* declared that the "most amiable tendencies and affections implanted in human nature" could be found in "the sister."[23]

After vigorous training in discipline, devotion, and self-denial as sisters and daughters, the young woman could enter "the sphere . . . which she is so exactly fitted to adorn and bless as the wife." Charles Burdett, author of *Blonde and Brunette,* thought that "woman is made for love, conjugal and maternal, and when the powerful sentiment which seeks this necessary completion of the end for which she was created has . . . been awakened . . . [h]usbands and children . . . become necessary to her moral organization." The *Ladies' Companion* praised "The Wife" as "we behold her in her domestic scenes, a mere passive creature of enjoyment . . . brightening the family circle with her endearments and prized for the extreme joy which that presence and those endearments are calculated to impart." But the "Christian Home," "that appointed shrine for woman . . . [where] she ministers daily in the holy works of household peace," needed more than a husband and wife. It required children. The "model of womanhood in its ideal excellence" could be achieved only if woman "was wife and mother both."[24]

"Oh, that sweet word Mother!" effused Dr. Chandler Gilman. "Is there a heart in any bosom . . . that does not throb thick and fast at the sound?" he asked rhetorically. "Maternal affection is inherent in the nature of women, it is planted within them," wrote one young man in the *Ladies' Literary Cabinet,* while another observed that the "mother has . . . from the constitution of her sex . . . gentleness and patience." Increasingly alluded to by her familial relations, the female was constantly instructed in the importance of being able "to excel . . . in a thorough and practical acquaintance with the arts and duties of domestic life." Woman thus became indistinguishable from "wife," "mother," "sister," "daughter"; and feminine domesticity emerged as the leitmotif of the womanhood myths.[25]

Simultaneously glorifying matrimony and denigrating singleness with ridicule, nineteenth-century authors urged women into a domestic life shaped by the complex needs of the age. T. S. Arthur thought that women should wed because "marriage is an orderly state" and the happiness of society depended upon "order." Other writers emphasized the assistance woman could give her husband "by relieving him of every care which she is capable of taking upon herself." The wife had to be ready to stay "beside his couch in the hour of sickness, enduring fatigue with uncomplaining patience." A painting by George Elgar Hicks, *Woman's Mission: Companion of Manhood,* shows the devoted, submissive wife giving solace to her grief-stricken husband. The black-bordered letter reveals that he has just learned of the death of a relative. With her loving, upturned face exuding tender compassion, the gentle wife clings to her spouse, trying to comfort him. But the husband, though deeply saddened, stands firm and erect. Even in sorrow he remains the strong tree; she, the clinging vine.[26]

Perpetually bombarded with the importance of wedlock, females learned with Florence, the heroine of T. S. Arthur's *Maiden,* "to think of marriage . . . justly; to esteem it the most important act of a woman's life, and as involving the most important results." Different facets of culture coalesced to force women into matrimony: the only avenue to personal fulfillment. Samuel Woodworth's comic opera *The Deed of Gift,* first performed at the Boston Theater on 22 March 1822, contained the following verse:

> Men may boast the bliss
> Of a *free* election,
> Women ask but this,
> Uncontrolled affection.
> Then we cheerly say
> Tutored by the pastor
> Honour, love, obey,
> To our lord and master.

Ladies' magazines became medleys of verses and refrains, serenading the bride "in gems and roses beaming." "Bring flowers, fresh flow'rs, for the bride to wear," intoned an air appearing in an 1843 issue of *Godey's,* for blossoms "were born to blush in her shining hair, . . . Her place is now at another's side, Bring flowers for the locks of the fair young bride."[27]

Plate IV. "Woman's Mission: Companion of Manhood," by George Elgar Hicks. The Tate Gallery, London.

The exaltation of marriage and its indispensability to feminine existence received further reinforcement from lyrics and stories that scorned those who remained single. In the tune "The Old Maid's Lament" an unmarried woman expresses remorse at her life. She confides: "When I was young and fair and gay, I passed my cheerful hours away." But now that it is too late for her to wed, she pleads: "O save me from that dismal stand, Where . . . old maids do land." In another melody, "My Grandma's Advice," an elderly relative admonishes her grandchild: "You'd better get married than die an old maid." The grandmother's exhortation seemed wise in a social milieu that mocked the concept of "single blessedness for woman [as] . . . a monstrous falsehood."[28]

Mr. Burton, a character in a short story appearing in the *Ladies' Magazine*, voiced the views of his real-life contemporaries when he declared: "I have an aversion to the whole tribe of antiquated maidens. . . . [I]t seems impossible they can possess the true feminine virtues and graces of character." Charles Burdett agreed that all women, regardless of interest or position, should marry. His *Blonde and Brunette* contains the following passage: "Old maidhood is a wretched, pitiable condition, to which the most unhappy marriage would be vastly preferable, as life, though wretched, is better than *annihilation*."[29]

Antebellum females, hurried into marriage by the dictates of the woman-belle ideal, did not always find the blissful happiness promised them. Tocqueville noted that "[in] America the independence of woman is irrecoverably lost in the bonds of matrimony. [The wife] lives in the home of her husband as if it were a cloister." The musical bachelor of a ballad declared that he "would not wed the purest soul, Unless her heart would bear control," and children studying from Alden's *Reader* found that lesson forty-four contained a quotation from Milton in which Eve tells Adam:

> My partner and protector, what
> thou bidd'st
> Unargued I obey; so God ordains;

God is thy law, thou mine; to
 know no more
Is woman's happiest knowledge, and
 her praise.[30]

The emotional subservience demanded of the wife to her husband dramatically increased as the nation struggled through the tumultuous years from 1820 to 1860. Similarly, the laws defining the position of the married woman, made flexible by the necessities of the colonial period, became rigorously enforced. Legal codes reflected the attempt to find a balm for the troubles of an anxious age in a complicated philosophy of womanhood. The severe execution of the laws concerning married women corresponded perfectly to the submissiveness, delicacy, emotionalism, and ineptitude insisted upon by the ethos of the perfect female.

Married women could not sign contracts; they had no title to their own earnings or to property even when they received it as inheritance or as dower; and they had no claim to their own children in the event of legal separation. The legislatures and courts repeatedly denied women's requests for divorce although the evidence detailed flagrant abuse. Males, however, had considerably more success in dissolving their marital ties, often for far less substantial reasons. The New York State *Assembly Documents* record that even in cases of "willful desertion and abandonment [by the husband] for the term of five years . . . accompanied by an entire neglect of all duties and obligations" women could not secure divorces.[31]

Warned that the status of a single woman equaled extinction, females were propelled into a married state that deprived them of any sense of independent competence or respect. Depicted as "toys," "ornaments," and "embellishments," women could not escape the message of their society: a woman's only worth, her sole importance, indeed her very existence, depended upon her connections to men. Only as daughter, sister, mother, and wife did a woman's life have any meaning or purpose. As an article in the Philadelphia *Public Ledger* made clear, "A woman is nobody. A wife is everything." The author of this journalistic proclamation urged the "ladies of Philadelphia to maintain their rights as wives, belles, virgins, and mothers, and not as women!"[32]

At once enervating her mind and paralyzing her powers, the myths about feminine character may have satisfied America's craving for a common ethos, but they eroded woman's ability to believe in herself as a complete individual. The postulation of one code of acceptable behavior and attitude for the entire sex gave support to the theory that "the peculiar characteristics of females, being less distinctly marked, are much more difficult to be delineated than those of the other sex." Whereas theorists believed that "men may hope to obtain happiness and distinction" by "various pursuits, . . . for women [only] one path" existed. Feminine "success in life depend[ed] entirely on her domestic education." The philosophers of woman's nature confidently predicted that even if "the education of women differs ever so much in *detail,* its *end* is the same, to qualify them to become wives and mothers, [for] in every station the object of female ambition is to marry well. This similarity of purpose produces a similarity of thought, feeling, and action, and consequently character, which no uniformity of training could otherwise bestow, and then the business of married women . . . is essentially alike:"

> To study household good
> And good works in her husband
> to promote.[33]

The single set of responsibilities and duties for all females applied regardless of position. Authors asserted that women do not "exhibit that variety of talent, or those prominent and peculiar qualities of mind, that distinguish men of different professions and dissimilar occupations." The "delicate sex" finds "earthly happiness only by subduing the heart of lordly men," wrote a contributor to the *Ladies' Magazine* in 1828. Another article proclaimed that "a virtuous woman is the same being in all stations, and in all ranks of life, she is called precisely to the same duties. . . . [W]omen have only to learn the common art of being good daughters, sisters, and wives." The reformer Robert Dale Owen described the situation of a woman as a being "of one occupation, one passion, one interest." And Francis Grund observed that "an American gentleman" views "a lady . . . as the representative of her sex; and it is to her sex, not to her peculiar amiable qualities, that she is indebted for his attentions."[34]

The theory that all females had identical obligations and responsibilities, shared the same interests, goals, and desires, and developed like traits and skills fostered a conception of women as interchangeable entities. It denied them the unique personality characteristics and special qualities that distinguish one person from another. Woman's sense of her individual worth evanesced as the nation absorbed this dehumanizing philosophy. An image of the consummate female emerged, insisting upon her inadequacy, domesticity, and abnegation. Refusing to acknowledge distinction or difference, the ethos of the woman-belle ideal spoke in the singular: to the female, never to females; to the mother, not to mothers; and to the wife, rather than to wives. The myths of womanhood strove to demonstrate the oneness of the entire sex, whose duties and privileges never changed because they flowed from an inferior and particular feminine nature. And this flawed being, who lacked individual autonomy, did not qualify to share in the natural rights of humanity.

5

The Butterfly in Amber

> She did nothing. She would stay in bed for hours, or dawdle over her toilette, sitting idly . . . and gradually a dumb misery crept over her like an icy mist. . . . She was neither angel nor brute. She was just a poor bored woman.
>
> —Romain Rolland, *Jean-Christophe*

Theorists obliterated woman's past with a distorted portrayal of her present. The image of a delicate female at home, happily and completely occupied with household and family, did not reflect the lives of a majority of women in Jacksonian America. This disparity between depiction and reality profoundly disturbed those forced to conform to a picture which bore them no resemblance.

The myths of the woman-belle ideal exercised their constricting canons on all women. They stifled the varying needs, aspirations, and activities of the diversified feminine population and, in so doing, denied the existence of many thousands of urban and rural working women. Prejudice against women laborers grossly limited available positions in rural areas. Caroline Dall related the successes of "two girls named Miller [who] carry on a farm of 300 acres, raising hay and grain, hiring labor but working mostly themselves. . . . [L]abor attracts them, as it would many women if they were not oppressed by public opinion." Similarly, few opportunities awaited an impoverished urban woman who could not survive without wages. She might take in washing or sewing, do industrial tasks at home, become a household servant, or work in a factory. Indeed, women and girls "formed from ⅔ to ¾ of the total number of factory workers in the first half of the nineteenth century." Victims of male resentment and of a system that fostered the fiction that a female devoted all her energy to domestic pursuits, women factory operatives, toiling thirteen to fourteen hours a day, received between fifty-four and ninety cents for seven days of grueling labor.[1]

A survey taken in 1831 indicated that "the number of women in Boston, New York, Philadelphia, and Baltimore who were self supporting was from eighteen to twenty thousand." The precepts of the woman-belle ideal, which insisted that females were incapable of all arduous labor, refused to recognize the vast numbers of the sex forced to earn a livelihood and inhibited serious attempts to ameliorate the plight of working women. "It is nothing that they can not get as high wages as men, when they can not do as much, or do it as well," justified Bushnell. "It is nothing that they can not get the wages of rugged . . . employments in such [jobs] as are gentle and delicate."[2]

Nineteenth-century myths of womanhood also failed to reflect accurately the position of middle- and upper-class city women, the *one* segment of society they seemed to describe. The effects of urban and industrial growth combined with the tenets of the woman-belle ideal to produce an anomalous sector of society: the useless lady. The creed of genuine womanhood glorified the home as it importuned woman to devote all of her energy and attention to the domestic sphere. Yet, while these dictates prevented the middle- and upper-class woman from following a profession or even a serious intellectual pursuit, the intricate synthesis of life in the nation's cities virtually denied her a fulfilling or satisfying role in the family.

Urban expansion, surpassing the city's ability to provide adequate public services, also exceeded the capacity of builders to furnish sufficient housing facilities for the surging population. With homes scarce and rents high, residents took apartments in hotels and boardinghouses. The City Hotel, Mechanics Hall, and Washington Hall, the leading hostelries of the period, had keen competition in the Waverly, Mansion House, American, Carlton, Clarendon, and Astor House. Built during the 1830s, these lodges offered luxurious accommodations to those unable or unwilling to find private dwellings. Boardinghouses, also, became increasingly popular; in 1842 Walt Whitman described the "Yankee nation" as "a boarding people." A character in a novel set in antebellum New York thought that "signs denoting boarding houses are almost as thick here as lawyers' shingles are in Philadelphia," for "any city family, even the wealthiest might at some time try this style of living."[3]

These public establishments assumed responsibility for all domestic chores. As Harriet Martineau observed, boardinghouses rendered women "totally idle. . . . On their husbands' departure to the counting-house after breakfast . . . the ladies sit for hours, doing nothing." Francis Grund also noted that New York's upper- and middle-class women did not perform household tasks, for "one-half live[d] in boarding houses, and the other half in houses kept by their servants." The influx of immigrants into the nation's cities provided urban residents with a steady supply of nurses, laundresses, cooks, parlor maids, and butlers. By 1855 nearly one-quarter of all foreign-born persons living in New York City had positions as domestics.[4]

The persistent craving for status in the urban milieu made the number and qualities of one's servants a matter of considerable significance. John Pintard expressed amazement at the "demand for help in this wonderfully progressive city." Advertisements similar to one in the *New York Tribune* of 30 June 1851 soliciting jobs "for about 70 excellent servants" appeared frequently. And, indeed, the entourage of workers washing, polishing, cooking, and cleaning provided the middle and upper classes of New York City with domestic necessities and luxuries.[5]

As they strove to differentiate themselves from the urban masses, as well as from one another, families of some means relinquished household responsibilities to servants and child care to nurses and tutors. Lydia Maria Child, visiting New York City in 1845, complained: "It is not genteel for mothers to wash and dress their own children, or make their clothing, or teach them." A contributor to the *Ladies' Repository* noted the frequency with which mothers entrusted their children to hired help. The short story "Mrs. Chaloner's Visit" described the "nursery [as] . . . the constant abiding place of . . . successive Irish nurses," while Maria McIntosh's novel *Two Lives* commented on the increasing reliance upon wet nurses among women of the wealthier classes. When one woman asked if Grace had become "more domestic" with "motherhood," the other replied: "Why should she, with excellent nurses and attendants of all sorts?" Originally, Grace had been "quite determined to nurse her own baby, but the fancy was so ridiculed by everyone who heard of it that she soon gave it up. Indeed, it would have been quite impossible as she soon found to fulfill the two characters of a lady of fashion and a nursing mother."[6]

Thus removed from domestic duties and inhibited from raising their children, middle- and upper-class urban women became "being[s] formed for no higher purpose than to be decorated." Mrs. A. J. Graves, an author, asked: "Do we not see females in every fashionable circle who fill no loftier station in social life, and who live as idly and as uselessly as the gorgeously attired inmates of the harem?" Barbara Bodichon, a British visitor and author, revealed that in no other country had she "been so much struck by the utter idleness of the lady class. . . . There is in America," she wrote, "a large class of ladies who do absolutely nothing." The groups of females who "throng the city promenades to exhibit their decorated persons or to make morning calls" constantly evoked comment.[7]

"There are hundreds of girls in every large city, who parade in the street in feathers, flowers, silks and laces, whose hands are as white as uselessness can make them," noted one writer. Another described "female characters who spend their time and talents in as useless a manner and with the same superficial appearance as the painted butterfly . . . particularly in [the] cities." The article "Young Ladies at Home" in the *Golden Keepsake* queried its readers: "Who does not see . . . scores and hundreds of young females . . . who are floating along on the current of fashionable life in our cities . . . without one useful end or aim?" While not suggesting any change in feminine activities, Jesse Peck ridiculed the stubborn decree of idleness: "The technical lady is *now* allowed to work provided what she does is perfectly useless! She may embroider, but not make a dress! She may make flowers, but not darn a stocking! She may make music, but not coffee! She may be an exquisite judge of viands on the table, but must carefully avoid the slightest claim to know how they are prepared! She may dismiss her cook, but she must get another or starve!"[8]

Carefully hedged in by custom and public opinion, the typical "New York or Philadelphia ladies [would] rise at eight or nine, breakfast at ten—then . . . potter three or four hours, – then have a chat with three or four women of their set, – then walk on Broadway or Chestnut Street or go shopping, – then sit down to dinner, then potter again until 6 o'clock – then take tea, and finally dress for a party." Few dared to estimate the number of women passing their lives so vacuously, but the *Ladies' Magazine* believed that several hundred thousand "young ladies" were being "brought up to do nothing." With "lives . . . consumed in utter frivolity . . . a little light reading, a little needle-work, a little shopping, visiting, dressing and undressing," women had no choice but to conform to the dictates of status in the urban environment, which declared "gentility . . . in exact proportion to . . . [feminine] uselessness." The formula for attaining an elevated social rank seemed to be that "those [women] only are entitled to the highest place in society, who have nothing to do."[9]

The dreary, monotonous life imposed upon these females rendered them extraneous members of society. It deprived women of making any important contribution to the domestic sphere, the sole area of activity granted as the feminine province by the precepts of the woman-belle ideal. Insecurities, manifesting themselves in ostentatious display of luxurious living complete with servants, nurses, and tutors, prevented those women enjoying a comfortable financial position from managing their households and raising their children. Similarly, economic necessity, compelling perpetual and arduous labor, precluded poor females from devoting attention to home and family.

The prevailing theories deeply affected feminine existence, although they contrasted sharply with the lives of most women during the antebellum era. Yet these myths of feminine nature were woven into the fabric of American thought. They cajoled, coaxed, and actually intimidated women into acceptance of a prescribed position that ultimately frustrated creative potential and thwarted efforts at self-realization. The rigidity of rules governing woman's behavior was obvious even to foreign visitors. Tocqueville observed that an American woman "upon her entrance into the world finds . . . notions firmly established; . . . she is not slow to perceive that she cannot part for an instant from the established usages of her contemporaries without putting in jeopardy her peace of mind, her honor, nay, even her social position." Harriet Martineau noted that the "whole apparatus of opinion is brought to bear offensively upon individuals among women who exercise freedom of mind in deciding upon what duty is, and the methods by which it is to be pursued."[10]

"With the female portion of [the] family there is but little room for fear; for they are so hedged round and guarded by the rules of society that to step over the boundary line is to win shame for life," wrote Dr. Charles Meigs of Philadelphia. Meanwhile his contemporaries were producing a body of literature to bludgeon women into submission by fulminations against unfeminine behavior. "Alas! that women should ever so mistake their natural means to influence and guide . . . with a sacrifice of womanly conduct and womanly grace," wrote James Fenimore Cooper in *The Ways of the Hour*. "The person who would draw the sex from the quiet scenes that they so much embellish to mingle in the strifes of the world, who would place them in a station that nature has obviously intended men should occupy is not their real friend." George Templeton Strong criticized those who "would unsex woman and destroy the Idea of Womanhood on Earth by removing their 'disabilities' and elevating them into a race of disagreeable, effeminate men in petticoats." The diarist thought that "special force of character or intellect are dangerous things in a woman . . . [for] they are apt to make her unhappy, and to be as scourges and scorpions unto that forlorn and woefull catiff, her husband."[11]

With a plentiful stock of pejorative terms in the semantic arsenal, nineteenth-century authors bombarded women with warnings against "unwomanly" and "unnatural" activities. "Let woman throw off her feminine character, and . . . her dignity, her own chief protection is lost," cautioned Rev. Stearns. "Beware then," he admonished his female listeners, "how you forfeit your peculiar advantages, beware how you do anything to diminish that delicate and chivalrous respect." He predicted that women would be the primary victims in a chaotic society that placed both sexes on an equal level. "Be assured ladies," Stearns warned, "if the hedges and borders of the social garden should be broken up, the lovely vine which now twines itself so gracefully upon the trellis, and bears such rich clusters will be the first to fall and be trodden under foot." "Women never aim so suicidal a blow against their own interest as when they try to do away with or revolt against . . . [the] doctrine of their inferiority," declared the *Ladies' Garland* in 1839. "They throw away their props, reject . . . guidance and guardianship and absolve the lords of creation from that protection which they are so willing to afford."[12]

Prophecies of certain disaster awaiting recalcitrant females coerced compliance with the era's conception of glorified womanhood. Yet, this vision of feminine perfection, a patchwork of ideas and theories unevenly sewn together from the unraveling social cloth of the antebellum era, enshrouded but never suited American women. It contained blatant contradictions and inconsistencies that would come to torment those made to wear the constraining and ill-fitting vestments of the woman-belle ideal.

The decrees authoritatively asserted woman's intellectual inferiority to man, while the same stipulations charged these mentally defective beings with determining "the happiness . . . of mankind." Women could never hope to understand the intricacies of public affairs, but they could do more "to bind society together than all the laws that legislations ever formed." Assaulted with evidence of their incompetencies while simultaneously burdened with the awesome trust of creating the crucial "bond of union between families," women became plagued with self-doubt and a deep sense of inadequacy.[13]

Antebellum females also found themselves pulled in antithetical directions by a creed that insisted upon extreme delicacy yet gave them the responsibility for presiding at sickbeds and witnessing the depths of human physical suffering. Dr. J. W. Corson in "Woman in the Chamber of Sickness," an article that appeared repeatedly in the leading ladies' magazines of the period, wrote: "I love to see her at the couch of sickness, sustaining the fainting head, offering to the parched lips its cordial, to the craving palate its simplest nourishment . . . and complying with every wish of the invalid." Not only was the frail, blushing female supposed to fulfill these physically and emotionally grueling duties without swooning or becoming ill herself, but she had to welcome these difficult tasks. "She is not only the most able to comfort the distressed, but she is happily the most willing. . . . Her kindness appears to be the natural prompting of an amiable instinct, without which she would not be woman."[14]

As woman's indefatigable ministrations to ill relatives and friends belied her "frail constitution," so too did the garments she wore. Women were told that they could never engage in strenuous labor and "that females are weak without the support of dress." Yet the current styles induced them to wear corsets and fabrics with yards of flouncing, which constricted breathing, confined activity, bruised their bodies, and often weighed as much as fifteen pounds. Feminine fashion required a considerable amount of physical strength to bear. It was still another area where women had to conform to the incompatible directives of the nineteenth century. Independent of the benefits of consumption to capitalism, individual men gained security and prestige from the indolent luxury they could afford to subsidize. They wanted their women to dress in magnificent and costly garments. Wives and daughters acquiesced in their role as consumer and some, no doubt, thoroughly enjoyed the splendid attire. But for others, absorption with fashion clearly represented a poor substitute for more interesting endeavor and came to be merely a way of occupying time.[15]

The impetus for fine female apparel was, then, supported on many levels and for many reasons. Yet women constantly received ridicule and criticism for their concern with dress. A child's schoolbook mocked:

> Fickle fashion! Why this fuss?
> Acting and behaving thus.
> Must the wife thy whims partake,
> And be fools—for fashion's sake?

"Vanity produces contempt and destruction," warned the author of the *Female Monitor.* But even if "vanity is one of woman's worst faults," she could hardly help herself because the "propensity to ornament in women is an instinct, it is universal and unvarying." At once urged into displaying fashionable garb, admonished "to carefully avoid ostentation," and told that vanity constituted an innate feminine quality, women experienced perpetual tension as they strove to accommodate to these and numerous other conflicting demands.[16]

Society dictated that woman "must make it the business of her life . . . her pleasure and constant employment to rear up her children" and insisted that "every married woman . . . should keep her own house." But women found that the differing economic and social realities of their respective classes barred them from dedicating time and energy to home and children. The era glorified motherhood and blandished females with praise of their special attributes for raising children. Yet the courts constantly denied the mother custody of her children in divorce cases. In the urban environment where women were deliberately and methodically prevented from fulfilling enterprise, little girls learned the axiom: "It is a great sin to be idle."[17]

The culture glorified marriage and taught that "[there] are two eventful periods in the life of a woman—one when she wonders who she'll have—the other when she wonders who'll have her." Nevertheless women heard themselves scornfully described as "man catchers" and received reprimands for developing accomplishments that "were merely lures for husbands." In a society that obstinately denied that decent women had any sexual drives, professional literature on the extent of masturbation existed in abundance. The writings confirmed that the "practice of masturbation is . . . more common and extensive . . . with youth of both sexes, than is usually supposed" and catalogued the numerous female "diseases," "both local and general . . . induced by masturbation . . . which have been attributed to other causes."[18]

The irreconcilable mandates of accepted feminine behavior also extended to matters of education. Consistent with the nineteenth-century refusal to recognize women as autonomous beings, they received an education for the benefit of others, rather than for their own needs. "Wish not to know what is improper for thee," cautioned one author, adding that women should learn "what it is fit thou shouldst know. . . . For those who venture too boldly forth lose themselves in the depth of their own reasonings." Another writer asserted that "a woman's knowledge of chemistry should extend no further than to the melting of butter; [and] geography to a thorough acquaintance with every hole and corner in the house."[19]

Women who found the smattering of instruction granted them insufficient to their interests and curiosity and who yearned for more knowledge, quickly evoked society's rebuke. The popular song, "The Clever Woman," advised all to "fly . . . from a woman dubb'd clever":

> She's coarse among females, with men she is funny
> She frightens the timid and tickles the strong;
> Intriguing in public, but cautious in private,

> The ice of her nature then only is known.
> Save, save, then O save me from women thus clever
> Who outrage their nature to gain but a name.

The Novel Reader, an engraving appearing in a literary annual, illustrated the alleged incompatibility of a woman's intellectual interests and her domestic responsibilities. The housewife, absorbed in her book, is impervious to the disorder enveloping the home, as husband and children try in vain to get her attention. The room is strewn with litter, a cat is drinking from the family pitcher, a dog is about to devour a large piece of meat intended for dinner, and a

Plate V. "The Novel Reader." Courtesy, Harvard University Library.

baby cries unnoticed in a basket. This scene of disarray left no doubt about the domestic damage females invited when they violated one of the cardinal principles of the woman-belle ideal. The woman who placed her own interests before the needs of the family and attempted intellectual fulfillment surely courted disaster.[20]

Constantly advised to temper intellectual interests and reproached for attempting to further her education, women at the same time received perpetual criticism for "petty" conversation and a "low standard of intellectual excellence." But while writers berated the entire sex for their inability to participate in engrossing discussions, they undermined the need for woman's intellectual endeavor by stressing that her knowledge "is not . . . to be reproduced in some literary composition, nor ever in any learned professions." Even if her studying revealed that "she possess[ed] talent," the model wife always "remember[ed] that to make a happy home for her husband and child is far more praiseworthy than to make a book."[21]

Antebellum females strove simply to maintain their balance, with the era's contradictory decrees pulling them in diverse directions. Yet, women might have found some compensation for this emotional hardship if they knew that their presence at home truly enriched their husband's lives. But the imperatives of livelihood and status combined with the variety of urban recreational facilities to keep men away from home for long periods of time. Man's absence underscored the hollowness of woman's existence.

For city men, "making money is the principal pursuit to which they are devoted; and which so completely absorbs their time, that between business and politics, they hardly find time for the cultivation of affection," reported one of Francis Grund's New York associates. Numerous observers remarked that "[men in] America [were] daily engaged from ten-twelve hours in . . . business." "[Man] is absorbed, especially in our great cities, in the taskwork of the workshop, the warehouse or the office from early morn to dewy eve," wrote one author. Another believed the male sex "too much occupied in the pursuit of wealth or fame to lend a willing ear or consoling voice." This masculine preoccupation with work gave rise to a slim, questioning body of literature that emphasized the need for relaxation, cautiously advising men to create and cultivate their leisure at home. Yet, as places for entertainment blossomed within the growing cities, men sought their amusement outside the domestic realm.[22]

"Shows, convivialities, [and] plays . . . do their part in turning men loose from home," noted a contemporary magazine, and Mrs. A. J. Graves observed that many wives "burn the midnight oil" waiting for their husbands to return from "societies or clubs." With so little time to spend with his spouse, a man might "marry a woman with tastes, disposition, and character essentially different from his," claimed one author. Yet the "points of contact are so few that he might become the father of a large family without discovering his mistake. He has no time to be unhappy."[23]

Man's varied and engrossing activities may have given him no time for reflection, but with women of the middle and upper classes, the reverse proved true. "Women are left all day to themselves: the life is monotonous," observed a writer, while one of Grund's companions commented: "Our women . . . with the exception of the time consumed at meals, [are] the whole day left to themselves." Another of Grund's acquaintances remarked that woman "seldom is . . . the intimate friend of her husband, the repository of his secrets, his true and faithful counselor." With no choice but to remain at home, women found themselves acutely isolated. It became increasingly apparent that men needed the *idea* of home and the *concept* of a peaceful, stable abode to ease their accommodation to perplexing social transition. But they did not choose to spend much time within the walls their theories had constructed. And women's prosaic existences filled the gap between the myths which told them that the well-being of family and, indeed, society depended upon their role in the house and the realities which nagged them into a slow awareness of the uselessness of their lives.[24]

Thus sequestered within the domestic circle, women experienced intense loneliness. Cut off from participation in the functioning of their communities and deprived of an effective or rewarding role in their homes, females also were taught that they did not have the ability to form friendships with members of their own sex. "The Friendship of Woman," appearing in the *Ladies' Magazine* of 1829, asserted that the "jealousy of love, the rivalry of beauty, the pride of accomplishments, or fancies of fashion . . . take possession of the heart," making it difficult for women to become intimates. A popular novel contained the following indictment: "A dog will lick away the sores and wounds of another of its own kind; man, tried himself in the crucibles of . . . suffering and temptation, has still some sympathy for a fallen brother; but woman . . . yielding to a mean spirit . . . can find in her heart . . . no feeling for the fallen and erring of her own." The nineteenth-century theories of womanhood, insidiously urging females to view each other with suspicion, attempted to keep women apart from other members of their sex. Repeated declarations by authoritarian figures that women did not know "what Friendship was, [because] they were hardly capable of anything so cool and rational as friendship," sought to prevent women's efforts to communicate fully with one another.[25]

Statements alleging that females were natural competitors, perhaps a projection of masculine feelings of rivalry, contrasted with the sermons, pamphlets, and public addresses of the colonial period, which helped women to take pride in the achievements of members of their sex and provided important models of feminine talent. Writings of the antebellum era denigrated those who excelled in areas beyond the stipulated sphere. "With all her renown, we think of Elizabeth only as the sovereign of England; . . . she has left no lesson . . . of enduring goodness to her sex, for if woman ever wins our love and insures our respect, it is not in the scenes of courtly power, . . . but in the sanctuary of home." The criticisms of well-known women and the derogatory remarks about feminine friendship inevitably had a negative impact on the way in which the individual female viewed herself. These assertions, insulating woman from intimate companionship with other females, also alienated woman from herself.[26]

Not only then did the prevailing concepts of the woman-belle ideal regulate feminine activities, duties, behavior, and attitudes, but they also governed woman's psychological life. Restraints imposed on the spontaneous expression of sentiment joined with specifications of one acceptable temperament for the entire sex to make women stifle their deepest emotions and question the validity of their feelings. Women constantly heard that they "are ever inclined to be gay and cheerful," for "women are naturally buoyant and light-hearted." *The Speaker* taught schoolchildren that "Married Ladies" should "be gay and good humored, complying and kind," and "Advice of a Father to his Only Daughter" included the admonition: "Never evince discontent." "Be not angry with your boy," scolded a popular song, while a contemporary author wrote: "How sadly is she deficient in natural feeling who thinks her infant troublesome." Indeed, the principles of exemplary womanhood demanded the constant inhibition of emotions.[27]

The constraining theories postulated a single psyche for all females. "You ought . . . to love home," decreed the writer Josiah Holland. An article in the *Ladies' Literary Cabinet* declared that "in the *household only* can she be happy." Tocqueville believed that women enjoyed being servile: "They attach a sort of pride to the voluntary surrender of their own will"; and Ralph, in an essay entitled "Domestic Happiness," agreed with the French reformer: "I have often had occasion to observe how easy the yoke of obedience sets . . . and how perfectly unconscious of its weight females seemed." Disallowing the possibility that any true woman could be discontent in her allotted sphere, authors propagated the view that "America is beyond dispute the Paradise of woman." Indeed, they asserted that "every American woman has reason to thank God every day of her life, that she was born into this happy country. . . . She is placed . . . in our own happy America, upon an equality with man."[28]

Disingenuous proclamations glorified woman's position. They combined with directives on cheerful behavior, creating a barrier to the unfettered expression of feeling. The unending cavalcade of irreconcilable demands refused to recognize diversity or individuality. Instead it presented the yardstick of the woman-belle ideal to measure the degree to which one adequately performed "the duties and responsibilities of woman . . . which [*she*] *must do.*" The myths of womanhood withheld from females the freedom to respond honestly and creatively to their lives, while declaring that they did not have the capacity to form friendships. Those women experiencing profound unhappiness were thus prevented from openly confessing their misery. The code of perfection compelled women to internalize their suffering.[29]

Not all females, of course, endured deprivation. Many, who lived surrounded by every possible comfort, appeared to accept and, indeed, to enjoy their situation. Some women liked being idle; others abhorred it. But the rigid stereotype of ideal feminine behavior disavowed the possibility that women, like men, had differing requirements, skills, aspirations, and psychological needs. All women were fenced together within narrow limits that controlled their existences and denied their interests and abilities a meaningful outlet. Vigorous women chafed against the confining boundaries of inferiority, abnegation, docility, and domesticity with their confusing dictates. Although few would have dared publicly to protest their condition, the conflicts in the vision of feminine excellence ultimately bred despair, anxiety, and anger. Middle- and upper-class women hungered for a more satisfying form of sustenance than the myths of the woman-belle ideal.

6

For Relief of the Body, Reconstruction of the Mind

I am bombarded yet   I stand

I have been standing all my life in the
direct path of a battery of signals
. . . .
. . . I am an instrument in the shape
of a woman trying to translate pulsations
into images   for the relief of the body
and the reconstruction of the mind.

—Adrienne Rich, *Planetarium,* 1968

> The greatest trial . . . is that I have nothing to do. Here I am with abundant leisure, and capable, I believe, of accomplishing some good, and yet with no object on which to expend my energies. . . . I cannot be happy without being employed. Alone as I am, my mind seems to prey upon itself until I am weary of life.[1]

With these words, one female expressed the sense of stagnation and misery that scarred the lives of many nineteenth-century American women. The decrees of genuine womanhood, tyrannically governing feminine existence, thwarted efforts at self-realization. Women could neither control their own destinies nor help to free one another from society's bonds as long as the myths of the woman-belle ideal remained embedded in the nation's consciousness.

The contradictory mandates generated severe tension. Intense inner turmoil sought an outlet and impelled women to ameliorate their intolerable condition. This search for personal fulfillment assumed different forms, sometimes even affording temporary abatement. But remaining individual and insular, it did nothing to improve the general plight of women until the interactions of the city brought a new understanding of woman's position.

Before the dynamics of urban growth would enable women to gain new insights and support from their shared experiences, nineteenth-century females suffered alone. Their numerous ailments became the observable symptoms of inner malaise. Visitors and residents alike expressed astonishment at the extent of ill health among American women. A British actress, Fanny Kemble, remarked that women in the United States "look old and faded" by the time they reach twenty-five years of age, while the "pallid and unhealthy complexions of the American ladies" struck her compatriot, Richard Cobden, with amazement. A journal reported that "foreigners who visit this country [comment] that American ladies have, almost without exception, a delicacy of complexion and appearance, amounting almost to sickness." Citizens concurred with these European observations.[2]

Both James Fenimore Cooper and Nathaniel Hawthorne expressed dismay at the precarious health of American females. Other, less eminent writers voiced similar views. Joel Hawes described the "puny forms . . . feeble frames and sickly faces," as well as the "dismal train of ills," which characterized women of the "higher classes." Rev. Anson Smyth thought the "health of [the] American woman poor compared to what it used to be," and his colleague, Rev. Dr. Hawes of Hartford, bemoaned the fact "that the muscular vigor and strength of our . . . women have, for a long time past been undergoing a melancholy change. . . . But a small proportion of our adult females enjoy complete health."[3]

Authors agreed that infirmity characterized "women in our larger towns [rather] than those of rural districts." Mrs. S. W. Benedict noted that the "fashionable often complain of bodily ill" and thought it "difficult to find a woman devoted to ease and fashion, who is not habitually . . . an invalid." George Burnap also commented on the prevalence of poor health among those leading "an idle, useless life." Some attempted casual assessments of the numbers of socially and economically comfortable women suffering from various maladies, but Catharine Beecher, author and reformer, appears to have been the first to make a systematic survey of the extent of feminine illness in America.[4]

Beecher's "extensive travels" revealed "the deplorable suffering of multitudes of young wives and mothers." When these informal observations convinced her that "there was a terrible decay of female health all over the land," she devoted herself to a thorough exploration of the numerous and diverse ailments that plagued her countrywomen. Using a questionnaire designed to determine relative states of health, Beecher asked her acquaintances in cities throughout the nation to report on the physical condition of the ten women they knew best. The startling replies confirmed her earlier desultory investigation and attested to the ubiquity of invalidism among nineteenth-century American women.[5]

In over two hundred towns and cities sampled, only two had a majority of healthy women among the ten questioned. In the remaining cities, the "habitual invalids" and "delicate or diseased" outnumbered the "strong and healthy" from 4 to 1 to as much as 10 to 1. Indeed Catharine Beecher claimed that she could not recall in her "immense circle of friends and acquaintances all over the Union, so many as ten married ladies born in this century and country, who are perfectly sound, healthy, and vigorous."[6]

Establishing the extent of feminine illness, however, proved much easier than agreeing upon its cause. Contemporaries offered discrepant hypotheses; numerous explanations for female malady filled antebellum literature. Some doctors and health experts spurned investigation completely, asserting that women merely feigned poor health to avoid responsibility. Edward Dixon, in his popular book *Woman and Her Diseases,* cautioned physicians and husbands that women often "pretend hysteric attacks in order to excite sympathy and obtain some desired end." But other writers made serious studies into the etiology of women's afflictions.[7]

George Burnap attributed female infirmities to the extravagant "mode of living" of "the more affluent classes." Catharine Beecher blamed both the constricting garments of fashionable attire and the lack of exercise for much of the sickness she observed. "Light, Air, Sleep, Food, and Clothes" seemed to her the essential keys to good health. She urged more attention to these salubrious ingredients, in spite of the medical profession's contention that the female diseases lay beyond woman's control.[8]

Doctors directed their attention to the womb, holding the reproductive system responsible for most female ills. Her uterus exercises a "paramount power" over her physical and moral system, and its grasp is "no less whimsical than potent," believed William P. Dewes, professor of midwifery at the University of Pennsylvania. Because doctors agreed that woman "is constantly liable to irregularities in her menstrua, and menaced severely by their consequences," they focused medical treatment on uterine and menstrual disorders. Female sexual organs bore the onus for headaches, nervous disorders, indigestion, insomnia, depression, and backaches.[9]

The pages of the *Water-Cure Journal,* a contemporary periodical heralding the benefits of hydropathy, document the nineteenth-century obsession with "uterine-related diseases." Articles on such topics as "chlorsis or green sickness . . . the non-appearance of the menstrual discharge . . . [which] inevitably results in the serious derangement of the general health," "menstrual cramps" to which the "luxurious and idle are more subject," and "leuccorrhoea and uterine catarrh" dominated the publication. The water-cure offered such novel therapy as "hip baths," "cold injections into the urethra," and "rubbing of the back, loins, and abdomen." Its remedies contrasted sharply with the practices of orthodox medicine, which often used "leeching" and "cauterization" to alleviate feminine discomfort.[10]

Much female physical anguish did indeed relate to the reproductive system, particularly as the prevailing codes of delicacy prevented physically sick women from seeking help. Dr. Charles Meigs "rejoiced" at the difficulty of making a "local examination" as it gave "evidence of a high and worthy grade of moral feeling." Women, conforming to the dictates of modest behavior, suffered in silence rather than endure the "mortification" of a gynecological examination, as propriety combined with ignorance to make the womb a source of much distress.[11]

The conventional wisdom of the era preached that "conception . . . is much more likely to happen from intercourse a few days before or after the menstrual period." Accordingly, women who wished to practice some form of birth control intentionally had sexual relations in the middle of the menstrual cycle. They no doubt found their repeated pregnancies not only surprising but physically difficult as well. The diverse ailments attending birth ranged from minor irritation, to severe infection, to prolapsus uteri, but doctors responded to all uterine disorders with the same antiquated and often harmful treatments. Even a normal, uncomplicated birth could prove debilitating. The traditional medical practices insisted upon complete inactivity for long periods of time following delivery. A Mrs. O. C. W. reported to the *Water-Cure Journal* that she was "kept confined to . . . bed nearly two months" with the birth of her first child, and "it was not until about the middle of the following summer that [she] attained [her] former health and strength."[12]

Clearly, childbearing did have painful and dangerous aspects.

Scholars seeking to understand the roots of feminine maladies have sympathetically suggested that women used the "pretext of being 'delicate' as a way of . . . closing the bedroom door," "an elaborate strateg[y] for limiting the occasions of sexual intercourse . . . and thus limiting their families." Undoubtedly some women fabricated illness to shield themselves from unwanted pregnancies. Others, obviously, were physically ill. Still others were merely dupes of subtle economic and social pressure to keep women nonproductive and dependent. But the prevalence of poor health among women of leisure, the comments of a few sensitive observers, and the strong psychological component of the various described afflictions, all combine to invite further investigation into the causes of feminine illness.[13]

George Combe, the Scottish phrenologist, believed that "nervous disease of which females of the middle and upper classes were the most frequent victims" could be attributed to "inactivity of intellect and feeling." Dr. W. A. Alcott, the noted nutritional reformer, urged that ladies be given "some employment . . . to save them from ennui, and disgust, and misery—sometimes from speedy or more protracted suicide." Harriet Martineau blamed the "vacuity of mind . . . among women of station and education in the most enlightened parts of the country" for a host of problems.[14]

Catharine Beecher, whose "extensive tours in all portions of the Free States" had "brought [her] into most intimate communion" with countless women, exclaimed "And oh! what heartaches were the result of these years of quiet observation of the experience of my sex in domestic life. How many hearts have revealed the fact that what they had been trained to imagine the highest earthly felicity, was but the beginning of care, disappointment, and sorrow, and often led to the extremity of mental and physical suffering." And, above all, Beecher wondered why she found so many women in comfortable circumstances "expressing the hope that their daughters would never marry."[15]

Some thoughtful individuals, therefore, stated or implied that many women's ailments had a psychological rather than physical origin, and the personal experiences of nineteenth-century females seem to support this hypothesis. The private journals, letters, and case studies of diverse women give expression to the dysphoria torturing antebellum females. They detail the symptoms of hysteria, severe anxiety, and constant depression. "I was quite ill, and my spirits depressed," wrote Sarah Connell Ayer often in her diary, revealing the perpetual mental anguish of this middle-class wife and mother. The phrase "my spirits were unusually depressed" covered the sheets of her journal. Ayer frequently confessed having to curtail activities because of her emotional state, "for which [she] could not account."[16]

Having little understanding of the causes or nature of their afflictions, women described anger and anxiety. In 1841, Elizabeth Payson Prentiss, who later became an author of children's books, wrote of her constant nervousness, which often made life "insupportable." "I . . . think mother would not trust me to carry the dishes to the closet, if she knew how strong an effort I have to make to avoid dashing them all to pieces," she confided. "When I am at the head of the stairs I can hardly help throwing myself down. . . . Tonight, for instance, my head began to feel all at once as if it were enlarging till at last it seemed to fill the room. . . . Three days out of seven I am as sick as I . . . can be—the rest of the time, languid, feeble, and exhausted by frequent faint turns, so that I can't do the smallest thing in my family."[17]

"My spirits are . . . depressed this forenoon," wrote Ann Warder countless times in her journal. Sarah Stearns suffered from "anxiety [and] vexation" and felt "quite unable to attend the concerns of [her] family." A brilliant student, Nancy Maria Hyde constantly complained that "[her] spirits have been unusually depressed, and [her] feelings have been those of languor and despondency." Susan Huntington's memoirs describe her perpetual battle with "distressing nervous depression," while Laura Clark's journal entries divulge a suffering so great that she states: "I sometimes . . . wonder that I am alive."[18]

This unending struggle with devastating afflictions they could neither understand nor relieve intensified the difficult plight of American women. In a letter that she did not dare to sign, one woman articulated her despair: "I am so . . . encompassed with infirmities that I long sometimes to flee away." Few women consciously expressed the wish to "flee" or escape from a life they found unbearable, but thousands of nineteenth-century females fell victim to a particular form of psychoneurosis. Manifesting itself in disabling symptoms, this illness gave women no choice but to retreat from their daily routines. The *Water-Cure Journal* disclosed the case histories of numerous females who had suddenly and inexplicably become totally incapacitated. Miss Elizabeth Pott was "an excellent scholar [who] had not been able to read or write for years," and Miss Isabella Thompson suddenly "could not do anything." These furnished but two examples of the thousands of women invalids who experimented with hydropathy. Among those who flocked to the flourishing water-cure centers was Harriet Beecher Stowe. Her case study provides an interesting illustration of the nature of much feminine malady.[19]

The daughter of Lyman Beecher, a fiery minister who infused his children with a passionate desire to reform humanity, Harriet suffered from a tormenting apprehension that she could not fulfill her father's expectations. To her sister Catharine she confessed the fear that she might not be "fit for anything." Fortunately Catharine, ten years her senior, had plans to open a school for girls and very much needed Harriet's help. The two young women worked together until 1836, when Harriet married Calvin Stowe, a classics professor. Demanding, domineering, and irascible, Professor Stowe expected complete obedience from his wife. Within their first ten years of married life, Harriet bore three children and agreed to have Calvin's aged and complaining mother live with them. Then, suddenly, at the end of this decade, which Harriet described as filled with "pain, confusion, disappointment and suffering," when all she "proposed was met and crossed and in every way hedged up," her right side became totally paralyzed.[20]

Harriet went to the famous water-cure sanitarium in Brattleboro,

Vermont, for therapy. There, the "shattered broken invalid, just able to creep along by great care," began to reexamine her life. In the serene atmosphere, removed from the perpetual exactions of a domestic martinet, Harriet Beecher Stowe started her slow recovery. "Not for years have I enjoyed life as I have here," she wrote, ignoring her husband's repeated entreaties to return home. After a year away from her life of "constant discouragement," of "hasty and irritated censure," Harriet came to realize that she could not make her family "my chief good and portion."[21]

During her stay in Brattleboro, Harriet gained the emotional strength to insist that her husband make certain concessions as a prerequisite for resuming cohabitation. He agreed to accept a teaching position at Bowdoin College in Maine and apparently pledged not to inhibit Harriet's fledgling career as an author. She began work on *Uncle Tom's Cabin* shortly after rejoining her family in Maine; her ailments, not surprisingly, disappeared. Until her death in 1896 at the age of eighty-five, she enjoyed vigorous health, free from all signs of her affliction.[22]

Harriet Beecher Stowe's paralysis emanated from deep emotional distress. Clinically called conversion hysteria, or conversion reaction, this crippling psychoneurosis is characterized by the tendency to represent inner psychological conflicts by means of symbolic somatic disturbances. Hysteria, then, as well as depression and anxiety, singularly or collectively incapacitated Jacksonian women. Stowe benefited from a stable childhood, an indulgent, if somewhat awe-inspiring father, and an ambitious and supportive sister. Additionally, she had a comfortable economic situation that enabled her to remain in Brattleboro for over a year, a conciliatory husband, occupying interests, and a strong will. Harriet Beecher Stowe thus managed to overcome the more obvious, debilitating symptoms of illness brought on by the conflicts of her life. But most women did not share this good fortune and languished in their chambers alone and afraid.

Contemporaries could not understand why females, with every comfort and no responsibility, became so desperately ill. Yet an abundance of psychoneurotic symptoms plagued American women. These ailments afforded visible evidence of stifled anger, unassuaged guilt, and unfilled emotional and physical drives. Fear of punishment and loss of love from the realization of repressed drives and wishes, the overwhelming feeling of stagnation, and the lack of self-esteem became manifested in profound psychological and related physical distress.[23]

Largely psychogenic, feminine illness represented a *symptom* of the internal conflicts rather than a *solution* to them. Nevertheless, invalidism did offer some compensations or secondary gains. For the ailing woman of the middle or upper classes, sickness generally meant repeated visits to various doctors and specialists. By evincing concern, the physician gave the female a kind of masculine attention that she missed at home. As Harriet Beecher Stowe reported: "The Dr. treats us with great kindness—seems interested in us." And, of course, by withdrawing to her room, the sick woman might become the focus of family attention and hence enjoy a fleeting sense of importance she would otherwise be denied. Severe afflictions usually required prolonged treatment at sanitariums or rest homes. For women who could afford such luxuries, the relative freedom and equanimity offered at these institutions proved favorable to superficial recovery.[24]

The beneficial side effects concomitant with infirmity, however, provided neither the inducement to become sick nor a cure for her ills. Invalidism, barely understood and poorly treated, did little to alleviate the strains and anxieties. But the plethora of afflicted women does much to illuminate the pervasive suffering of females in Jacksonian America. Similarly, women's diaries and letters illustrate inner turmoil, ambivalence, and anger, as women spilled their deepest feelings into cherished and confidential writing.

Female journals of this period reveal both woman's struggle to accept and comply with the era's concept of feminine nature and behavior and the harvest of unhappiness that her efforts inevitably reaped. The persistent vigil to conform to the precepts of the woman-belle ideal produced severe tension: "How soon one is wearied of the constant exertion to be agreeable, even when conscious of admiration!" complained one woman. Another believed that "it is the struggle to be patient and gentle and cheerful, when pressed down and worn upon and distracted that costs so much."[25]

Taught from childhood that the true woman always sacrificed her self-interest for the happiness of others, women worried incessantly that they might not have these angelic virtues and blamed themselves for their apparent failings. "I think that to give happiness in married life a woman should possess oceans of self–sacrificing love and I, for one, haven't half of that self-forgetting spirit which I think essential," confided Elizabeth Prentiss to a friend in 1843. The introspection of one diarist exposed her "fear that this power of enjoying myself makes my pleasure too independent of others, and consequently renders me too little solicitous about them," while her contemporaries berated themselves for similar "shortcomings."[26]

Another axiom of feminine nature—woman's innate desire to tend the sick—demanded compliance. Antebellum females constantly ministered to ill friends and family. Their diaries disclose irritation with these tasks and also the strain women experienced from the need to perform these duties with the cheerfulness required of them. Elizabeth Prentiss frequently confessed vexation at having "to drag one's self out of bed to take care of a sick baby," and Harriet Beecher Stowe complained that her choleric son acted like a "great fellow who thinks women [were] made for his especial convenience." The conflict between society's vision of the female happily and indefatigably caring for the sick and woman's resentment at these chores finds full eloquence in the diary of Hannah Backhouse. Feeling an overwhelming sense of repugnance at ministering to sick relatives, Hannah struggled to cultivate the "appropriate" feelings. When her brother became ill she had an opportunity to test her endurance. Her diary records a mixed success. "I often felt my aversion to trifles, and the want of employment and ideas made me feel it a great cross; this sometimes overcame me," she admitted.[27]

Yet this young woman ardently hoped she would develop the requisite qualities: "Beginning to act from duty in such cases, one may end by acting from affection, and then it becomes necessary to one's satisfaction to do so. A woman who cannot suffer the confinement of a sick room, leaves unfulfilled one of her most marked duties and can never be fit for a wife. It is a difficult task when one is not spurred onward by the continual impulse of the heart, or in short, when self is a dearer object than the invalid. . . . I could often wish my heart were more susceptible of kindness and compassion than it is."[28]

Secretly protesting the demands made upon them, women also writhed under the decrees of the era that fettered their activities. "How painfully sensitive am I to not being free to act as I like," asserted Hannah Backhouse. She admitted that as a child she most enjoyed "using the hammer and saw with dexterity, and [found] the greatest pleasure [in] being victorious in a game of trapball." When admonished against the unladylike nature of her amusements, she wrote: "I fell into a sulky mood in my own mind, growling over the misery of . . . restraint. I sometimes feel my want of freedom rather galling."[29]

Other women perceived their bondage differently. Catharine Sedgwick, who later became a noted novelist, ironically came to express her views on women in a letter to a friend requesting fabric for dresses. Absorption with fashion surely would have been considered a fitting topic for a twenty-one-year-old woman, but Catharine evidently found the subject stifling. "I wish there was some philosophy in vogue that would free us. . . . Nothing less than the 'genius of universal emancipation' would effect it, and I am afraid that even this wonder-evoking genius has no microscopic eye to discern the pigmy chains that bind us in this debasing dependence."[30]

Feminine thralldom assumed many forms, but economic deprivation emerged as one of the most visible signs of oppression. With opportunities for employment severely limited, impoverished women, as well as those whose families had recently suffered financial reversals, found themselves victimized by the prevailing legal and social codes. Nancy Maria Hyde, considered by her contemporaries to have been an exceptionally able student, endured great hardship after her father's death. Creditors pressed upon Nancy and her mother for the payment of debts, and "neither in the family of her father, her mother, or herself, was there a son or a brother, to stand up as their helper." Writing a plea to the Connecticut General Assembly on behalf of her mother, Nancy articulated the plight of the single, widowed, or abandoned woman who lacked the aid of a male relative: "I find myself not only deprived of support in my declining age, but likely to be left wholly destitute of a home for myself and children."[31]

This appeal evidently did not bring the desired assistance. Nancy left school in an attempt to relieve her family's monetary problems. Teaching was one of the few occupations open to women, but even entry into this field proved difficult. Desperate for an income and unable to find work as a teacher, Nancy took a job painting artificial fruit. But as she explained to her journal: "Choice would never have instigated me to this employment." Other women, similiarly situated, tried to support themselves by writing. Yet, like Hannah Adams, the gifted author whose scholarly works included *History of Religions,* they found that the "penalties and discouragements attending authors in general fall upon woman with double weight. To the curiosity of the idle, and the envy of the malicious, their sex affords a peculiar excitement."[32]

The ethos of the woman-belle ideal prohibited women from most forms of financially remunerative endeavor. It also denied the value of independent feminine achievement and criticized females for developing pride in their accomplishments. The prevailing codes deemed few tasks ladylike. Embroidering, painting, playing musical instruments, and perhaps writing some trivial verses probably did not appeal to most women. Yet those who demonstrated talent and an eagerness to follow these limited, acceptable pursuits had still other restrictions. The perfect female never exhibited self-assurance nor even allowed herself to feel confident. "The love of painting has been uppermost in my mind for some weeks past," wrote Hannah Backhouse. After completing a canvas that gave her special satisfaction she admitted: "I did so well that I felt most uncomfortably elated with it. . . . How I disliked myself. . . . I strove much against my feelings."[33]

Similarly, Susan Huntington wrote: "Pride has been my constant foe." "Once when I was the mere child of fiction and romance, my ambition was to distinguish myself by poetizing and shining as an authoress. After I was married and was taught some sharp lessons, my great desire was to be . . . a good wife, good mother. . . . But pride besets me still." Several years later Huntington expressed the forbidden yearning to display her knowledge when "thrown into an intelligent circle, capable of estimating all that was commanding and all that was attractive in [my] character, and whose qualifications would ensure [me] the respect and constant attentions of that circle." Indeed, she envied the woman of a "humbler and more retired . . . station . . . as it furnished a comparative exemption from . . . [these] temptations."[34]

Women could expose neither mental ability nor knowledge, but the craving for intellectual stimulation forms a constant litany running through their private journals and letters. "Write me a long letter," Sarah Ayer begged her friend Maria. "Tell me everything . . . what books you have been reading, your opinion of them, and indeed everything that interests you." Before sealing the letter, Ayer enclosed a proposed reading list and asked Maria to comment on her selections. Hannah Backhouse records the "delightful hour" she spent "reading Locke," and Catharine Sedgwick's correspondence with her women friends contain frequent references to current authors.[35]

Not surprisingly, most women could not satisfy intellectual needs within the narrow limits allowed them. And many anguished over insipid conversation resulting from women's lack of education and involvement. "I cannot bear talking about trifles," exclaimed Hannah Backhouse. Other women echoed these feelings. In a letter to her confidante, Sarah Ayer wrote: "I hate large parties, such as we have both frequently attended, where . . . improving conversation, and all intellectual enjoyments were banished, and trifling amusements fit only to please a child supplied their places." "How much more real pleasure and advantage is to be derived from solid and refined conversation," she continued, "than from that empty, unmeaning *chit-chat* which I am sorry to say so frequently forms the greater part of female conversation."[36]

Elizabeth Prentiss, raised in the blossoming seaport city of Portland, Maine, disclosed a similar dissatisfaction to her diary on 1 December 1841: "I went to the sewing circle this afternoon and had such a stupid time! Enough gossip and nonsense was talked to make one sick." Apparently concerned about the frivolity of her female companions, she added: "I can't think the girls are the silly creatures they make themselves appear. They want an aim in life, some worthy object; give them that, and the good and excellent which, I am sure, lies hidden in their nature will develop itself at once." Yet, her sense of separateness plagued her: "Oh, what is it I *do* want? Somebody who feels as I feel and thinks as I think."[37]

Susan Huntington, feeling as Elizabeth Prentiss did, conducted a private campaign against the strictures imposed upon feminine intellect. Reacting to the statement that "thought is the characterizing feature of men, and feeling of women," she wrote: "Will not women infer that, if the case be so, it is not necessary for her to cultivate her mental powers; that she may as well confine her views and her thoughts . . . [to a] contracted sphere."[38]

Women who tried to "cultivate" their "mental powers" in a social milieu that mocked their attempts and undermined their efforts often experienced profound frustration and, ultimately, resignation. "My mind grows inactive and lethargic," complained Sarah Stearns, and Elizabeth Prentiss had the same grievance. "Don't ask me if I have read anything else," she wrote shortly after her marriage and subsequent relocation in New Bedford, Massachusetts. "My mind has become a complete mummy, and therefore, incapable of either receiving or originating a new idea." Wedlock had brought the end of her previous attempts to indulge intellectual curiosity. "Just what I expected would befall me has happened. I have got immersed in the whirlpool of petty cares and concerns which swallow up so many other and higher interests, and talk as anxiously about good 'help' and bad, as the rest of 'em do. . . . I sometimes feel really ashamed of myself to see . . . how my time seems to be wasted if I venture to take up a book. . . . [W]ives who have no love and enthusiasm for their husbands are more to be pitied than blamed if they settle down into mere . . . [household] managers."[39]

Substantially barred from satisfying the requirements of her mind, the middle- and upper-class woman had to endure the agony of relentless boredom. "There is such a sameness in my life . . . that the particulars of it are hardly worth the pains of writing," recorded one young woman. And Ellen Parker of New Hampshire grieved that "another long day has passed into eternity. How slowly time passes to me." Mary Peacock's diary reflects her disgust at having to "sit idle," considering it as "the most tiresome thing a person can do." Hannah Backhouse, describing her friends who came to tea, exclaimed: "What dull worldly people they seem to be!" "Having done nothing all day, and being all assembled in the evening, vacancy pervaded the whole room to such a degree, that I wished I had been obliged to work for my bread, that my duty might not be in the listless inactivity of a parlour." [40]

Forced leisure generated an oppressive sense of uselessness and caused the nineteenth-century woman to "[wonder] why [she] was made, and if anybody on earth [would] ever be a bit happier for it." Plagued by feelings of worthlessness, but immersed in the ethos of the woman-belle ideal, she could not appreciate the intricate origins of her anguish. She therefore accepted the wisdom of contemporary theorists and attributed all unhappiness to her individual failings. This self-blame ultimately intensified her conflicts and sense of isolation. Elizabeth Prentiss confessed to feeling "mentally and spiritually alone in the world," and Sarah Ayer, writing in Concord, Massachusetts, complained: "[I have] lived so much in solitude . . . that my mind has become somewhat enervated."[41]

As women attempted to meet society's expectations, they resolved to become more self-sacrificing and patient and endeavored to enjoy their sickbed duties. They restrained themselves from exhibiting wit and intellect and tried to find meaning in a life of futility.

And throughout this lonely search for fulfillment women entrusted their troubled emotions and thoughts to personal diaries. The myriad of confidential writings provided an outlet for stifled feelings but did little to enable women to challenge the womanhood myths. The persistent urge to find understanding could not be absorbed by scattered pages of private journals. And the need to communicate came streaming forth, eventually eroding the carefully constructed dam of male authorship. Feminine anguish flowed into countless novels and short stories; woman's creative literature emerged as a confluence of anger and sadness, hope and despair.[42]

The astonishing outpouring of writing by females at once annoyed and amazed those accustomed to dominating the literary field. Predictably, resentment against women authors rose up to meet their hesitant efforts. Nathaniel Hawthorne damned the entire "mob of scribbling women." Articles warned women that they could not "be too cautious in assuming the privilege of presenting their thoughts to the world." And essays, cautioning those who "[devoted] themselves to studies and research" that they would soon "despise their duties and neglect them altogether," appeared frequently.[43]

One author, Mrs. Farrar, tried to diminish the prejudice she had encountered. Farrar reminded aspiring writers that "they are responsible to their sex . . . for not bringing literary pursuits into disrepute by neglecting their personal appearance." She warned that the "connection, in many minds, is still very close between blue stockings and dirty stockings." Knowing that contemporary opinion was arrayed against them, women frequently justified, explained, or apologized for their literary attempts. Some attributed their careers to financial necessity. Catharine Sedgwick spoke for others when she explained that she "wanted some pursuit, and felt spiritless and sad." "My books have been a pleasant occupation and excitement in my life," she wrote. "[They] have relieved me from the danger of ennui."[44]

The existence of voluminous printed material signed by women afforded evidence that middle- and upper-class females did not find domestic life engrossing or enriching. The theme of feminine tedium dotted the pages of woman's writings. "Oh, the weary years of unused life to which so large a portion of the human race is remorselessly consigned!" bemoaned the author of the novel *Three Sisters*. Written in the first person, this tale traces the maturation of three women. The author indicted the system that created and encouraged the useless lady: "I returned home . . . to find my elder sisters leading that living death to which it is the fashion to consign females of the wealthy middle-class . . . an aimless life."[45]

Vesta, the courageous heroine of Charlotte Chesebro's *Children of Light*, sighed: "I'm tired of reading, and tired to death of embroidery; and one can not be forever praising the work of another." She asked her companions if they would "acknowledge that idle persons are, of all, most miserable?" Chesebro infused her character with a yearning for excitement and fulfillment. "If I were a man, I would very soon discover what there was for me to do. . . . I would be clear of dragging out my life in the kitchen, or of putting myself down to the mending of old clothes, or of finding my recreation in walking over the lawn and garden, for all the world like a stupid animal, . . . a well-trained dog! When I feel like rushing out—strong enough to fight all the battles of the world, and with some little disposition that way too." Yet, Vesta had to face the reality of her existence:

> But here I am, only a woman—a housekeeper, the mistress of an hospital as I might say, to be kept in my 'proper sphere' and 'place,' and never to stir an inch out of it in any direction, for fear that all creation would turn against me, and hunt me down, as they would a wild beast! Oh, these laws of propriety—these ridiculous customs.[46]

In one of her many novels Catharine Sedgwick frequently expressed her sympathy for urban women of leisure. Sedgwick wrote that "a woman of two-twenty, like Grace Herbert, if not occupied by an engrossing affection, is in this fine world . . . much like a locomotive off the track. If she had been absolutely poor and friendless, she would have found a safety-valve in employment. If her destiny had been cast in the country, its unmasked life and healthy simplicity would have tended to a serene existence." But alas, because Grace had money and lived in the city her days would be passed in idle misery.[47]

A character in the story "Truth in Fiction," published in the *Evergreen,* sardonically noted: "I think I may . . . claim to the virtue of usefulness, for no other individual in all the wide world, I believe, has done so much for the encouragement of manufactures as I have." Another fictitious young woman, reading from a book that called females "flower-crowned victims offered up to the human lords of creation," agreed that although "men have a thousand objects in life . . . , if a woman succeed not in the sole hope of her hazardous career, she is utterly lost to all purposes of exertion or happiness."[48]

Women writers recognized the era's insistence upon matrimony as the only acceptable path to feminine fulfillment, but many attempted to invalidate this decree through their literature. Mary Howitt, author of "Single Sisters," printed in the 1845 edition of the *Keepsake,* objected to "fairy tales which portray 'old maids' as cruel and ugly." Indeed, Ada Lester, in a story bearing her name, did not marry and achieved much recognition. Leopoldine of Julia Delafaye-Brehier's "Two Sisters" claims that she does not regret being single for "that condition, which appears to you so frightful, has its happiness. . . . I have called into my aid the arts and letters which it is so difficult for married females to cultivate with constancy." In another tale, the married Emily confesses to her spinster sister: "You have had years of happiness while I have never felt a single moment of unalloyed felicity." On her deathbed, Emily pleads: "My sister, teach my children the moral of our story."[49]

Emily's small children might have required an explanation of their mother's dying words, but the countless stories of females forced into marriage by a deleterious dictate made the message clear to antebellum readers. The *Amulet* of 1846 relates the sad history of a sixteen-year-old girl "who abides her parents wishes and marries a man she can't love." An autobiographical sketch appearing in the *Ladies' Wreath,* "A Life Without Love," tells of a woman who never loved her husband-to-be and whose wedding day, rather than bringing her joy, filled her with dread and a feeling of "strange repulsion." And Catharine Sedgwick expressed her opinion by writing that Grace "will soon be married, and then, like Eleanor, mere wife and mother to the end of her life."[50]

The ethos of the woman-belle ideal deemed marriage and the promise of a fashionable life the only appropriate aim for the true woman, as it insisted on the oneness of the entire sex. Although this philosophy prevented theorists from acknowledging the existence of countless working women, female writers, some dependent upon their earnings, understood and wrote of the realities of economic hardship. "Poor Mrs. Stephens," the sewing woman of Harriet Beecher Stowe's "Tea Rose," had "to live in one coarse room, and wash, iron and cook, . . . [and] had to spend every moment of [her] time in hard toil, with no prospect from [her] window but a brick side-walk, or a dirty lane." The *Ladies' Casket* of 1848 carried the tale of "Polly Bush who . . . had not been able to get her scanty earnings out of the clutch of the hard miser Latham." And Blanch, a washerwoman forced to provide for her blind father, saddened readers of the 1845 edition of the *Rose*.[51]

While the suffering of women born into poverty furnished a popular theme for female fiction writers, the plight of women from comfortable backgrounds who suddenly had to support themselves also evoked compassion and attention. Two schoolgirls in the novel *Live and Let Live* protested the prevailing theories that left woman utterly destitute of the means of survival. "Great pains were taken to make us attractive in a drawing-room and amicable in our domestic relations. But as to the actual business of life we were as little trained for it as if we had been born in the royal family of Persia." Alice Montrose of Maria McIntosh's popular novel, *The Lofty and the Lowly*, suffered greatly after her husband's death. "Before I could teach, I should find it necessary to become a learner." Totally devoid of skill and of confidence in herself, Alice concluded: "I cannot go forth into the careless world and enter upon the business of life." "Men give to their daughters neither trade, profession, nor fortune, and to further their own interests, even take from them what properly they may possess," lamented a young woman of another novel after learning of her father's financial losses. "The son must be educated to a trade—the daughter pillaged for the son's advancement—the weak left weak and defenseless—the strong strengthened."[52]

The fear of a life of pauperism drove some women into marriages consummated solely for economic security. The middle daughter of *The Three Sisters* had to endure this unhappy fate:

> With strength, ability and energy beyond the average of either sex, simply for want of training and definite pursuit, a recognized sphere of action, this competent human being, thus rendered incompetent, cast the burthen of mere existence on a husband, and, in exchange for the means to live, gave life itself. . . . She married a man she had twice refused during [her] father's lifetime, never pretending to herself or to him that she loved him.[53]

The dominant theories, which left females economically destitute, also impoverished them intellectually. In "Cousin William," Harriet Beecher Stowe related Mary's unhappiness when "she saw a library of books in his room, that made her sigh every day when she dusted them, to think how much there is to be known of which she was ignorant." Mrs. A. J. Graves told of "the little girl that steals away to some quiet solitude that she may indulge her fondness for books, or fill her imagination with visions of future intellectual eminence." And two schoolgirls discussing Madame Eugene's "very 'awakening' and edifying . . . sermon last evening at prayer" thought it "unfortunate and deplorable that she was not a *man*." "I am sure," remarked one, "[that] Madame would shine in the Roman forum."[54]

The narrator of *The Three Sisters* longed to become a doctor and as a child performed operations on dolls. "Had I been a boy instead of a girl, these early indications would have been hailed with satisfaction as pointing unerringly to my future vocation. As it was, they procured me only reprimands and punishment for mischief; and as I could not play properly with my dolls, they were taken from me altogether." Eliza Woodson of Eliza Farnham's fictionalized autobiography had no books for her own. Desperate for reading material, she "devoured" congressional debates, political newspapers, and cabinet reports brought in by the men in her family. But her relatives, finding these pursuits "curious," ostracized Eliza and labeled her a "fool."[55]

Fear of derision and exclusion forced women to hide their knowledge and skills. "Amelia's frosty reception in the best Philadelphia drawing rooms" led this character of the novel *Ferdinand and Elmira* "to warn her friends to display no learning or sentiment, for the moment it is discovered, your reputation is lost forever." Ruth Hall, the literary creation of the indefatigable Fanny Fern, aroused the curiosity of her friends. They "wonder[ed] . . . why she took so much pains to bother her head with those stupid books, when she was every day growing prettier" and would not be able to use or exhibit her imagination or learning.[56]

"The Mysterious Picture," appearing in the 1832 edition of *Affection's Gift*, is a sensitive study of one young woman caught between her own needs and society's dictates. Josephine Vericour had "an ardent ambition to excel" in the painting of miniatures, but she "was the victim of a painful and unconquerable timidity, and entire want of confidence in herself." Josephine could not believe she was capable of producing anything of value. And, indeed, the work done under the scrutiny of her instructor was quite mediocre. Then one night a miraculous event happened. When Josephine awakened, she found the unfinished painting she had left on her easel transformed into a magnificent work of art. At first the startled young woman said and did nothing about this extraordinary occurrence. But she arose on several subsequent mornings to discover that more of her own undistinguished miniatures had been changed into truly beautiful paintings. Baffled, Josephine decided to stay awake and catch the artistic intruder who furtively worked in her bedroom each night.[57]

When darkness gave way to dawn and no one appeared, the confused and tired Josephine confided these mysterious incidents to a friend and begged that her schoolmate keep vigil the next night.

The friend agreed, and the scene she witnessed astonished her. In the dead of night Josephine, sleepwalking, approached an incomplete canvas and worked with a proficiency and talent never displayed in public. With the first rays of morning, the young artist finished her work. She crept back into bed and slept, having no awareness of her marvelous accomplishment. At first Josephine refused to believe her friend's story. Finally, however, when convinced of its authenticity, she "made vigorous efforts to conquer her timidity in the presence of her master. . . . [In] time she was able to paint as well under his inspection as she had done when alone and asleep in the gloom of midnight."[58]

The story of Josephine Vericour seems to be no more than a charming tale of a gifted schoolgirl. But its author, Eliza Leslie, skillfully wove together many separate strands of the rope that bound her countrywomen. Josephine's master symbolized the antebellum male who watched, instructed, and inhibited the talents and needs of women. Josephine, the legitimate child of the woman-belle ideal, felt acute inferiority. Although wishing to excel in a loved activity, she could not perform well in her teacher's presence. She knew that a woman who displayed talent evoked scorn and contempt. Her artistic impulses, unable to be denied, manifested themselves in such a manner that they neither brought credit to Josephine nor enhanced her self-image. Yet Leslie implied that if woman could somehow be numbed or made impervious to the prohibitions against her abilities, the long-stifled talents would surely burst forth. Ironically then, somnambulism aroused Josephine's dormant skills. Confronted with the reality of her achievement, she was able to develop the self-assurance to shield her from society's disapproval. But most of Josephine Vericour's living counterparts did not share this good fortune and passed their lives unfulfilled and unhappy.

Predictably, fiction written by women told of this feminine sorrow. "Ah! Could we lay bare the secret history of many a wife's heart, what martyrs would be found, over whose uncomplaining lips the grave sets its unbroken seal of silence," wrote Fanny Fern in

Ruth Hall. Isabella of *The Lofty and the Lowly* lamented: "Such is the heroism often demanded of woman—the heroism of the martyr not the soldier"; while Eliza of *The Gamesters* asked her friend: "Why . . . did the God of nature endow us with such exquisite feelings, to have them so constantly wounded?"[59]

A mixture of hope, sadness, and resignation, woman's literary efforts vivify both her struggles for happiness and her ultimate defeat. "Let him be morose and dark, if he will; I will not follow his example. I will not be the slave of his mad caprices," proclaimed the recently married heroine of *Ernest Linwood.* But she had hardly uttered these determined words before an angel, appearing over her right shoulder, whispered: "You will be the forebearing gentle wife who promised to endure all." The angel thus reminded the misguided bride that women had to accommodate to their fate. This insistence upon acquiescence "had cost the woman's heart of Mrs. Marvyn some pangs," wrote Harriet Beecher Stowe in *The Minister's Wooing.* Yet, "after a few tremulous movements, the needle of her soul settled and her life-lot was accepted, [but] not as what she would like or could conceive." In "A Simple Tale of Love," appearing in the 1848 edition of the *Amaranth*, Amalie Winter summarized the underlying questions of tormented feminine existence: "They ask themselves—why was I loved, and why am I no longer loved? What availed the beatings of my heart, and my dreams of happiness?"[60]

Unable to answer these questions, a woman could neither identify nor articulate the roots of her unhappiness. But a profound dissatisfaction with her life, blending with an intense craving for fulfillment, manifested itself in two distinct, although related, themes: masculine despotism and feminine potential. These dual motifs at once revealed her misery and her hope. "Women are abused all the world over," wrote Stowe in one of her novels, as her colleagues poured forth streams of literature depicting males grossly mistreating women. As gamblers, alcoholics, philanderers, and even murderers, men paraded through female fiction, the embodiments of woman's long-repressed anger. By consistently presenting men as villains, women writers could find some release for their stifled rage.

Moreover, their position as authors enabled them to mold and determine masculine life, albeit only a fictitious existence. Symbolizing hostility, the desire to control man's being as he controlled woman's, and perhaps also the wish for retaliation, male characterization assumed a singularity that approached the stereotyped portrayal of antebellum woman.[61]

"Oh, it is a terrible thing to be a drunkard's wife! How many thousands of virtuous and noble hearted women have perished in the agony of such a situation," sobbed Flora of Lydia Jane Pierson's tale, "The Wash-Woman's Story." Here the laborer detailed a marriage of "hopeless and useless . . . pleadings, upbraidings, [and] reproofs" for which she received horrible "abuse [and] . . . more frequent and prolonged desertion." Like Flora's husband, Edward Grey in a short story by Emma C. Einbury became "reckless alike of wife or children" when alcohol seized possession of his mind. Originally "a poor, but honest farmer," Grey became a drunkard, lost his farm, and moved his family to the city where "they were shut up in a close room, in one of those squalid haunts of misery and vice." Similarly, inebriety ruined a harmonious family in *The Gamesters.* When Anderson "returned from his midnight orgies, the amicable woman who had chosen him for a guide and protector was treated with scottish brutality. . . . His home, his prattling infant, his domestic blessings, were turned into curses; and when insensibility had eradicated feeling, he beheld them with horror."[62]

Alcoholism did not provide the only obstacle to domestic tranquility: the antebellum era abounded with enticements to lure masculine attention and resources away from the family. Women writers frequently focused on speculation and gambling as productive of much feminine suffering. In "Straws of Destiny," contained in the *Forget-me-not* of 1850, Mrs. M. A. Felter related the history of a poor young woman: "[Her] story was a painful, but not uncommon one. Her father, involved in speculation, had lost every farthing of his large fortune, and had died from dejection and sorrow in consequence. Her mother had followed him, and left her an orphan, to struggle as best she might with bitter poverty."[63]

In 1839, the *Baltimore Book* told of Alice Howard's mother, who "had lived to see her fortune dissipated by [her] husband." The lust for money drove men to perpetrate demonic deeds, as the story "Julia Nelson" demonstrates. In this tale by Maria Williams, appearing in the gift book *Amethyst,* Tremone seduces Julia. But he soon squanders her wealth and "long[s] for the death of his innocent spouse, that by a union with the famous Madame A of immense estate, he might repair his fallen fortunes." The villain is thwarted in his dastardly act; Julia manages to escape destruction. But other heroines of women's fiction did not have this happy fate.[64]

The pages of nineteenth-century literature overflow with the sad tales of females forced to endure a destiny worse than physical death: the ruination of their reputation by callous and profligate men. In *The Gamesters* "fiendlike Somerton, with hellish industry, plotted the destruction of Eliza." "No penitence, however exemplary and sincere, can meet acceptance at the world's tribunal, the wounds of female reputation admit no unitives and resist all healing application," wrote Caroline Warren in this novel. In the 1844 edition of the *Rose,* a woman tells of her "desertion and despair" after a romance with a man of wealth and family background. When, years later, she sees the immoral Mr. Davis again, she cries out: "In beggard and abandonment [I] reared the child [I] bore you."[65]

If women fell victim to reckless men, they could not be blamed, according to Mrs. D. Clarke, author of "Grace Brown," as society pardoned males' unscrupulous behavior and made it impossible for women to know a single man's true character. But women married to "profligate men" could have no delusions about their husbands' conduct and often had positive proof of their infidelity. Mr. Hayman of the novel *Constanta Neville* orders his wife to nurse his illegitimate child; and Mrs. Wood's heroine, Lady Stanley, is forced to accept and care for her husband's bastard offspring.[66]

To be sure, not all fictitious females found themselves married to alcoholics, gamblers, murderers, or philanderers. Many wed men free of these vices. But that in no way assured women of blissful lives. Indeed, stories that described unhappy marriages proliferated. "He had been 'a brute of a husband' to the meekest and gentlest of wives, a harsh master in his household, and a tyrant to his child," wrote Camila Toulmin in "The Painter's Revealing." Chesebro reported that Mrs. Weld had been "mated, nay, united with a man who distrusted her, misunderstood her, and attempted . . . to control her by mere 'brute-blind force.' "[67]

Mrs. Latham, in a story appearing in the *Ladies' Casket* of 1848, "had a great many trials. . . . [She] had a multitude of thorns in her flesh, which prickled and tormented her continually, and one was . . . the fact that she was so *scrimped* for money by her avaricious husband." The *American Keepsake* displayed the woes of a young woman who asked her husband's assistance in a difficult matter and was all but ignored. "This was about the extent of aid I ever received from my husband in any of my domestic difficulties," she complained. In *Married or Single?* Grace asked her sister: "Tell me, honestly, Eleanor, do you really think that your husband had any right to speak pettishly to you, because his pocket-handkerchiefs were not where his lordship expected to find them? to flout you, because your laundress happened to put too much starch in his shirts? or to make you wait an hour for your dinner, with more discourtesy than he would have used toward the keeper of a lodging-house?"[68]

Along with the theme of masculine villainy, another current of thought circulated through the fiction written by Jacksonian females. Arousing feminine imagination to the glorious potentialities of women, these literary motifs enabled writers to express cherished dreams for their sex. At the same time they provided antebellum females with role models from fiction, which society had consistently denied them. Stories describing women of courage, creativity, and strength took their place beside the tales of male scoundrels: the one representing woman's despondency, the other symbolizing her hidden aspirations.

A single narrative often contained both themes, as male abuse offered women an opportunity to demonstrate fortitude and perseverance. "The Wife's Promise" by Mrs. Lydia Jane Pierson combined these two subjects. "Did you not *promise* in the presence of God to obey me?" cried a furious husband, John Evans, to his pale trembling wife. He condescendingly informed her, "Let me tell you, Madam, that a wife is by the laws held in all respects in subjection," and jeeringly asked: "Was not woman made for man?" Yet, Mrs. Evans does not demurely accept this treatment. She declares: "I do not contend about the laws that were framed by *men*, and we know that since the world began, the strong have oppressed the weak and deemed all resistance treason. . . . The framers of the marriage act were men also—fallible men. I know that all our laws bind women down to slavery."[69]

In a "Sketch from Real Life," written by Maria for the 1826 issue of the *Forget-me-not*, unsuspecting Rosalie married Edgar Mandlebert and bore him a son before discovering that he was already married. But Rosalie knew "she did not merit her bitter fate" and refused to think of herself as a social misfit. Determined to manage without a husband, she worked long hours and "was rewarded with health, peace and cheerfulness." "Widow's Daughter," appearing in the *Amaranth*, also details the achievements of an audacious young woman, Eva Mortan, who manages by "the mighty force of will" to support her family after her father's suicide. Similarly, Elsie Grey shows her resolution and courage when her father's alcoholism leaves the family destitute. For "it was entirely owing to the constant exertions of the little girl, that the whole family were preserved from starvation."[70]

The women of this body of fiction were capable, imaginative, and successful. They shaped their own lives and decided upon behavior appropriate to their skills and needs. When Elsie's father is cajoled into committing a forgery, the remarkable young woman goes with him to trial. Fully convinced that her father acted against his will, Elsie travels to Albany by herself and through her persuasive arguments procures a pardon from the governor. Ellen, the courageous orphan of another tale, became determined to locate her lover, a soldier in the Continental Army. "She conceived the design of adopting a disguise and travelling on foot to the Capital. No suggestion of danger could shake the resolution of the heroic girl," who at age seventeen set out from Germantown to Philadelphia through "scattered parties of British troops."[71]

In "Cousin Lucy" an imaginative young stepmother dons a disguise to help her stepson. His father strongly objects to his marrying a woman of the "mechanic class." But by using her ingenuity and refusing to listen to the husband's intolerance, Margaret follows her own conscience and resolves the family dispute. Her husband, upon learning of the scheme, remarks: "As my wife was . . . the instigator of this plot against my pride and prejudice, and as it has been so successful and happy in its issue, I must pardon the aiders and abettors as well as the chief conspirator herself—Ah! My sweet Margaret."[72]

While the resourceful stepmother of "Cousin Lucy" ultimately wins her husband's approval, the heroine of Mrs. Shelley's tale, "The Parvenue," does not. In this story, published in the *Amaranth* of 1848, a poor woman marries Lord Reginald. She is repelled by the extravagance of wealth. Refusing to spend money on clothing, she distributes it to the needy. The young bride knows that these actions will bring her rebuke, for she has been taught that "to please [her] husband and do honor to his rank, was [her] first duty." Nevertheless, she continues to follow her own impulses. By sharing her riches with her parents and with other impoverished citizens, she incurs her husband's wrath but feels secure in the justness of her course.[73]

Women writers implicitly urged females to have confidence in their decisions, even when confronted by male opposition. Their stories maintained that women could determine appropriate actions because they possessed both judgment and intelligence. And woman's intellectual interests and abilities captured frequent literary attention. The hero of "The March of Mind—A Fragment of Fact" has quite a surprise when he visits with women friends in the hope of hearing some "unadulterated feminine nonsense." To his astonishment he relates: "I peeped over Millicent's shoulder, hoping to find the book in her hand [to be] the last new novel, I found her examining the notes she had taken of a chemical lecture." Eleanor of

Married or Single? had an important virtue that "was not merely feminine endurance. She relieved her husband of the drudgery of his researches and often aided him with suggestions of her sound judgment."[74]

Examples of feminine intellect studded the pages of women's magazines and gift books. But few females of literature enjoyed such glowing accolades as Beulah received when she delivered her school's commencement address. This heroine of a novel by Mrs. Augusta Evans "ascended the platform, and surrounded by men signalized by scholarship and venerable from age, . . . she began her address. The theme was 'Female Heroism,' and . . . she sought among the dusty annals of the past for instances in confirmation of her predicate, that female intellect was capable of the most exalted attainments. . . . The reasoning was singularly forcible, the imagery glowing and gorgeous, and occasional passages of exquisite pathos drew tears from her fascinated audience, while more than once, a beautiful burst of enthusiasm was received with flattering applause."[75]

Woman's intellectual might was equalled in literature by her physical strength. Nineteenth-century female characters demonstrated phenomenal endurance and energy as they accomplished their numerous chores. Mrs. Stowe's Katy "could harness a chaise, or row a boat; she could saddle and ride a horse; she could cut any garment that ever was seen or thought of; [and] make jelly, cake, and wine." Ellen of *The Wide, Wide World,* the first book by an American author to sell over a million copies, had to perform countless gruelling tasks. Nevertheless she found the time to study. One of her friends reported: "Mamma, [Ellen] beats me entirely in speaking French, and she knows all about English history and arithmetic." Mrs. Hale boasted of her fictitious Mary Grey: "She spins, she knits, she feeds the poultry, weeds the garden, makes all [the] clothes, helps . . . at . . . lessons, and in the evenings leads her poor blind parents through the green lanes." Fleda, of Susan B. Warner's popular novel *Queechy,* cheerfully did the work of three hired men as well as teach, nurse, and cook. She arose before dawn to do the chores and tend the livestock, yet found time before breakfast to study the latest agricultural methods. Through her efforts she transformed a run-down farm into a model of agricultural excellence. Additionally, she cared for guests, revived the ailing health of her family, and found time to read extensively. These miraculous accomplishments placed Fleda among those extraordinary feminine creations of woman's imagination.[76]

Fictitious women, infused with vitality, ambition, and initiative, projected a vision of feminine capability quite unlike the prevailing images of womanhood, for these creatures of literature abounded with qualities the male sex allegedly monopolized. By endowing their women characters with traditionally masculine traits, female writers fashioned heroines from their unfulfilled drives, their unspoken aspirations for themselves and other women, and their beliefs in the unrecognized potential of their sex. By controlling the context in which their protagonists lived, authors implicitly expressed their conviction that in a different, more just social setting woman would be allowed to demonstrate her abilities.

Through their females of fiction, women writers could verbalize thoughts they themselves dared not utter, achieve feats they could never accomplish, and enjoy a freedom their society had consistently forbidden. Yet they avoided the painful consequences that these bold endeavors would have brought them in the real world. Their persistent characterization of the male as villain alleviated, to some extent, their feelings of hostility and sense of injustice. And their countless vignettes of woman struggling against the privations of her life enabled authors to articulate and acknowledge the conflicts of their own existence.

The abundance of literature written by nineteenth-century woman was a complex fusion of fantasy and reality. It emerged as yet another reaction to the tensions and contradictions inherent in the womanhood myths. But unlike illness and diary writing, both of which remained as essentially isolated and private manifestations of unhappiness, the deluge of fiction, occupying the idle hours of countless educated women, undoubtedly affected its readers. However, the nature and extent of the response among literate women of leisure is problematic. Tales of courageous, accomplished females may have encouraged some to become more assertive, but most women only vicariously enjoyed their heroine's successes or empathetically wept over her hardships. They found compensations and outlets in fiction for personal frustration and did nothing to improve their own lives.

Yet, the impulse to share feelings and ideas, and the need to resolve conflicts, persisted. The craving to find the sense of self amidst confusion and emptiness, revealed in illness and in different forms of feminine writing, could not be quelled. This yearning for fulfillment and sharing exploded into networks of female voluntary associations in cities across the nation. In the pulsating urban milieu, women found a profound form of communication and expression and a compelling purpose for their energies. Through female benevolent societies women slowly and painfully comprehended the meaning of their collective experiences.

As they gained an awareness of the depth, subtleness, and pervasiveness of their oppression, they ultimately came to perceive women as autonomous beings, complex and different from each other, but alike in that they shared a common humanity so long denied them. They began cautiously. First determining the nature of their duties and responsibilities to themselves, to other women, and to society, they would ultimately begin to claim possession of their own lives.

Ironically, the industrializing city played a dual role. The dynamism of urban life contributed heavily to the masculine insecurity and anxiety that coalesced into a monolithic philosophy of womanhood. Yet, it was this same social context that impelled women first to identify, but later to challenge and defy, the confining tenets of the woman-belle ideal.

II

TOWARD FEMINISM

Woman will learn the power of association and she will learn the value of herself. . . .

—New York Working Woman's Protective Union, 1863

7
Association

> Association makes the whole world kin:
> O'er laping time and space, its magic powers
> Can bring the future and the past within
> The scope and feeling of the present hour
>
> —author unknown, *Association*

Woman's voluntary associations arose in combined response to personal needs and social demands in the growing cities. Through organization, upper- and middle-class women confronted and evaluated their lives. They created a vibrant feminist ideology, which in turn sparked the demand for woman's rights.

Throughout the first part of the nineteenth century, voluntary organizations proliferated. Alexis de Tocqueville noted the immense variety of associations—"political," "commercial," "manufacturing," "religious, moral, serious, futile, general or restricted, enormous or diminutive." He explained that "[in] democratic nations . . . all the citizens are independent and feeble. . . . They all, therefore, become powerless, if they do not learn voluntarily to help each other." The French observer found the impulse inherent in the American political system. But twentieth-century writers, focusing more narrowly on urban charitable societies, have interpreted the plethora of associations during the Jacksonian era differently.[1]

Some scholars emphasized the potential effectiveness of charitable associations in assimilation and acculturation. They have viewed organized benevolence largely as a reponse to an unstable and threatening social context. Voluntary societies became a means by which the "wealthy and respectable old town [could] absorb and digest its chaotic and dangerous environment, to inculcate the entire city population with its attitudes and values." Raymond Mohl stated in *Poverty in New York 1783–1825* that "charity and benevolence [were] . . . important agents of social and moral stewardship." With harmony and docility as their paramount concerns, "middle class men and women consciously promoted moral reformation and religious indoctrination as a method of restoring order to the urban community." Authors accentuating the integrative and indoctrinating aspects of charitable work have stressed the value of evangelicalism in maintaining social control. Clifford Griffin, in *Their Brother's Keeper*, believed that "religion and morality as dispensed by the benevolent societies throughout the seemingly chaotic nation became a means of establishing secular order." And Keith Melder asserted that the "evangelical movement appeared . . . as a potent weapon in . . . [the] battle for stability and order."[2]

Predictably, this concept of "moral stewardship" elicited divergent opinions. In *Revivalism and Social Reform*, Timothy L. Smith argued that evangelists and perfectionists led the way in both expounding and applying the doctrine of Christian responsibility to the poor. The sense of duty emanated "from the zeal and compassion which the mid-century revivalists awakened for sinning and suffering men," rather than from the need for social control. Similarly, Carroll Smith Rosenberg, author of *Religion and the Rise of the American City: The New York City Mission Movement 1812–1870*, wrote that social welfare agencies "saw religion as a principal impetus towards respectable self sufficiency for the poor." Urban benevolent societies "did not develop solely or even primarily because of the alarming growth of urban problems . . . [but] such works were the product of an optimistic, truly 'Jacksonian' belief in the perfectability of man."[3]

Social control and religion afford persuasive arguments for understanding nineteenth-century voluntarism. Undoubtedly the desire to maintain a stable society based upon traditional patterns of deference and morality, as well as the conviction that eternal life was the best gift to be given to the poor, provided important motives for benevolent organizations. Yet, an intensive study of more than one hundred fifty female associations in American cities during the period from 1800 to 1860 reveals that neither of these interpretations is adequate to explain the massive outpouring of energy into female societies.

Although Raymond Mohl's study is not directed primarily toward women's groups, he considers them to have been motivated by the same attitudes as men's organizations. To substantiate this interpretation, Mohl notes that several charities conducted by women imposed restrictions on the recipients of their benefaction.

The Society for the Relief of Poor Widows with Small Children, for example, would not aid a woman unless the managers had evidence of the husband's death or proof of at least twelve months' absence from home. Moreover, a widow could be removed from the pension list for "intemperance" or "immorality."[4]

Mohl finds evidence of social control in such regulations and states that "the Society for the Relief of Poor Widows mirrored contemporary currents of urban philosophy." There are, however, other explanations for the deliberate distinctions made among the society's beneficiaries. The managers repeatedly defend and lament the need to limit the recipients because of a lack of funds. In a report written in 1816 they note that "at present" they are giving alms to "202 widows and 500 children." "[By] allowing only 3 dollars a month for 6 months the sum is $3,636," and this total did not reflect the society's policy of providing unlimited assistance during periods of illness. Statements of other female associations reflect similar financial shortages that required economy in charity.[5]

Nevertheless, even acknowledging that women's charities could not afford to aid all the indigent females in their respective cities, one might reasonably question the criteria used to deny aid to potential recipients. Did it imply a condescendingly moral judgment that some women deserved assistance more than others? While it is true that many female voluntary associations in the first few decades of the nineteenth century explicitly favored "respectable women," or "females of fair character," it is by no means certain that these rules evolved from the wish to discipline potentially unruly segments of the population.[6]

The lives of the women who worked as members, managers, and officers of the early female societies had been molded by the precepts of the woman-belle ideal. Their sense of themselves and of other women had been shaped by a philosophy that insisted that only one kind of woman existed. They were taught from childhood that a female's worth came from purity, piety, docility, domesticity, and willingness to sacrifice for her male relations. Thus, upper- and middle-class women who pioneered in organized benevolence could not easily relate to females who seemed so grossly different from themselves. Alcoholics, prostitutes, and criminals all appeared so alien, so beyond the realm of comprehension, that they could hardly be considered women.

Practical considerations also directed feminine attention to the more acceptable females on the fringes of society. Fearing their unprecedented activities would call forth hostility and derision, women in early voluntary associations aided the least "socially offensive" members of their sex. This pragmatic decision made it possible for their followers to pursue wider and more audacious schemes of benevolence and attract broader support. Raymond Mohl's analysis ends with 1825. Had he continued his study he would have found that as women absorbed the lessons of urban life, they came to recognize and respect the diversity of their sex. Willingly, they reached out to females so entirely different from themselves that their only bond lay in gender.

Moreover, the activities and attitudes described in the reports of female societies flourishing in the first part of the nineteenth century give little evidence of moral stewardship. Not only do the extant records fail to disclose significant social-control motivation, but examples abound of women risking their person, property, and reputation to assist less fortunate members of their sex. Theories that established classes in American cities consciously used organized benevolence to impose their vision of society on the urban masses might possibly be applicable to male organizations. But they have little relevance to the female voluntary associations of the years between 1800 and 1860.

Historians who have viewed religious enthusiasm as the impulse for organized benevolence have emphasized the clerical support given to some urban charities. They also have asserted that the language and style of antebellum philanthropic associations reflected deep and sincere piety and have noted the impact of the Second Great Awakening on the nation's cities. The religious argument appears to have a certain cogency. Yet, when one tries to explain the rise of female voluntary societies within the context of pious fervor, flaws in the interpretation become apparent. These invite further investigation into the relationship between religion and feminine urban philanthropy: one must question whether religiosity and clerical persuasion actually hastened women into benevolent associations.[7]

Numerous clergymen commented on the propriety of feminine societies. Their remarks tell much about the nature of charitable work they considered appropriate for the "fair sex." Some religious leaders, particularly those of the traditional denominations, vehemently opposed women's involvement in any organization as it meant "laying aside the delicacy . . . and decorum which can never be violated without the most corrupting effects on themselves and public morals." Bishop Hobart of New York believed that the "progress of *female demoralization* amongst that portion of the *sex* which has fallen prey to Bible Society beguilements could . . . be traced by [any] one who had the daily registers of the period within his reach." Another minister condemned woman when, "impatient of her proper sphere . . . and forsaking the domestic hearth, her delicate voice is heard from house to house . . . expecting to put down every real or supposed evil . . . by the right arm of female power and clamorous for the organization of a female society for this specific object."[8]

Other clergymen accepted the formation of feminine societies but tempered approval with large doses of caution. An article appearing in the *Panoplist* for 1816 advised a secretary of one charitable organization, a female cent society, on behavior appropriate for women. "It is very important to adhere strictly to the Holy Scriptures," the author wrote as he reminded females of the apostolic prohibitions on feminine conduct. Nevertheless, although women could not "set themselves up as public teachers, and [take] the lead in religious exercises, and in other important discussions, and so [usurp] authority over man," the writer thought it acceptable for "a few females assembled in private . . . to meet together for prayer." Rev. J. K. Brownson, addressing the young ladies of the Oakland Female Seminary, admonished his audience that "the proper dignity of woman consists not in aspiring to . . . wield the reforms of the day. Ambition for this in the female sex is preposterous." Brownson asserted that women had a role in "promoting the great moral reforms of the day, but not to *lead* and *guide* them."[9]

Religious leaders who thought female associations admissible generally agreed that women could enter benevolent work as long as they primarily conformed to the principles of the woman-belle ideal. Clergymen addressing women's societies endorsed the limitations on both feminine prerogative and behavior. Rev. Moses Stuart announced to the Salem Female Charitable Society that "the management of funds" lay beyond the proper sphere of women and that "the aid of men who are skilled in these matters [should be] . . . procured." Some clergymen viewed woman's charitable involvement merely as a stage for the display of traditional female attributes. They continually lectured the volunteers on the importance of separate realms for men and women.[10]

While speaking before women's voluntary associations, ministers sometimes discoursed upon the female role in spreading the Holy

Gospel. Again these clerical directives closely followed the dominant nineteenth-century thinking on womanhood. Rev. Samuel Worcester told a group of women in Massachusetts that those "who hold the interesting situation of mothers of families, may shew their love to Christ, and render him service and assistance, by making it their care that their children should be His."[11]

Rev. Matthew La Rue Perrine in a sermon delivered at the first annual meeting of the Female Missionary Society for the Poor of the City of New York on 12 May 1817 claimed that "[woman] is satisfied in being an *assistant* of man," for "there is not one among us who feels disposed to indulge the thought that the duties of women in the Church of God are . . . the same as those of men." Yet, women "may . . . form associations among themselves to support men who are spending their time, their talents in evangelizing the poor. . . . [I]t will become the present members of this Society to exhibit a pattern of Christian modesty, meekness, submission . . . [as that] which are of the ornament of your sex must be observed, and must shine in all your deliberations, resolutions, and actions."[12]

Ministers who agreed to such speaking engagements were, no doubt, among those most in accord with the aims of feminine benevolent associations. Yet even these relatively sympathetic clergymen imposed rigid boundaries on the nature and extent of philanthropic activity a female could pursue. The sermons delivered before numerous women's societies indicate that although religious leaders might tolerate or even endorse these organizations, in most instances they did not supply the impetus for their formation. As long as women remained docile, subservient, and unthreatening, doing nothing to disrupt the myth of the essential difference between male and female natures, clergymen accepted their societies. The church, sincerely appreciating the willingness of women to give their time to religious endeavors, might make use of feminine energy, but it would not countenance any activity that caused woman to leave her "limited circle." Indeed, the pulpit refused to support those societies that it believed took her beyond the allocated sphere.

These repeated and specific clerical strictures necessitate further inquiry into the hypothesis that religion exercised the prevailing influence in the development of female voluntary associations. Historians who make the religious argument have failed to differentiate between male and female societies. They have thus postulated a causal relationship between all organized urban benevolence and piety. In her study of religion in New York City, Carroll Smith Rosenberg discusses the Female Missionary Society for the Poor of New York within the same context as two seemingly similar male associations. All founded in 1816, "these societies were an integral part of the Second Great Awakening's missionary and millennial enthusiasm," writes Rosenberg. Yet the subsequent history of the Female Missionary Society must raise serious doubts about clerical endorsement of feminine philanthropy.[13]

Rev. William Gray, addressing the organization's members in 1821, told of "the impression which has rested on the minds of many, that you had engaged in an enterprise beyond your appropriate sphere, . . . [for many] questioned the propriety of females managing in the capacity which this society has done." He informed the women of the Female Missionary Society that "the active management of [their] Institution has been wholly transferred from the hands of the Ladies into those of the Gentlemen." Although Gray believed that "these are certainly events of a promising character and appear well adapted to give strength and permanence to the mission," it is by no means certain that the women agreed. But, powerless to protest, they evidently complied with the clerical decision.[14]

Not all female societies, however, demurely accepted the treatment they received by the clergy. For many complex reasons, the American Female Moral Reform Society strenuously resisted clerical objections to its work. Although this society will be studied in greater detail in following chapters, it is worth examining briefly here. Rosenberg includes it in her group of "New York's earliest true city missions" arising in response to the Second Great Awakening. A thorough analysis of the enterprises of the Moral Reform Society over a period of fifty years makes it difficult to accept the label of "city mission." To be sure, in the later years of the association, the members organized a directory to help poor women find work, established a home for the friendless, and became increasingly responsive to the problems of slum life. These activities, however, would seem to render the name "settlement house" more appropriate than "mission." Nor is it clear that the genesis of the Moral Reform Society lay in revivalism. Dedicated to the abolition of prostitution and to the ostracism of male profligates, the society published a journal, the *Advocate of Moral Reform*, to assist in its campaign.[15]

The early issues of the *Advocate* explained the association's origins: "This work must be begun with ladies. They are the injured, and they must rise and assert their rights. . . .[I]f licentious men are to be admitted into virtuous society we shall ask the same for licentious women. All we ask is equal privileges where there is equal guilt; we think our claim is righteous, and in this day of pleading for equal rights we trust it will be acknowledged." In 1835, the women wrote in their journal that the "virtuous daughters of America ought to regard the existing state of licentiousness, systematized as it is in our cities, . . . as a regular crusade against the sex, and they ought to rise in their own defense."[16]

Rather than being impelled to action by religious prodding, the Moral Reform Society repeatedly criticized religious leaders for impeding their cause. In the first volume of their paper they note that they applied to "six editors of religious journals in the city to publish circulars" and all but two refused. In a subsequent issue the *Advocate* carries the following indictment: "Yes, 'tis true that these heralds of the cross refuse to give publicity to a society of *ladies* (of course nothing political about it) engaged in saving the country and church from general prostitution." And, in an open letter to the famous revivalist minister, Lyman Beecher, they ask: "If the cause of Moral Reform should fail, will it not be because the influence of such men . . . [as Rev. Beecher] is withheld?" Indeed, the countless objections "advanced either from the pulpit or in articles furnished by clergymen for . . . periodicals" that moral reform efforts "tend to debase and corrupt the mind, by the familiarity with vice which they necessarily occasion," make it difficult to accept the theory that this important woman's society flourished throughout the nation because of evangelical enthusiasm.[17]

Nevertheless religion did play a part in organized benevolence. Many women active in charitable work were deeply pious, and the rhetoric used in their publications may reflect a profound religious commitment. Yet, to view urban female philanthropy in the years after 1830 largely as a response to the Second Great Awakening is to ignore other motives. While a religious dimension did exist, the clergy stipulated an essentially limited role for women even in those societies dedicated to spreading the Gospel. Religious leaders were opposed to many significant feminine organizations. Moreover, the proliferation of female voluntary societies in urban areas some thirty years before the Second Great Awakening, giving the later societies important models and precedents, suggests that piety played a limited role in organized philanthropy. It is, therefore, necessary to look beyond religious fervor for an explanation of the network of woman's voluntary societies in the years between 1800 and 1860.[18]

An analysis of the ways in which women experienced and perceived their deteriorating status from the start of the colonial period to the early years of the nineteenth century sheds new light on female voluntarism. Such a study strongly suggests that the dynamics of urbanization, contributing strongly to the creation of the woman-belle ideal, also became the unwitting midwife of female benevolent societies. Women's charities responded to many of the same problems and pressures that called male associations into being. Both were touched by an acute sense of individual impotence to effect social change and by pervasive feelings of isolation. But female societies had a heritage uniquely their own and developed along lines quite distinct from their masculine counterparts.

Urban man did join voluntary societies of all kinds. Yet these organizations comprised only *one* of many ways the male city dweller could pursue community and personal fulfillment. Urban woman, in contrast, was substantially barred from all rewarding endeavor. She had virtually no alternatives. Chained to a futile existence fraught with profound conflicts, her discontent manifested itself in illness and in diaries and works of fiction.

Finally, as boredom, loneliness, and the craving for identity coalesced into a driving force, women founded networks of societies throughout urban America. The records of these associations reveal much of the motivation behind their formation. "It is not to listen to beautiful theories or flowery paragraphs on education that these meetings take place. . . . The experience of one may, when imparted, be of service to many others; and the peculiar trials of one will, when shared by a sister hand, be deprived of half their bitterness," proclaimed an article urging the formation of maternal associations.[19]

An essay appearing in the journal of a prominent women's society wrote of experiencing "Solitude in Cities" when "the sense of [isolation] settled down . . . as the clouds often seem to press the earth, making the air heavy, oppressive and stifling." The first directress of the Society for the Relief of Poor Widows emphasized that the organization could be "very useful to those ladies who have sufficient health and leisure to engage in it." And a report of the Association for the Relief of Respectable, Aged, Indigent Females stressed the benefits that women received from joining an association that enabled them actually to perform works of charity, rather than sentimentally "sigh[ing] in the parlour over pictures of ideal misery. Ours must be an active . . . benevolence."[20]

Numerous publications of female societies advocated organized benevolence as the antidote for a tedious, useless existence. One paper quoted a woman as saying: " 'I should be thankful to know of some way in which I could employ my time and means for the benefit of some one.' " The female author of the article, noting the many widows desperate for assistance, expressed astonishment at "this Christian lady . . . languishing for the want of 'something to do!' " The writer was certain that if women would be involved in benevolent activities, they "shall be forever delivered from the fashionable ennui of 'nothing to do.' "[21]

In the short story "A Cure of Low Spirits," Mary S. Graham described the "cloud upon [her] feelings": "I could not smile . . . nor speak in a tone of cheerfulness." But when she visited a widow and sick child, "all changed." "Sympathy for others and active efforts to do others good, had expelled the . . . [low] spirits from my heart . . . and I sung cheerfully as I prepared . . . a basket of provisions for the poor widow." At a testimonial for a member of the Orphan Asylum Society, a co-worker asserted that a "well-spent life" of active benevolence should serve as an example to other females of "the various talents of wealth, of influence, and of leisure, [used] for the end for which they were given."[22]

Although the literature of female voluntary associations urged women to organize, it understood that they "would be glad to lift up their hands and do something, but the chains of custom and fashion are upon them. A false social position has made them timid and fearful." And indeed, diffidence made some females reluctant to join an organization. Yet the unremitting inner tensions drove others to become active in associations dedicated to helping members of their sex.[23]

In one sense, then, feminine involvement in voluntary societies represented a multifaceted quest for identity. In another, it formed a plausible response to urban problems. The closeness of city living brought upper- and middle-class women into unavoidable contact with lower levels of society. Aged and indigent women, underpaid and sickly laborers, alcoholics, and prostitutes were all visible; their presence disturbing, their needs compelling. An annual report of one society recorded that "in the latter part of the year 1813, a few ladies, moved with compassion, associated themselves for the purpose of relieving the necessities and distresses of aged females." Another organization asserted that the "social duties" of the "women of our city . . . lie among the population of the . . . city," for "New York City . . . is a great world of itself. . . . From year to year its teeming thousands multiply, and whatever may be found of human suffering . . . may be seen, in some phase, within the precincts of this vast city."[24]

Catharine Sedgwick, the author who later became active in New

York's charities, wrote to her sister of the "confusion and dismay" the economic reversals produced on "those who have been accustomed to live upon the fruit of their labors." Sarah Martyn, a leader in the Moral Reform Society, regarded New York as a "great city, . . . though of the extremes which constantly meet and pain the eye, the extremes of princely magnificence and squalid penury, of reckless extravagance and abject want, nothing but actual observation can give even a faint impression."[25]

The Female Benevolent Society asserted that "[one] of the motives which led to the formation of the Society was the . . . wretched condition of thousands of abandoned females in the city of N-Y." Reports of organizations from other developing urban areas reflect the same concerns. "Consider a moment some of the causes for such an association," advised a speaker before the Newburyport Orphan Asylum, founded by women in 1803. "It is well known that in populous maritime districts, a greater inequality prevails in the condition of the people, than in those of the same extent whose inhabitants subsist chiefly by agricultural pursuits." These blatant social and economic disparities necessitated concerted action on the part of the female sex. Noting that "it is not the duty only of *large* cities to provide for the destitute sufferer," the members of the Newburyport Orphan Asylum agreed that the "HONOR of the TOWN requires it." The urge to organize in Newburyport was particularly strong because the "neighboring towns of Salem and Portsmouth . . . furnished worthy examples" of feminine benevolence.[26]

The members of the Female Charitable Society in Salem believed that city dwellers had a responsibility to help one another, for the poor must derive some advantage from where they live or "they would experience the same inconveniences and privations when living in the crowded city as in the depths of the forest." The women who established the Orphan Asylum of New York thought their work had a special urgency because "the subjects of misfortune and misery multiply in large commercial towns." And an 1821 report of the Boston Female Refuge recorded that "cities swarm with a mixed population, instances of poverty [and] distress . . . meet the eye."

In Troy, New York, a group of women instituted an orphan asylum "to afford assistance to indigent women and children," while their counterparts in cities across the nation responded similarly to the combination of social and personal pressures.[27]

In emerging urban areas throughout the country, female benevolent societies blossomed forth, cross-fertilizing one another as they sowed the seeds of American feminism. The history of the activities, aspirations, ideas, and lives of the women who joined associations devoted to helping others of their sex is the chronicle of the origins of woman's emancipation. It is the story of her attempts to find freedom from the bonds of an imprisoning ethos that thwarted her efforts at self-realization, denied her autonomous nature, and refuted her common humanity.

Through their work in voluntary societies women became aware of their oppression. They began, first for themselves and then for other females, to challenge the precepts of the woman-belle ideal. In so doing, they slowly came to recognize a unity of all women, which was based on respect for individuality. Each woman, as an independent being, was entitled to human dignity and basic natural rights. The feminist thinking that emerged from female voluntarism evolved gradually, as generations of urban women learned of and assimilated each others' experiences.

In 1800 the fear of social ostracism prevented most women from participating in organized benevolence. Mrs. Isabella Graham, who founded the Society for the Relief of Poor Widows with Small Children, likened a group of "young ladies" about to form a charitable association to the "great general in ancient times, [who] in search of glory landed his troops on the hostile coast, and then burnt all his ships; thus it became necessary for them to conquer or die." Graham told the assembled women that once they had "embarked in this design, there is no remaining neuter. . . . Your names and undertaking are in every mouth; you must press forward and justify your cause; . . . it cannot be otherwise." She recalled that her own society, which distributed firewood, shoes, and clothing to widows and provided them with work, "was a new thing in this country. It was feeble in origin; many treated it with ridicule; many raised against it the standard of opposition. The men could not allow the [female] sex the steadiness and perseverance necessary to establish such an undertaking."[28]

Isabella Graham, who had been "blessed with a spirit of philanthropy, with an ardent and generous mind, [and] a sound judgment," did indeed possess the determination to stand firm in the face of opposition. In 1797 she became the founder of the first benevolent association managed by women in the United States. Three years later, the aroused sympathies of another courageous woman gave shape to a second pioneer society. Mrs. Stillman of Boston became interested in the plight of orphaned females when she heard a tale of "a little orphan girl, who, having no one to protect her had easily become a victim of the designs of an unscrupulous man." Stillman wanted to provide an asylum for girls. But the women of Boston had never before combined for a public purpose and the idea's "novelty occasioned objections and delay."[29]

The *Boston Gazette* carried a long anonymous correspondence on the correctitude of the plan. Finally, the women sent out private notices and "one hundred subscribers were obtained." "With comparatively few friends, and slender resources, its founders . . . struggled against the prejudices and obstacles which an undertaking so novel and so little understood was calculated to excite," a later report of the society noted. But "this was not a scheme of visionary enthusiasts, fading at the touch of examination, and destroyed by the test of experience." The Boston Female Asylum, established in 1800 by an assemblage of daring women, endured for over one hundred years. And the female populations of other cities found inspiration in the efforts of these early activists.[30]

Within the first decade of the nineteenth century, female asylums appeared in numerous urban areas. Troy, Salem, Newburyport, and Portsmouth—each boasted of an orphanage founded and managed by women, while in 1806 women of the Empire City associated for the "pleasing task of ministering to the wants [of] . . . parentless children." Developed under the tutelage of the Society for the Relief of Poor Widows, the Orphan Asylum of New York arose because of "the pain which it gave the ladies of the Widows' Society to behold a family of orphans driven on the decease of a widow to seek refuge in the Alms House."[31]

Graham's daughter, Joanna Bethune, who had gained experience in benevolent work as the third directress of the Society for the Relief of Poor Widows, agitated for the formation of the new charity. She won election to the post of treasurer, while Mrs. Sarah Ogden Hoffman, one of Mrs. Graham's associates, became the first directress. Mrs. Sarah Startin, "the widow of a wealthy English merchant, holding a high place in society," also became an officer. The "estimation in which [Mrs. Startin] was held . . . enabled her to commend the work" of the organization to the public. Yet the members of the original benevolent associations still had to contend with the many who refused to support an "institution . . . entrusted to *females*."[32]

Ever cognizant of the precarious position they occupied, the women of the early associations exercised extreme caution that their activities provoked no unnecessary criticism. The reports of these first societies reflect the members' misgivings about the propriety of their work and their capability to perform it. The 1814 constitution of the New York Female Society for the Aid of Foreign Missions hoped to allay apprehension by acknowledging that "it is not the province of Females to go forth in a public capacity and preach the Work of Life." The annual report for 1826 of the Brooklyn Female Bible Society gave an apologetic explanation for the association's origin and hoped it would not give "any just cause for either . . . sneers or . . . censure." The Association for the Relief of Respectable, Aged, Indigent Females called upon "those [men] superior in intellect to come and assist us in our work, for encouraging *us* in our limited sphere, may lead to . . . [enlarged] plans of benevolence." And members of the Penitent Females' Refuge of Boston, long accustomed to masculine direction, believed that "the house could not be successfully managed without the presence of a Gentleman as Superintendent."[33]

Woman's self-doubts combined with social pressure and legal restrictions to shape the actions and regulations of many early female benevolent organizations. To enable their associations to hold property, most societies eventually organized in corporate form. The wish to avoid legal complications arising from a husband's right to control his wife's money led numerous organizations to follow the example of the Newburyport Female Charity. This society decreed that "the treasurer . . . should always be a single woman of the age of 21 years upwards." Because the dictates of convention deemed it unladylike for women to solicit funds, some associations, including the Female Missionary Society, depended upon a "committee of gentlemen . . . to obtain subscriptions." As the code of feminine decorum also prohibited unchaperoned ladies from walking in their cities' poorer neighborhoods, some of the original associations insisted that members be "accompanied by men" for the purpose of "visiting from house to house."[34]

The necessity of compliance, or at least of the appearance of compliance, with the prevailing social mores limited members' activities. Yet even in their hesitant, infant stage, voluntary associations helped women to escape from the bondage of the woman-belle ideal. The determination to initiate an organization or to join an existing society represented, for many females, an important step toward self-assertion. This was particularly true because the decision often provoked the opposition of friends and family. Providing women with a sense of community and involvement, the associations' meetings and activities presented a compelling alternative to the monotonous and often sickly life of the useless lady. And the functions of the different societies gave women feelings of responsibility and importance denied them in the domestic realm.

Membership in an association provided the upper- and middle-class woman, traditionally isolated at home, an opportunity to relate to other women of similar background in an unprecedented manner. Acquaintances and friendships assumed a dimension not found within the stylized tedium of "social calls." Energized by a sense of mission, the women of the respective societies drew together. They shielded one another from ridicule and scorn, exchanged ideas on methods, worked hard and long hours to meet deadlines and avert crises, and supported each other in the many difficulties arising from work in organized benevolence.

Sarah Ayer, a member of numerous female voluntary associations in Portland, Maine, recorded her acute sense of loss when she moved to Eastport. Although continuing to miss her friends, Mrs. Ayer apparently assuaged her loneliness by attending prayer meetings, for she wrote: "We had an interesting female prayer meeting. I do generally enjoy these little social meetings." Yet these gatherings could not replace her friendships in the Portland voluntary societies. She writes of the women she left: "We shared each other's joys and sorrows, and found the one heightened and the other alleviated by sympathy." From the intense and continuous involvement with females similarly situated, urban volunteers came to rely upon each other. Slowly piercing the isolating myth that "women could not form friendships," the members began to see each association as "one small link in a chain of female union."[35]

Voluntarism also illuminated and developed hitherto hidden skills. The members of each association drew up their own constitutions and bylaws, elected officers, arranged for meetings, assigned duties, managed funds, and wrote and published annual reports on the society's progress. Most organizations stipulated that "the direction of the affairs of the society shall be vested in a first and second Directress, a Secretary, a Treasurer, and twelve managers, all of whom shall be chosen by a plurality of ballots at the annual meeting."[36]

Those societies that distributed alms typically divided their respective cities into districts. A manager, assigned to each area, had the responsibility to assess the number of destitute women in her division and to determine the kind and amount of relief necessary. Associations required their members to make accurate accounts of the aid given and to keep careful records of their visits. They urged volunteers to consult with the board of directors "in particular situations of embarrassment or distress."[37]

The membership dues varied with the different societies, but each organization published a precise accounting of its funds. The Female Bethel Association of New York, established "in the winter of 1832" to aid "the destitute and suffering families of the Seamen, their widows and orphans," decreed that "the treasurer shall receive and have in charge all the moneys belonging to the Society." The treasurer had to "keep a full and correct account . . . make all disbursements and render an account to the Board at its first meeting each month." Numerous societies imposed fines for failure to follow rules and for absenteeism. The regularity of the meetings, the significance attached to them, and the promulgation of specific regulations imparted structure and importance to vacuous lives previously passed in promenades down Broadway or Chestnut Street.[38]

As female associations proliferated in the years after 1820, women's options and opportunities increased dramatically. The kaleidoscopic milieu of the cities presented ever changing and challenging needs to a female population desperate for a chance to be useful. Some associations, like the Brooklyn Orphan Asylum housed in "Jackson Mansion of the Heights," arose after a specific urban crisis: "The ravages of cholera in 1832, by which many children were left orphans, suggested to the minds of a few benevolent ladies the necessity of an Orphan Asylum." Other organizations originated because of the devastating poverty concomitant with urban growth.[39]

The Female Association aided numerous "sick poor," while in one year the Female Assistance Society relieved over 1,500 impoverished women. During the same period, the Association for the Relief of Respectable, Aged, Indigent Females distributed alms to 150 women over the age of sixty. And some 254 widows and 667 children under ten years of age received the bounties of the Society for the Relief of Poor Widows. In 1823, a group of women formed the New York Asylum for Lying-in Women, established "to afford an asylum to women in a state of pregnancy, who are destitute of the means of support, and who are unable to procure the necessary medical assistance and nursing during the periods of their confinement." The Society for Employing the Poor of Boston, the Ladies' Depository, and the Society for the Promotion of Industry, the latter two of New York City, distributed work to indigent females. And widows and orphans of sailors found helping hands in the Boston Seamen's Aid Society and the Female Bethel Association of New York, both formed in the early 1830s.[40]

As the widespread poverty, crime, and disease of urban society compelled woman's entry into organized philanthropy, female voluntarism developed a momentum of its own. The existing associations, needing auxiliaries to enhance their efforts, pressed for their formation. Yet, the most ardent promoters of the new societies were the members themselves. When a family move forced a woman to leave her associations, she frequently tried to initiate another society in her new home. Sarah Ayer recorded in her diary: "A number of us met together with a view to the forming of a maternal association, similar to the one in Portland. I had long felt anxious for the formation of such a society and rejoiced in the prospect of succeeding so well." Similarly, Susan Huntington hoped to sponsor voluntary organizations in Boston and asked her friends in other cities to send her detailed information about their associations. Indeed, societies frequently helped each other by exchanging reports, proposals, and ideas.[41]

The ever increasing number of female voluntary associations induced women to become active in more than one organization. At the time of her death in her mid-thirties, Susan Huntington had been a life member of the Female Orphan Asylum, vice-president of the Graham Society, director of the Corban Society, corresponding secretary and one of the visitors and distributors of the Female Bible Society of Boston and Vicinity, an annual subscriber to both the Widow's Society and the Boston Female Education Society, and a member of the Boston Maternal Association. Joanna Bethune was a dedicated worker in the Society for the Relief of Poor Widows, the Orphan Asylum, and the Society for the Promotion of Industry. She also organized the New York Female Union Society for the Promotion of Sabbath Schools, an interdenominational group that brought some eight thousand children of the city into its classes, and in 1827 founded the Infant School Society. Her mother, Isabella Graham, had an equally extensive and diversified record of benevolent work. Of course, not all women devoted every minute to charity. But most females entering the field of public philanthropy committed their time and energies to more than one organization.[42]

The differing aims and activities of female associations provided the woman of the middle and upper classes with opportunities to perceive and express her individuality. The antebellum woman, so long the victim of a narrow, defining creed that imperiously told her what she *must* and *must not* do, now found herself with numerous options. For the first time *she* could decide for herself how she wished to spend her time and energy. By giving her a myriad of choices, benevolent associations encouraged the woman of means to express her uniqueness. She did so by affiliation with a society that suited her particular interests and aptitudes. Yet this association neither limited nor defined her. She could be a member of several different organizations simultaneously and could exercise different talents in each.

In one society a member could visit and assist desolate families. In another, she could work as a treasurer responsible for substantial resources. And in a third she could function as a manager, supervising the members and helping the board of directors to determine policy. She might teach young girls, obtain work for poor women, and meet with the city merchants to secure supplies. Each position offered different responsibilities; her personal contacts varied greatly; a range of alternatives awaited her. The economically secure urban woman could at last begin to realize the special capacities and concerns that contributed to making her distinct from other women in her class. While developing new skills and interests, she worked intimately with the members of her society, experiencing a sense of closeness with other females.

Benevolent societies were slowly creating change. Whereas the woman-belle ideal had insisted that all females had the same needs, abilities, and aspirations, voluntary organizations enabled their members to recognize that they were not alike. And, rather than the isolation or alienation that often accompanies the realization of individual differences, a sense of community with other women developed. Awareness of individuality grew out of unity and would have important implications for the development of feminism.

Female voluntary associations also enabled women to demonstrate physical strength and emotional fortitude. Of her mother, Joanna Bethune wrote: "It was often her custom to leave home after breakfast, to take with her a few rolls of bread and return in the evening about eight o'clock. Her only dinner on such days was her bread." Other women shared Mrs. Graham's determination. During the yellow fever epidemic in 1798, four members of the board of the Society for the Relief of Poor Widows "at the risk of their lives remained in the city, steady in the exercise of their office." Similarly, women remained at the Orphan Asylum of New York to care for sick children during a cholera epidemic in 1834. At least one member contracted the disease and died.[43]

In other ways, also, did women in benevolent societies prove their courage. Although some females succumbed to pressure and sought male protection when they walked in their cities' poorer areas, the overwhelming majority of women visited in wretched neighborhoods alone. Disregarding the inherent risks, they entered districts conspicuous for disease, alcoholism, and crime. As they met the challenging and often excruciating responsibilities of their organizations, women in charity work also had to "experience much painful banter." "Indomitable perseverance" was required, for each novel enterprise called forth new opposition.[44]

The members of the Boston Seamen's Aid Society recalled that their "effort was met with a very ready response by many; some spurned the idea of ladies being associated with such outcasts as seamen or their families, but a few [volunteers] were determined to accomplish their object. This they did." One report recorded that "it has been asserted by a disparager of our sex, that women are unfit for the detail of business which requires method and exactness—that they always prefer fancies to facts, and detest all figures save those of poetry and dance. But I trust we shall show that, in the prosecution of the benevolent plan, we have not shrunk from the duty of investigating facts, or the labor and care of exact calculation." The endless charges of incompetency were no doubt demoralizing at times. But they challenged women to prove their abilities and invigorated the members with a crusading zeal.[45]

The persistent lack of revenue also stimulated the imagination and urged women to increased endeavor. For "these enterprising women did not sit . . . waiting for the manna to drop into their outstretched hands, but . . . arranged for ways and means to obtain relief." Fund-raising efforts included holding bazaars, selling subscriptions, arranging for speakers to address groups of women, soliciting donations from prominent citizens, and petitioning the government. The requests for governmental assistance were frequently productive of aid, but they had an importance that transcended the additional capital.[46]

Once women breached the mythical barrier and entered the "public arena" by exercising their right of petition, they continued to work with municipal and state officials. In so doing, they became knowledgeable in matters of city administration. The members made valuable suggestions for programs that would benefit the female populations of their respective communities. Gradually they gained confidence that "the weaker sex" had the intelligence to understand the intricacies of government and the potentiality to effect important social change.

Emboldened by frequent favorable responses of public officials to their financial requests, women began to bring their problems and plans to governmental authorities. When members of the Boston Seamen's Aid Society indicted the public education system for failing to offer poor female students technical training, the magistrates gave the situation prompt attention. The society also criticized the "General Government" for contracting with those "who, . . . not obliged to work for a living, . . . furnish . . . [goods] at the lowest rate." The women charged:

> Large quantities of the clothing for the navy are made in the towns around Boston, by the farmers' wives and daughters . . . [who] do

> not have their board, house-rent, or fuel to pay for, so they can live. It is not, however, the loss of this work which alone causes the distress of the poor females in the city. . . . The irresistible influence of the Government, by its agents, is brought to operate directly to beat down the price of wages on the only kind of labor which a considerable class of females in every large city can perform, and on which their families, usually the aged and sick, or young children are entirely dependent for a subsistence.

Their activities on behalf of poor women had revealed that "except [for] domestic service and washing, [government work] is the only one open to the sex." The members of the society therefore proposed that "it be an indispensable condition that the making of these garments . . . shall be given to those females who are most in need of such employment."[47]

The Seamen's Aid Society, after its initial year, concentrated almost exclusively on the condition of working women: its "object was to correct the evil of insufficient wages to poor females." Arranging to provide work for needy women, the association's members recalled that the "most delicate part of our duty was to fix the scale of prices for our work. We thought it a righteous principle that the person who labors steadily and faithfully shall receive as wages sufficient, at least, for . . . her support."

Paying their employees substantially more than the average salary given to women, the volunteers joyfully wrote: "Already our example has had an influence for good. Many of the Slop-shops have raised their rate of wages; on some garments ⅓, . . . And all the work is, we believe, better paid. This increase of wages for sewing is benefiting other poor females, therefore, besides those whom we employ. This is the consummation of which we aimed, to secure to our own sex the profits of the needle."[48]

Heartened by their successes, the volunteers became infused with a sense of assurance. The societies' reports reveal this growing faith in their enterprises and in themselves. Speaking of the Society for the Relief of Poor Widows with Small Children, Mrs. Graham happily proclaimed that its "fame is spread over the U.S., and celebrated in foreign cities, who have followed the laudable example. This fame is not more brilliant than just. The hungry are fed, the naked are clothed and shelter is provided for the outcasts, and medicine for the sick, and the soothing voice of sympathy cheers the disconsolate." On another occasion she declared: "The ladies of New York rendered themselves truly deserving of applause for their zeal in this benevolent undertaking."[49]

The seventh annual report of the Orphan Asylum of New York proclaimed: "Your Managers are increasingly alive to the importance of the station they occupy." The ladies of the Seamen's Aid Society boasted of their administrative competence and sound fiscal management. In the third annual report they proudly stated: "We have not since we began, met with any loss of any kind." The report of another association noted that the "high importance of the object proposed by the society has commanded the attention and regard of the benevolent; its extensive usefulness has been proved by 14 years experience."[50]

Woman's sense of the significance of her actions received some reinforcement. Female organizations won sporadic endorsement from popular magazines, and although most men withheld praise, some civic-minded males commended the efforts of female voluntary societies. Rev. Timothy Alden, addressing the members of the Portsmouth Female Asylum, noted: "The ladies of Portsmouth having been so public spirited in their charitable exertions for female education, the gentlemen of the town have paid a becoming deference to their good example by making provision, this year, for 3 female morning schools, which are handsomely attended." John Pintard, whose letters to his daughter reflect his intense interest in the Empire City, exuded praise for women's charities. He believed they proved the breadth of women's capabilities and earned the indebtedness of the city for their efforts.[51]

Through association, women began to find a sense of respect, importance, and appreciation, all of which were generally absent from their personal lives. As women in voluntary societies became aware of the value of their accomplishments, they published the memoirs and eulogies of their co-workers. The reality of feminine attainments became diffused throughout the country, providing the sex with important role models and awakening many women to their long-stifled potential. In *The Life of Mrs. Isabella Graham,* published in 1839 and read widely, her daughter wrote: "She was so happy in the execution of her trust, as to acquire the respect and the confidence of the ladies who acted with her, as well as the affections of the poor." When Miss Sarah W. Ogden, a member of the Orphan Asylum of New York, died, the association noted her passing in their annual report: "To an intellect strong, prompt, and persevering were added a highly cultivated mind and a discriminating judgment rarely to be found in one of her years." While frequently emphasizing a particular woman's intelligence and fortitude, most tributes also stressed the member's boundless compassion: "Her whole time was occupied in searching out the distresses of the poor and devising measures to comfort and establish them to the extent of her influence and means," lauded a typical encomium. Thus, through benevolent activities the urban woman of means became enmeshed in the plight of those females below her on the social scale.[52]

Voluntarism exposed many facets of woman's oppression. It brought into sharp focus those abuses that generally had the greatest impact on the lives of poorer women. Whether they distributed firewood to widows, shelter to orphans, medicine to the sick, Bibles to the unconverted, or education to young girls, the women in philanthropic organizations visited with and listened to hundreds of thousands of destitute females in cities across the country. Their collective experiences vivified the depth and extent of feminine suffering. The records of the first thirty years of benevolent work illuminate the volunteers' collision with two distinct, but related, aspects of woman's maltreatment: the inequity of her economic position and her subjugation to masculine brutality.

The proximity of urban life compelled upper- and middle-class women to be the perpetual witnesses of abject poverty in their cities. While the desolation remained impersonal, females could accept the convenient excuses that the "poor are lazy," "the poor don't want to work," and "in America anyone can make money." But as women came to know and share in the daily existences of their wards through their societies, they gained an awareness of the injustices perpetrated upon their sex. The Association for the Relief of Respectable, Aged, Indigent Females early complained of the lack of job opportunities for women. In 1815 the Society for the Relief of Poor Widows asserted: "An attentive observation has thoroughly convinced us that it is an impossibility for a widow, with the labor of her own hands, to support her infant family . . . even if work abound."[53]

Denying the traditional rhetoric of "lazy poor," the volunteers ascribed the prevalence of female poverty to the few jobs available and the low wages paid to women. Associations noted that "the only means of earning money for those who cannot go out to labor in families, nor take in washing, is by needlework. . . . [T]he price allowed these poor women would 'hardly pay for candle-light.' . . . With the most diligent industry, a poor woman can not earn more than from 60¢ to one dollar per week."[54]

During the first three decades of organized benevolence, most female charities began to perceive the correlation between feminine poverty and a discriminatory system that kept women at the bottom of the economic scale. But few organizations had the audacity of the Seamen's Aid Society, which angrily lashed out at what it considered the sources of oppression. "Combinations of Selfish Men are formed to beat down the price of female labor; and then . . . they call this diminished rate the market price. The slop-shopkeeper grows rich, and adds house to house, while the widow and orphan who toil in his employ, are pining in want and misery. . . . [It is] a shame and disgrace for any one, who writes himself *man*, to make a fortune out of the handy-work of poor females!"[55]

In a later report the volunteers of the Seamen's Aid Society attacked the "associations of rich men, who are adorning the city with splendid palace-like dwellings for the wealthy" and who expect impoverished females to pay their exorbitant rents. The members urged the formation of "an association . . . to build some neat, commodious, comfortable houses, prepared purposely to accommodate" the poor in order to solve the problem of inadequate housing facilities. In their fourth annual report they wrote that "the poor now pay from 20–100% more for groceries and fuel than the rich. The latter can purchase in large quantities, and favorable periods." They argued for the starting of "an association to purchase fuel when it is cheapest, and keep a sufficient stock to sell to . . . poor laboring . . . women, at only such advance as shall be necessary to cover the extra expenses of dealing it out in small quantities."[56]

As the volunteers listened to the woes of destitute women, they heard of masculine abuse in forms that most of the members had never personally experienced. Or, if they had, they refused to reveal it for the shame and disgrace that would have inevitably followed. Yet now they were faced with hundreds of women speaking openly of alcoholism, beatings, and abandonment. These accounts evoked pity and anger. The tales built upon and seemed to sanction the repressed hostility many of the members already felt toward men but dared not express before. Beginning in the second decade of organized feminine philanthropy, women started to publish narratives of masculine mistreatment in their annual reports. Members thus indirectly, even directly, blamed men for feminine suffering, while finding a socially acceptable mode to express their own resentment.

A publication of the Society for Employing the Poor of Boston wrote of the husbands who desert "mothers of families . . . and leave them the task of maintaining their children and themselves." The twenty-third annual report of the Female Assistance Society described a woman who had been in "comfortable circumstances, but was reduced to a state of dire need by the intemperance of her husband." Visitors' reports printed in the societies' literature detailed countless instances of male abuse. Readers frequently learned of cases similar to that of a woman who, shortly after the birth of her child, had been "cruelly beaten by her husband. . . . [He then] took off with . . . the scanty furniture and abandoned her, leaving her only two sticks of wood, a pail of water, and some ship-bread."[57]

The volunteers hoped they would be accepted as "friends" and wrote of the recipients of their aid with sympathy and understanding. "How can one expect that the worn and wearied woman, whose every moment is passed in hard or hurried work, who scarcely can spend time to eat her scanty meals, lest she should not complete the garment, or carry home the washing in season to obtain money for the next day's subsistence, . . . [could] give to her young children that . . . attention which every human being requires in early life?" queried one report. Another addressed itself to the plight of impoverished girls who "frequently have not the clothes decent to attend the city schools; and they stay at home to avoid . . . ridicule."[58]

The members' continuing relationships with destitute females over a period of three decades broke through the anonymous mass of urban poverty and gave names and faces to feminine desolation. The volunteers began to appreciate the human worth of the females they assisted. "The occurrences which come under the observation of the Managers in the discharge of their duties, are not such as are likely to attract the attention of the gay and thoughtless, who regard nothing as precious which had not a glittering exterior. . . . But they possess a real interest in the eyes of those who have learned to judge things according to their real value," proclaimed an annual report for 1826. The document implicitly rebelled against the artificial criteria traditionally used to appraise women while it explicitly defended the essential humanity of the recipients of aid.[59]

This growing concern and identification with poorer women had significant implications for the development of feminist ideology. Numerous reports emphasized the similarity between the backgrounds of the benefactors and some of the beneficiaries. These observations impressed the socially and economically secure women who formed the societies with the fragility of their position. Surely, some became empathetic toward those desolate women because they realized a financial loss or sudden death might lead them to share such an unhappy fate. But for others, the intense contact with the countless privations endured by impoverished females dramatized society's cruelty toward their sex.

The experiences of the volunteers gave them the context in which to understand their own frustrations and oblique feelings of dissatisfaction. The reality of their personal oppression became inescapable. No longer could they accept the isolating myths. No longer could they believe that their unhappiness, their anxieties, their "unwomanly interests" emanated from some individual failure. For now, tens of thousands of women like themselves were searching for identity, direction, and fulfillment through benevolent societies. And, even more compelling, hundreds of thousands of others were struggling alone and unnoticed on the city streets.

These perceptions, scattered and incipient, subtly suggested a unity of all women emerging from the common bonds of oppression. But after only three decades of organized benevolence, women had neither the discernment nor the strength to forge these inchoate elements of thought into an analysis of feminine inequality. Their belief that woman's problems could be solved through benevolent organizations, while demonstrating the importance volunteers attached to their involvement, reflected this yet immature state of awareness.

Nevertheless, the first thirty years of female voluntary associations did much to free women. Enabling them to transcend the limitations of personal experience, benevolent societies impelled urban females of the middle and upper classes to confront the enslaving ethos of the woman-belle ideal. It was charitable involvement that allowed women to break out of their domain and begin to infiltrate the masculine sphere. And in the course of their work, the volunteers demonstrated courage, fortitude, and acumen, contrasting sharply with the antebellum theory of a pale, irrational creature who was too delicate to leave her house and too mentally feeble to understand the intricacies of the "public arena." This proof of woman's competence undermined the myth of the total dissimilarity between male and female natures.

Moreover, the multiplicity of societies and positions provided women with the opportunity to recognize and utilize their diverse abilities while permitting them to express their individuality through a unity with other women. Varied duties gave members a sense of importance and extended their personal relationships. The numerous difficulties encountered by the volunteers and the significance they attached to their work inevitably evoked strong feelings of camaraderie. As women banded together to help impoverished females, they began to understand their personal thralldom. From this grueling and gradual recognition of their own tyrannized status, the volunteers eventually came to identify with females entirely different from themselves. Ultimately they would articulate a kinship with *all women* as the victims of society's oppression.

8

The Deviant Woman

Women to cards may be compared
we play
A round or two; when used we
throw away
Take a fresh pack; nor is it worth
the grieving
Who cuts or shuffles with our
dirty leaving

—author unknown, 1844

But most thro' midnight streets I hear
How the youthful Harlot's curse
Blasts the newborn Infant's tear,
And blights with plagues the Marriage hearse.

—William Blake

Oh! Woman! rouse thee from the sleep
Which all thy faculties would keep
In dormant state! dare to be free
From custom's fond idolatry!
Dare—dare to think! assert the mind,
That is in woman's form enshrined,
Was never meant a toy to be,
A play thing for the mastery
Of greater souls!

This verse, which appeared in an 1848 publication of the American Female Moral Reform Society, expressed the assertive and ultimately emancipating thought that emerged from those feminine voluntary associations dedicated to helping outcasts of their sex. Experiences in these organizations at once heightened members' awareness of society's oppression of women and deepened their compassion for other females. Through their work, the volunteers gained a sense of themselves as accountable beings who shared with men and with women of differing social and economic backgrounds an identical nature and a common humanity. This special synthesis of ideas and perceptions gradually evolved into a theoretical basis for woman's rights campaigns. From a blend of their past role in organized philanthropy and their growing knowledge gained in societies concerned with deviant females, urban women planned a future free from the shackles of the woman-belle ideal.[1]

After 1830, three important voluntary societies were formed in New York City to care for aberrant women: the Female Benevolent Society, the Female Moral Reform Society, and the Women's Prison Association. To be sure, efforts to reform "fallen females" developed in part from the insecurities of urban existence. But woman's assault on the double sexual standard and her criticism of society's treatment of erring females had deeper meanings. The defense of the deviant female grew out of woman's hostility to man, the wish to control masculine behavior as he dictated hers, and a hesitant claim for equality.

At their inception these associations followed the patterns of activity established by women's philanthropic organizations in the early decades of the nineteenth century. Yet, feminine attempts to assist wayward members of their sex were unprecedented in antebellum America and aroused vitriolic opposition. This resistance further induced women to confront and reevaluate their own lives, forcing them to a new understanding of woman's position in society.

Increasing concern over the atomization of the family, the absence of the male from the home, and the prevalence of crime and vice fused to produce a wealth of printed material on lewd behavior. "Then could be seen the miserable street-walkers taking their nightly round up and down Broadway; . . . painted, tinseled creatures. . . . There are at the very least 15,000 of these wretched creatures in [New York]," wrote a popular novelist, who asserted that his "book [was] intended to be a mirror of life as it is in this city." It is doubtful if this work of fiction justified the author's claim of authenticity. But the numerous exaggerated accounts of prostitution appearing after 1820 do accurately reflect the city dweller's growing despair about urban conditions. Novelists, journalists, and municipal officials—each contributed to the literature. Yet, the works of few individuals evoked the response aroused by John R. McDowall's descriptions of harlotry in New York City.[2]

A young divinity student who spent the summer of 1830 visiting tenements and distributing Bibles and tracts, McDowall became so interested in the problem of prostitution that he decided not to return to school in the fall. Instead, he devoted himself to a thorough exploration of licentious conduct. McDowall publicized the results in *McDowall's Journal* and in two pamphlets, *Magdalen Report* and *Magdalen Facts*. "Not less than 10,000 . . . malevolent, cruel and revengeful" harlots preyed upon the population of the Empire City, he claimed and threatened to reveal "these sinks of iniquity . . . disguised under the mask of boarding houses . . . and shops of various kinds." Predictably, the publication of McDowall's research heightened the city dweller's uneasiness and called forth severe opposition to the continued circulation of his study.[3]

Philip Hone labeled the *Magdalen Report* "a disgraceful document." Civic-minded New Yorkers met at Tammany Hall to discuss the insulting accusations. The *Commercial Advertiser* on 24 August 1831 reported that the participants at the meeting had resolved to punish "these base slanders." And other sources condemned *McDowall's Journal* "as a nuisance which calls loudly for the interference of the civil authorities."[4]

The combined weight of opposition, ill-health, and meager resources eventually forced John McDowall to retreat from his crusade against promiscuous behavior. And the New York Magdalen Society, which was managed by men and had employed McDowall for a time, also ceased to operate. After such events, one would expect urban residents to eschew campaigning against illicit sexuality. But during the early 1830s, two societies concerned with the problems of prostitution appeared in New York City. Women founded and administered both.[5]

Although some members of the Female Benevolent Society and the Female Moral Reform Society had previously worked with John McDowall, upper- and middle-class women found a special significance in the institution of prostitution and its explicit acceptance of a double standard of sexual behavior. The prostitute was the metaphor of woman's oppression. By selling her body she became the ultimate commodity, a mere object. The harlot epitomized that form of subjugation common to women of different classes. Considered as appendages lacking autonomy, all women experienced the pain of the nonentity.

Moreover, the prostitute was crucial to the continued existence of myth of the woman-belle ideal. Antebellum theorists, insisting that purity formed the essential requisite of the true woman, decreed that respectable females, unlike their male counterparts, did not have sexual drives. They used this assertion to support the argument that men and women had totally different natures. As long as the middle- and upper-class man could gratify his sexual needs away from his home, he could cling to the fiction that his wife was an ethereal, aphysical being. As for the prostitute, man considered her a creature so degraded that she did not and could never deserve the glorious name of "woman." Seen as a negative image of the quintessential female, the harlot, then, became an unwitting participant in the ethos of the idealized woman. She attracted the attention of numerous urban women, impelling them to organization and lending a distinct importance to their ideologies.

Implicit in their wish to eradicate prostitution was the yet unidentified discontentment of upper- and middle-class women with their prescribed position. This dissatisfaction colored the programs and philosophies that emerged from their organizations. The Female Benevolent Society, evolving from the combined efforts of women in the Laight, Spring, and Carmine Street Churches, "intend[ed] to prevent as well as to remedy the evil of licentiousness . . . by rendering assistance to females who . . . manifest a desire to return to the paths of virtue from which they have swerved." Finding that "these females, . . . [b]y the general consent of the church, and of the world, . . . were left to perish in their sins," the volunteers decided to erect an asylum. And, "with the enemy behind and the Red Sea before them, they . . . resolved to 'rise and build.' "[6]

The members described their refuge, situated in "Yorkville four miles from the City-Hall," as the "first and only permanent Magdalen institution in the city of New York." There, in that secluded spot, the women hoped to show the inmates "by the love of kindness . . . that they may begin to learn, what they now despair of; that it is possible for them to be rescued from their crimes, and that there are those who will aid them in their attempts at reformation." Anticipating the eventual departure of inmates from their home, the volunteers instructed repentant women in various skills. "Everything she earn[ed] over 1 dollar a week [was] deposited for her use in the Greenwich Savings Bank. . . . The one dollar per week [was] for board and [was] applied to the support of the asylum."[7]

The society prospered. By 1838 the women enlarged the scope of their organization to assist the "friendless female orphan, when no way is left for her to obtain a livelihood but that of prostitution." In the same year, the annual report listed over six hundred female subscribers to the organization. The treasurer recorded a donation of $400 from the "Honorable Corporation of New York" and included the "avails of a fair," "work of the inmates," "subscriptions and donations" as some of the other sources of income. Contributions to the association flowed in from women living in New England and in upstate New York: "Ladies of Greenwich," "Mrs. Gould from Litchfield," "Miss Comstock of New Haven," and "Mrs. C. Clarke of Utica" sent money, while "Mrs. Williams of Springfield, Connecticut" gave the asylum two pairs of stockings.[8]

Assured that feminine support and sympathy for the association extended beyond the city on the Hudson, the members of the Female Benevolent Society articulated attitudes differing substantially from masculine opinions on prostitution. John McDowall believed it "indeed undeniable" that a prostitute's "suffering [was] self-inflicted, . . . that it [was] the necessary result of voluntary vice." Rev. Ralph Wardlaw, whose *Lectures on Magdalenism* received great publicity, referred to harlots as "depraved women." He asked: "How many of our young men, the inexperienced and the thoughtless, the light hearted and gay, are . . . haplessly led astray [by immoral women]?" And Charles Christian, in *A Brief Treatise on the Police of the City of New York*, asserted that "the vast number of loose women that infest the streets of the city . . . are . . . so totally bereft of shame, that they are . . . beyond the possibility of reform."[9]

Contrasting sharply with these sentiments, the published views of the Female Benevolent Society demonstrated both their acutely felt compassion for women and their hostility to men. Describing "deep-laid schemes of treachery against female innocence," the members boldly declared:

> It cannot be concealed that the treachery of man, betraying the interests of . . . woman, is one of the principal causes, which furnishes the victims of licentiousness. Few, very few . . . have sought their wretched calling.

They urged society "to brand the seducer with the infamy that he deserves." The volunteers then initiated an attack on the double standard, which revealed their anger, their wish to influence masculine behavior, and their still undefined protest against the abuse of women. Upon the man, "upon *his* head should rest the shame and wretched consequences of his criminal conduct. These . . . have hitherto been heaped upon [woman]. . . . [L]et every virtuous female utterly refuse to associate with [profligate men], let her feel herself to be polluted by their presence, let them be regarded as enemies to the sex."[10]

The Female Benevolent Society continued to function for the balance of the century. Yet it soon became overshadowed by the dynamic Female Moral Reform Society. Assuming control of *McDowall's Journal* and renaming it the *Advocate of Moral Reform,* this organization had much in common with the Female Benevolent Society but criticized the latter for failing to give widespread publicity to either its programs or its theories. The Moral Reform Society asserted: "We believe in doing and saying too. . . . [But] the great good must result from *saying.*" And the upper- and middle-class women who began the Moral Reform Society in 1834 wasted little time in promulgating their activities and philosophies.[11]

The semimonthly *Advocate of Moral Reform,* edited by members of the society, circulated throughout the nation. It lashed out against the accepted distinction between immoral men and women and carried countless articles calling for an end to the double standard. An essay in the first volume declared that the "great object of Moral Reform is to shut out . . . the *men* who are licentious, and oblige them to have no society. . . . The work of exclusion is *done* for the women; let Moral Reform do it for the men." "Level your artillery at the head and heart of the debauchee. Fix an eternal stigma upon . . . every man who will sport with female virtue," commanded a second author.[12]

The all-female editorial staff of the *Advocate* queried: "Why should a female be trodden under foot, and spurned from society, and driven from a parent's roof, if she but fall into sin—while common consent allows the male to habituate himself to this vice, and treats him as not guilty?" "Has God made a distinction in regard to the two sexes in this respect? Is it any where said that what is sin in one, is not sin in the other? . . . Whence has this perversion of truth arisen?" they asked. Their reply that the "perversion" results "from a corrupt state of society" is significant. It hints at the conclusions these women would eventually draw from their probing inquiry into the differing criteria for men and women.[13]

The women of the society utilized the *Advocate,* as well as pamphlets, letters, and annual reports, in their campaign against the double standard. They found a dramatic illustration of the inequitable treatment accorded male and female profligates in the murder case of Helen Jewett. On Saturday night, 9 April 1836, this young prostitute was murdered with an axe at Rosina Townsend's "Palace of the Passions." Attempting to prevent detection, the criminal set fire to the corpse, but Miss Jewett's body remained identifiable. The lurid details of the slaying attracted widespread notice. James Gordon Bennett, reporting the case in the New York *Herald,* called the killing "one of the most foul and premeditated murders that ever fell to our lot to record." In the ensuing weeks the members of the Female Moral Reform Society, along with New Yorkers of every background, followed the trial of the alleged nineteen-year-old slayer, Richard Robinson.[14]

Robinson eventually won an acquittal, although most city residents agreed with Philip Hone that the "weight of evidence was against [him]." Hone's diary entry for 8 June 1836 recorded that Rosina Townsend admitted the accused to Miss Jewett's room the night of the murder and brought them a bottle of champagne one hour later. A piece of the tassel from the young man's cloak had been found on the murder weapon, and the New York *Sun* reported that a miniature seen in Helen's room on Friday was in his possession two days later. Everything linked Richard Robinson to the murder; yet, he escaped conviction.[15]

The court viewed Rosina Townsend and the other prostitutes who testified against the youth as so corrupted that it did not accept their accounts of the fateful evening. The New York *Sun* reported that "His Honor Judge Edwards charged the jury to consider the character of the persons brought forward as witnesses. . . . '[W]hen persons are brought forward who lead such lives their testimony is not to be credited.' "[16]

As the focus of the trial shifted from the heinous act allegedly committed by Robinson to the integrity of the women witnesses, the editors of the *Advocate of Moral Reform* bristled with outrage. They wrote:

> The learned counsel for the prisoner spoke with . . . contempt and abhorrence of these prostitutes, but is his moral sense so blinded that he sees no guilt and degradation on the other side? . . . [W]e confess ourselves entirely unable to see any reason why the testimony of Mrs. Townsend and her inmates is not worth as much as that of the young men, who by their own confession are in the habit of visiting her house constantly. . . . The same degree of guilt which sinks a female beyond all hopes of redemption, makes the young libertine a *hero*, who has manly courage enough to throw off the shackles of virtue and dares to think and act for himself.

The facts of the Jewett-Robinson case faded in time, yet the women of the Moral Reform Society would not soon forget its lessons. The life of a woman who happened to be a prostitute had no value. Yet that of a man—who not only engaged in similar activity but was also the probable perpetrator of a brutal murder—would be preserved at any cost, including even a sacrifice of justice.[17]

Increasingly sensitive to society's inequitable attitude toward females, the volunteers channeled their resentment into a program that provided a release for their stifled anger: they decided to publish the names of men engaging in immoral activity. The *Advocate* became a weapon in their battle against a male-dominated society. Its editors warned: "Young men in the country! beware what you do when you come into the city; . . . should you be detected . . . coming out of haunts of impurity, our missionaries are not . . . so wonderfully delicate as to keep it still.[18]

Members visited and kept vigil at numerous brothels, always reporting their findings in the journal. They identified patrons of illicit establishments and continually reminded the public of their power by threatening to reveal the names of other customers. A notice entitled "Licentiousness in High Places" warned that the women even had names of public officials. This unprecedented expression of feminine anger and audacity inevitably evoked the wrath of substantial portions of the city and the nation. The volunteers' resolution aroused attempts to stifle the "outspoken females." But the relentless criticism forced the members to draw together, engendering profound introspection. Confronting the reality of their own oppression, upper- and middle-class women began to defend their activities and programs within the context of their new awareness of society's denigration of woman. As the volunteers reflected upon, discussed, and wrote about their involvement in moral reform, they started to articulate their commitments to other women, to themselves, and to society. Identifying, and then challenging, the theories of woman's inferior and particular nature, they slowly began to defy the paralyzing precepts of the woman-belle ideal.[19]

The forthright conduct of the women who formed the society generated abuse and scorn. In the first volume of the journal, the editors reported that postmasters had been instructed to "suppress or destroy" their publication "as incendiary matter." In subsequent issues they informed readers that numerous groups "did not approve of [women managing] the *Advocate of Moral Reform* . . . [and] thought the ladies had better resign it into the hands of the gentlemen, as they are much more capable of conducting a public paper." The members also acknowledged the vehement and widespread opposition to "separate societies of ladies." They printed countless articles refuting the charge that moral reform was "utterly unsuitable for them as being destructive of female sensibility."[20]

The *Commercial Advertiser* on 8 August 1836 castigated the members of the society as "females . . . so blinded by their fanaticism, as to forget the delicacy and reserve of their sex—to overleap the modesty of nature—and enter upon a course . . . from which we are free to proclaim, every pure minded woman . . . would have recoiled." "In this city the admonitions of their journal have too often but pointed out where 'the haunts of death' were situated and aroused the curiosity of heedless youth," declared the New York *Sun*. The *Commercial Advertiser* agreed: "We are indebted for the increase of . . . vice to . . . those who par excellence have assumed themselves the title of Moral Reformer." And, the *Evening Post* believed "certain individuals of the M[oral] R[eform] S[ociety] [to be] possessed of a diseased activity of mind, such as association frequently develops . . . remarkably in the female sex."[21]

Initially the women, still uncertain of the propriety of their work, reacted cautiously to the charges against them, urging men to join and support them. "How long shall Christian women wait the movement of their pastors in the great work of Moral Reform? . . . And how long shall we wait for their approval?" they asked. In an attack on the clergy for failing to endorse their efforts, they queried: "Where are our religious papers on this subject? Are they not all like dumb dogs that *dare* not bark?" Apologizing for their involvement in such an "unladylike" enterprise, the editors wrote: "If ever there was a field from which the timid nature and shrinking delicacy of woman should move her to retire, or one that imperiously demanded the strength and wisdom and courage of man, this is the one: the cause not only demands the aid of men, but men of strength and bravery. . . . [T]he work belongs to men, and when they will come up and take the mighty labour off our hands most gladly will we retire."[22]

In time the women began, hesitatingly, to defend their role in moral reform. They appealed to precedents established by organized female benevolence between 1800 and 1830. In 1837, the editors of the *Advocate* asked: "What is the duty of females with regard to the benevolent enterprises of the present day?" Their reply was lengthy and cogent:

> If the sphere of action is limited to private life exclusively, then we have long since left our province and entered that of the other sex.

> . . . Women have organized associations, held meetings, published reports, appointed solicitors and resolved themselves into committees without alarming the guardians of the public welfare or outraging public sentiment. They have gone still further, women have ascended the editorial chair, and if may be judged from the favorable reception of their publication, they have filled it with dignity.[23]

Reviewing the animosity to their work, they continued: "We have been reproached in the cant language of infidelity for leaving the kitchen and nursery to meddle in matters that concerned us not. . . . Why . . . should we be stigmatized as amazons, who have committed an unprecedented breach of decorum, when we appear as advocates of the cause of moral reform?" Moreover, they sought to understand why the opposition was greatest "when we wish to unite together to take measures for the protection of our own sex."[24]

Questioning the basis of masculine antagonism, the members slowly perceived that the scathing objections to their work did not actually relate to their involvement in public philanthropy. Rather, the criticisms were in some way tied to their relationships with other females and, perhaps, to the competence and self-assurance they now displayed. As the volunteers realized the fundamental nature and cause of the opposition, they no longer apologized for or explained their endeavors. Instead they wrote with great conviction: "*We burned the bridges* behind us, and there is no alternative between victory or death."[25]

No longer would they appeal to precedent or to men for assistance. "We are . . . impelled to action by a [just] sense of our duties and responsibilities," they declared. "We *must* claim the privilege of thinking and acting for ourselves." This argument, based on woman's right to individual conscience, had important implications for the development of feminist thought. It appeared frequently in the *Advocate*, as the members' successes strengthened their confidence, in both their theories and their work.[26]

Although they had originally vowed they would gladly leave the field to men, the women demonstrated their firm resolve to continue their activities. When the powerful, male Seventh Commandment Society suggested that the Moral Reform Society become its auxiliary, the women refused and defended their prerogative. "We feel ourselves solemnly bound to wage open war with a vice that is making such sad havoc of our sex." "Our course is designed . . . for the benefit of females," the women explained in another issue of the *Advocate*. "We hope to reach them in a variety of ways; . . . by securing their confidence and [through] freedom of communication." An essay appearing in 1837 argued that it was "the Province of Woman to take the lead in . . . Moral Reform . . . [because woman] understands her own sex best." In another article, published the same year, the editors wrote: "We wish it distinctly understood that we have no idea of relinquishing our paper. . . . *Never.*"[27]

The volunteers passionately defended themselves against charges of inferiority and inadequacy. "The remark has often been made by some of our brethren that women have neither education nor intellect sufficient to enable them to manage successfully a public society, and conduct a public journal. . . . [T]hough women's education . . . has generally been miserably defective, they have in repeated instances, risen to eminence in spite of the obstacles to be encountered." Members admitted that once they had "been terrified into silence by the cry of 'indelicacy,' " but now they remained steadfast. The "war which we are prosecuting is that of extermination," they asserted. "We have enlisted, and we are determined not to lay down our arms until our bodies lie in the dust; or victory is obtained."[28]

Women from different parts of the country sent countless letters of support to the Moral Reform Society. A woman in Ohio praised the efforts to elevate prostitutes: "I tell you that the female is sunk low enough already. . . . So long as the slightest deviation from the rules of propriety in females (men being judges) is put in contrast to the most artful deception man can invent to seduce woman, he will never feel his guilt or responsibility." The author of a letter appearing in an 1840 edition of the *Advocate* urged "tear[ing] away the artificial restraints which perverted feeling is endeavoring to throw around us." "A Friend to Equal Rights" reported that she had wanted to buy a copy of the *Advocate*, but her husband controlled all the money and prohibited the purchase. "I know it will be said that we have food, and clothing, and everything essential to comfort, . . . and that having this we ought to be content. But I cannot consent to this view of the subject. I am a rational creature, bound to think and act for myself and I claim the privilege of subscribing for a paper which my conscience and reason both approve, or giving to an object in which I am specially interested."[29]

Underlying woman's justification of her involvement in moral reform work was a vital premise. She had a right to determine her responsibilities to herself and to other women. This was true regardless of the fierce opposition her novel activities might engender. The volunteers argued: "We must speak out or do violence to our own consciences." "Duty" impelled women to correct this evil causing such misery "among our sex." They urged: "Dear sisters, let females maintain their rights, and bring truth and reason to bear on the minds and consciences of men." "With all deference to the opinons of others, our own [opinion] is unalterably fixed," proclaimed the editors.[30]

Thus determined in their efforts, the members of the society devoted themselves to preventing illicit sexual conduct and the concomitant abuse of women. Simultaneously agitating for the better treatment of all females, they struck a respondent chord in hearts and minds throughout America. In the summer of 1836, a committee of the board of managers visited with women "in a portion of 5 of the New England States." Breaking all custom by traveling unchaperoned, the group reported to the *Advocate* on 15 October: "Since leaving New York the 12th of July, we have met with ladies in 15 different associations and have stopped . . . [in approximately forty cities and towns]." Their discussions and observations convinced the managers of the importance women attached to moral reform activities: "Young ladies . . . are coming up to this work with a decision of character that seems to say 'The world will be the better for their having lived in it.' " The members of the New York society wanted women throughout the nation to view one another "as a band of sisters, affectionately united."[31]

The *Advocate of Moral Reform* became an important means of strengthening the harmonious ties among women. Three years after the formation of the society, the women reported that they printed 20,000 copies semimonthly. They received approximately 160 new subscribers each week and distributed the *Advocate* across the nation. The periodical stimulated interest in the New York society, encouraged the formation of auxiliaries, and gave women living in countless cities and towns a sense of belonging to an important and cohesive cause.[32]

To reinforce this feeling of unity, the parent society asked females to take an oath that they would shun profligate men. The fourth annual report, reprinted in the *Advocate,* declared: "By the operation of the pledge voluntarily adopted by thousands of females, a line of demarcation is drawn, over which the libertine . . . cannot pass." The solemn taking of a vow added gravity to woman's commitment to the society while intensifying her allegiance to the volunteers. Rejoicing that a "union of sentiment and effort [existed] among so many thousands of virtuous females from Maine–Alabama," the women expressed great confidence: "The mothers and daughters of our land are coming up to the contest and their motto is 'Extermination or everlasting battle.' . . . Man may quail at persecution, women never. Courage is called a masculine virtue, but . . . *virtues* like vices *know no distinction of sex.* . . . [M]ore than 20,000 warm hearts are beating in union on this subject and pledged to each other."[33]

Although the assault on licentious behavior and its crusading, unifying appeal remained important aspects of the society's work through 1848, the women lent their energies to a variety of other endeavors. To assist poor women, often with no alternative but prostitution or starvation, the organization established an employment service. It urged "teachers, seamstresses, or domestics who . . . wish to enter their names on the Register . . . [to] do so by making application at no. 13 Vandam Street any day during the week." In a related effort, the Moral Reform Society established an evening school "for the gratuitous instruction of domestics." In addition, they supervised a group of women who walked throughout the city seeking destitute females to assist.[34]

The members also wrote and published stories for children in the *Advocate* and recommended books to women. Charlotte Elizabeth's *Wrongs of Woman* received the following notice: "A . . . sketch designed to illustrate the wrongs and oppression to which the . . . apprentices of the milliners and dress-makers of England are subjected." A critique of Margaret Fuller's controversial feminist treatise, *Woman in the Nineteenth Century,* declared: "We cordially recommend it to the reading or rather thinking public, confident that it contains so much that is truly valuable, that every intelligent reader will be profited by the perusal." Other books discussed in the *Advocate* included the reminiscences of prominent members, as well as selections sent in by the auxiliary societies.[35]

Shortly after formation of the New York Female Moral Reform Society, the members avowed their "intention to operate in every city and village town in the United States where [they could] get an auxiliary society to operate through." By 1836 the New York chapter boasted 66 associations auxiliary to it consisting of three thousand members; two years later the number of local agencies jumped to 325; and in 1840, 555 organizations considered themselves linked to the New York Female Moral Reform Society. As the association became more national in character, the volunteers voted to change the name to the American Female Moral Reform Society. In 1839 they proclaimed that their "grand object was to reach and influence the heart of woman through the length and breadth of the land." Officers elected for 1840 reflect their more diversified membership. Although the president, Mrs. Hawkins, lived in New York City, the vice presidents were located in cities throughout the country, including Providence, Pittsburgh, and Chicago.[36]

The women who joined the auxiliary societies frequently met one another at quarterly, semiannual, and annual meetings and kept in close contact through the exchange of letters. Learning of one another's activities, they also shared hopes and disappointments. The president of the Utica society wrote to the New York chapter that "with you are identified every member and every effort of this great moral association." Another woman declared: "My heart bleeds for you, and that is why I address you by the name of Sister—I love all who are engaged in this cause as *Sisters.*" A chapter president wrote: "My dear sisters. . . . Have we not seen crooked things made straight, and darkness light before us? If the cause had been of man, it would long ago have come to naught."[37]

In May 1838, a volunteer from Salem maintained: "Dear Sisters, *our* cause is *one*. . . . [C]onsequently the same reproach that is cast upon *you* reaches *us*, the same difficulties oppose and the same ground of consolation are equally applicable. Does one member suffer? All the other members suffer." And from Rockford, Illinois, came the following note: "We feel that the Moral Reform cause belongs in common to us all. Every woman is, or ought to feel herself identified with it. Yes, dear sisters, when you suffer, we suffer with you, when you rejoice we are made glad."[38]

Forming a network of feelings and ideas, joining the many societies together, the letters provided a sense of community and a unity of purpose. Some societies specifically emulated the activities of the New York chapter. When the Boston auxiliary opened an "Office of Direction for Female Domestics," the editors of the *Advocate* wrote: "It is an encouraging fact that sister societies in five of our large cities, are now giving attention to this subject." But other associations, in smaller cities and towns, did not sponsor any significant programs. Rather, they seemed to hold meetings as a way of reaching and communicating with other women. The society of Gallia County, Ohio, did not initiate any reform measures but, like many others, wrote to the *Advocate:* "We have ever found it pleasant and profitable to meet."[39]

It is doubtful that the women of Rodman, New York; East Salisbury, Massachusetts; Elgin, Illinois; Webster, Michigan; or Rindge, New Hampshire, founded associations because of the injustices that rampant illicit behavior exposed in their communities. Yet, each of these towns and countless others across the nation formed moral reform societies. They served as forums where emotions and thoughts could be shared with other women. Moreover, enabling females to feel part of an important cause, the associations helped them develop both a sense of personal worth and a pride in their sex. A letter written in 1837 to the New York society from a Greenfield volunteer articulates the meaning women attached to their work in moral reform:

> I have long felt more and more impressed with the importance of your enterprise and have seen more of the difficulties raised to obstruct your progress. . . . Woman though weak and timid when relying upon her own strength, and supported by her own energies, has a soul invincible when duty calls. She is undaunted by sneers, unsubdued by reproach, and unterrified by alarm. I rejoice my friends that I am woman; and I never gloried more in my sex than I do now.[40]

Before 1830, benevolent societies had vaguely perceived a feminine existence separate from the possible relations of her life as wife, mother, sister, and daughter. But the belief in women's full autonomy, with the right to individual conscience and judgment, did not take form until later. The meaning of experiences in societies concerned with female deviance had first to be understood before woman's new identity could emerge. Members of the American Female Moral Reform Society explored their novel ideas about woman's position and nature in numerous publications. The *Advocate* became a vehicle for female discussion. "The paper is . . . needed to afford a channel of communication, in which the thoughts and feeling of females throughout the country may more freely mingle than they could do in any other way," the volunteers wrote in 1837. "It will be obvious to all, that this can only be accomplished . . . in a paper conducted exclusively by ladies, and devoted to their interests."[41]

In keeping with the intent to discuss topics relevant to the lives of their readers, the editors published essays both questioning and challenging the traditional role of woman. One entitled "The Condition of Woman," which appeared in the third volume of the *Advocate,* expressed the need "[to convince] man, who was designed to be [woman's] compeer, not her superior, . . . that her talents are in no degree inferior to his own." "Why will not man, instead of daily forging new chains (none the easier broken for being silken) endeavor to assist her in stemming the tide of flattery and prejudice which has been and still is the bane of her life?" asked the author, who signed her name "A woman." "From infancy to maturity . . . everything conspires to divert her from the path of real greatness and usefulness. She is taught to consider it immodest and entirely out of her sphere, to aspire to any thing beyond the toilette, domestic affairs, and the smiles of man." The essay ended with the plea:

> Hoping that some far abler and better abilities may be enlisted in a cause, than which none can be juster or nobler, and that woman will awake from the stupor which at present enshrouds her noblest powers of mind and exercise her own energies and talents for her own emancipation. . . .[42]

Writing on the "Province of Woman," the editors of the *Advocate* asserted: "We wish our sex to feel that they have a personal responsibility in *all* that concerns the . . . good of society, and that they can no more transfer this responsibility to their fathers, husbands, sons, or brothers than they can relinquish their own personal identity. . . . [Women] are capable . . . of thinking for themselves, judging for themselves, and acting for themselves." "We have substituted external accomplishments for useful knowledge and cultivated the imagination and affection at the expense of the judgment and intellect," continued the journalists. "Such has been . . . the education of woman. . . . If even under all the disadvantages of the present system, the intellect of woman has in so many instances shone forth with a brilliancy which has cheered and enlightened the world, what might not be expected from it were the education of the sexes conducted on the same general principles?"[43]

The editors urged readers to use their own judgment in evaluating a letter from their "respected and beloved sister," noted reformer Sarah Grimké. They added: "It is of immense importance to our sex to possess clear and *correct* ideas of our rights and duties, and we trust every reader will comply with the request so frequently and earnestly preferred by the writer of the article before us, to *search* the *scriptures* and decide the question for themselves." Grimké's essay, devoted to a discussion of "the duties of woman at the present time," challenged the scriptural decrees that women hold a subservient position in society.[44]

Grimké exhorted women to "read all the precepts of the Bible as addressed to woman as well as to man, and [to] lose in [their] moral, intellectual and immortal nature the consciousness of sex." She asserted that "nothing has enveloped the mind in more ignorance . . . than the false idea that the mere circumstance of sex . . . is to be the criterion of duty, intelligence, responsibility, superiority and inferiority. . . . Duties belong to situation, not to sex. . . . [B]ut the rights and responsibilities of men and women as moral beings are identical and must necessarily be so if their nature is the same."[45]

Predictably, this attack on Biblical authority aroused a flurry of responses from female and male readers. Although the editors declared that they stood "as impartial spectators of the combat," their introduction to "Delta's" rebuttal of Grimké's argument suggests where their sympathies lay:

> We suffer our correspondent, Delta, to speak for himself and his brethren in the foregoing article, for we would not have it supposed that if the 'weaker sex' seem to have the best of the argument it is because no one has been allowed to take the field against them. We regret for the sake of those husbands whose endangered rights he is endeavoring to defend, that their champion seems so unskilled in the use of the lance, and we recommend him to the mercy of the powerful antagonist against whom he has entered the lists, should this communication chance to meet her eye.[46]

This forceful presentation of views reflected the volunteers' growing self-assurance. Females in moral reform societies throughout the nation began to refer to themselves as women, eschewing the identity-negating terms of wife, mother, sister, and daughter. Essays and letters dotted the pages of the *Advocate*, articulating a newly found respect for females. The esteem each woman felt for her sex grew out of, but also heightened, her sense of individual value. A woman from Verona, New York, wrote that "woman has obtained the proud prerogative to act, feel and think for herself." Another urged: "When satisfied you are in the way of duty, do not be moved by the scoffs and sneers of the giddy multitude."[47]

An article discussing the importance of holding conventions for the auxiliary societies asked the women to "pledge [them]selves to sustain one *annually* in some of the large cities of the North." The gatherings served a symbolic purpose:

> The assembling of *women* in general convention meeting, for the specific purpose of furthering a philanthropic enterprise . . . betokens on the part of woman a clearer discernment of the capabilities of these mental powers . . . which have been for ages . . . *lost to the world.* It indicates an increasing recognition of those fearful, but ennobling, moral obligations, which grow out of her nature as a moral and accountable being . . . [and] the *glorious*, the *heroic* bursting of . . . iron limits. . . . When . . . I regard . . . the influence which they will exert in raising woman from the lowly path in which . . . she has hitherto walked . . . I experience sensations of peculiar joy; *for I am a woman.*[48]

The pride in womanhood expressed everywhere by those who worked in benevolent societies evolved from a fundamental view of woman's nature totally at variance with the precepts of the woman-belle ideal. Woman's new self-awareness gave her the courage to set out on an uncharted course. In delineating proper masculine conduct and establishing the criteria for social acceptability, the women in the Female Benevolent Society and the Female Moral Reform Society formed programs and policies that incurred the wrath of men across the nation.

Yet the volunteers knew that for decades women had organized themselves, initiated programs, instituted reforms, worked with civic leaders, written charters, elected officers, managed finances, and maintained records. Cognizant that women in early charities had demonstrated attributes long considered the exclusive property of men, the beleagured volunteers rejected the argument that women lacked the capability or strength to direct their projects. They came to suspect that the opposition originated instead from the concern that women *did indeed* possess the requisite qualities for success and would in time appreciate their effectiveness.

As women gained confidence, they perceived the antagonism as part of a system of oppression that objectified the entire sex and denied all females the basic human rights. This understanding gave the members a greater sense of unity with other women and enabled them to defend their ideas and activities on new grounds. The volunteers refused to accept the dictum that man and woman were totally different, with dissimilar duties and talents. They began to postulate that woman, like man, could determine her responsibilities for herself, for she was a *morally accountable, autonomous being with the right to independent judgment and conscience.*

This theory, set forth with increasing conviction and strength, crystallized the nebulous thoughts of the first thirty years of benevolent activity and fostered an intensive inquiry into the causes of woman's subservient status. The belief in woman's essential dignity as an individual molded the programs and ideas that evolved in future years of female benevolence and significantly influenced the development of feminism.

9

The Deviant Women

> The merciful wife of my poor neighbor, the shoe maker, would make as a legislative woman, a Duchess of Sutherland, were she in her castles with her income and I have no doubt their inmost daily experiences would be found very similar, could they be closely and honestly compared.
>
> I rejoice in you, as it is rarely given to one woman to rejoice in another.
>
> —Eliza Farnham

Women of moral reform societies across the nation basked in their new identity. The belief that they were autonomous individuals, who shared with men the right to independent conscience and judgment, spurred creative action and thought. Gradually realizing that their subservient position did not result from a unique or particular feminine character, the members intensified their inquiry into the causes of their subordinate status. If woman's inferior condition did not derive from basic failings in her nature, then its origins lay in an unjust society. This perception rendered the volunteers increasingly disaffected from their social milieu. As the century progressed, the manifestations of their estrangement changed and matured.

The first stage of dissatisfaction appeared in the late 1830s. Women conducted a vigorous campaign against men, customs, laws, and educational and employment systems that thwarted their efforts at self-realization. Simultaneously, they produced literature exalting the members of their own sex, disseminating the achievements and ideas of the volunteers to women throughout America. Attempts to secure better treatment for one group among them—prostitutes and criminals—produced an unexpected result: as their commitments to these women merged with their increasing estrangement, they began to view deviant women as sharers in their humanity. And even more remarkably, they came to see themselves as the aberrant female's sisters in alienation.

The editors of the *Advocate of Moral Reform* understood the importance of the press in articulating their new consciousness. "As the present course of public opinion was directed by men of the last generation, so the public opinion of the coming generation is now in the hands of us who are now acting upon the stage of human life." The members wrote and published articles both implicitly and explicitly challenging woman's traditional sphere. Nevertheless, essays glorifying the home persisted and appeared alongside expressly feminist tracts. The former revealed both the staff's ambivalence over their radical stance and their wish to appease the more conservative among their readers. Yet, by the end of the 1830s, treatises examining different aspects of woman's emancipation dominated the periodical and indicated its future direction. "We do not admit any but a *physical* inferiority in our sex," wrote one contributor. "[Woman is] not a slave to be trampled under foot; . . . but . . . [man's] equal in every social right," declared another, who clearly expressed the new trend.[1]

Although it would be many years before the editors of the *Advocate* published an exposition similar to Sarah Grimké's direct attack on the Bible, they did search the Scriptures for implications of woman's competence. Articles appeared frequently noting that

"Miriam, the prophetess, was associated with her brother as the leader of the tribes of Israel" and that "Deborah, the prophetess, . . . led not the women, but the men to successful combat." Through the *Advocate* the members could circulate articles displaying woman's abilities from Biblical days to the present. The periodical reported that numerous women were inspired to new endeavor by the volunteers' feats. Moreover, some men acknowledged the association's successes. A "gentleman" admirer of the Moral Reform Society asserted: "There is so much talent and so much wisdom enlisted as to withstand all the assaults of raillery." And the New York *Tribune* complimented the society in 1843 as being composed of "heroic women."[2]

As the members of the association came to understand their importance to other women as models of female ability, they shared their thoughts and experiences with readers. At the semiannual meeting of 1846, held in Clinton, New York, the volunteers spoke of the ways in which moral reform work had affected their lives. Margaret Dye, active in the New York chapter, "owed to [the] Society . . . enlarged views of woman's sphere and destiny," and Mrs. Barnes of Troy, New York, had found an outlet for her talents by opening "an evening school for domestics."[3]

The minutes of the meeting, published in the *Advocate*, also included the account of Mary A. Hawkins, who at the age of twenty-six became the first president of the association; she revealed that "so much opposition was raised against the [society that] her husband objected to her laboring in it." Nonetheless, she persevered and "though . . . entirely unused to writing for the public, the 3 first numbers of the *Advocate* were got out by [another woman] and herself." Augmenting these casual, personal narratives, the American Female Moral Reform Society published several books that detailed its members' accomplishments.[4]

Both *Our Golden Jubilee* and *Walks of Usefulness* recounted the life story of Margaret Prior, the first female missionary of the society. A member of the board of managers of the Orphan Asylum of New York and founder of a refuge for half-orphans, Mrs. Prior assumed her position in 1836 and held that post until her death six years later. During the period of her employment by the society, she "stepped fearlessly" through the "Five Points, in the Old Brewery, [and in] Murderers' Alley." The numerous accolades bestowed upon Margaret Prior were equaled by the praise accorded Mary Hawkins. The society's first president was "calm, self-collected, far seeing," recalled Sarah Ingraham Bennett, editor of the *Advocate* for more than a quarter century. *Wrought Gold,* a biography of Mary Hawkins prepared by the members, recounted that her "personal labors were incessant. . . . The widow, the orphan, the fatherless, penniless, and homeless, found in her a friend in need."[5]

Replete with descriptions of "usefulness" or "walks of usefulness," the memoirs and biographies formed a dramatic contrast to the image of ideal feminine perfection envisioned by antebellum theorists. The qualities detailed in the portrayal of Mrs. Hawkins, as well as of countless other women, were the antithesis of those female attributes insisted upon by an insecure era. "Her keenness of perception, her decision, her maturity of judgment, were traits so manifest that none could be associated with her without feeling her influence." Calling Mary Hawkins the "complete embodiment of true Womanhood," her co-workers found in their first president a woman to emulate, as they attempted to repudiate the woman-belle ideal.[6]

The identification with gifted and dedicated women imbued members with thoughts of their own unfulfilled potential. And the stories heightened their anger and bitter resentment of man, whom they saw as woman's oppressor. Lashing out through their periodical, the women criticized, lectured, and instructed men in a manner unprecedented in American history. Originally they had channeled their hostility toward males into the more socially accepted form of an attack on profligate men. Now, however, the women in moral reform associations were confident that multitudes of other females shared their views. They poured their frustrations and animosity into a scathing body of literature.

In "Evils of Despotic Government," appearing in the *Advocate* on

15 February 1838, they wrote: "We allude to the tyranny exercised in the Home department, where lordly man, 'clothed with little brief authority,' rules his trembling subjects with a rod of iron, conscious of entire impunity, and exulting in his fancied superiority." The authors continued:

> The man we are describing is not a gambler, a drunkard, a libertine, or even a man of the world. . . . He is kind and affable to those who are not under his immediate control, but the ebullitions of his anger and self-will are reserved for the helpless beings who are dependent on him.

Most men regard their wives "as a useful article of furniture, which is valuable only for the benefit derived from it, but which may be thrown aside at pleasure," asserted the writers. "[And] if [woman's] inferiority is only an artificial one, the mere inferiority of *station*, then surely it is the height of arrogance and presumption for him . . . to assume the exercise of despotic government."[7]

Provoked by the continuous stream of printed material reminding females of the obligations encumbent upon them, a woman retaliated with her "Counsel for Gentlemen," which had been "suggested by reading J. P. Y.'s 'Counsel for Ladies.' " "Much is . . . made about the duty of wives and much advice is given to make them what is thought by their counsellors they ought to be. . . . Woman is taught to look upon man as a superior being. She believes him so, until experience teaches her better," declared the author.[8]

Many other articles in the *Advocate* chided men for their behavior toward women and exhorted them to be more responsive to their wives' needs. "A Chapter to Young Husbands," published in 1842, analyzed the reasons why men take wives: "Was it simply to darn your stockings, mend your clothes, take care of your children, and watch over your sick bed? Was it simply to conduce to your own comfort? Nor is it a sufficient answer that you give her a home. . . . You do this for your help." And the article concluded that "in a large majority of the instances of domestic misery, the man is the aggressor." "There are husbands who not only refuse to help their wives in the thousand little ways which their leisure moments would permit, but will even throw obstacles in the way of the mother herself," declared another treatise.[9]

Countless writings refuted the decree that a woman's only value and happiness came from her married status. With the reprint in 1845 of "Love and Courtship," an article postulating the prevailing view of matrimony, the editors of the *Advocate* created the framework in which to express their thoughts on marriage. The objectionable essay had defined the character of love: "It is woman's all—her wealth, her power, her very being. Man . . . [has] ever an existence distinct from that of his affection . . . but woman centres all in that one feeling and 'In that she lives, or else she has no life.' " The journalists protested both the thesis of the article and its ramifications for women. "She who entertains this sentiment . . . lives . . . [not] for herself. . . . [H]er own existence is absorbed by the interests of another. . . . [W]oman as well as man . . . has an existence distinct from her affections. . . . Look where we may in society our sex are found in large numbers having a sterner work to do then simply leaning on a protector and guide."[10]

Another article dissenting from the theories articulated in "Love and Courtship" claimed: "By the sentiment alluded to [in 'Love and Courtship,' the] large class of single women are summarily blotted out of existence. They may continue to vegetate but cannot be said to live. . . . Alas for such women as Hannah Moore . . . , Harriet Martineau, and . . . our own Catharine Sedgwick, if the propositions of this writer be correct. One thing, however, must I think be conceded, that though *dead* these ladies have done far more for society, than very many who are *living* in the full enjoyment of . . . affections." Urging that "daughters . . . be taught to look forward to marriage with rational hopes and expectations," the author appealed: "Let them be made to feel that love and marriage are not essential to their respectability, usefulness and comfort."[11]

Although they might rail at theories stipulating the centrality of matrimony to woman's happiness, the all-female staff of the *Advocate* remained acutely aware of economic realities that often drove women into marriage. Their work with prostitutes and the other impoverished women who registered at the society's Office of Direction made it blatantly clear that a life of "single-bliss" was an impossibility in industrial, urban America. Society was so prejudiced against women laboring for remuneration that it denied the means of survival even to those completely dependent upon their own wages. Woman's freedom to accept or reject the marriage proposal and her ability to determine how she wished to conduct her life unequivocally related to her economic status. The members of the American Female Moral Reform Society attacked the system that they believed had kept their sex in a state of dependency.

"It is a fact universally admitted that the ordinary rate of wages for female labor is unjust and oppressive. In this single fact lies the germs of woman's degradation in unnumbered instances," proclaimed the *Advocate of Moral Reform* in 1845. An article entitled "Tailoresses and Seamstresses" told of "10,000 females in this city dependent upon their needles for support. . . . [A] valuable, worthy, and indispensable class of the community . . . laboring under a cruel and iron handed oppression . . . , [they are] [d]riven by the hand of a merciless oppression into the cellars and garrets of old, worn out, leaky . . . tenements, for which they have to pay an exorbitant rent, and there compelled to toil from 16–20 hours a day to gain a bare subsistence. . . . Here is labor without compensation—labor extorted from our own sisters . . . whom every principle of honor calls us to protect."[12]

"Must our poor and sickly females be compelled to give away so much time for nothing?" queried one writer in 1843. Another expressed astonishment that "this oppression [was] carried on . . . in the City of New York, the great commercial metropolis of the nation—the mistress of the arts—the seat of science . . . whose proud sons boast of their chivalrous and philanthropic doings. . . . Here it is that woman . . . is oppressed." "There is a strange and cruel mockery in the conduct of the lords of creation to the weaker sex," proclaimed an author from Philadelphia. "They are fond of speaking in extravagant terms on the excellence of women . . . [but] [w]hat support or encouragement does the widow . . . or the friendless female receive from man. How is her labor requited? How are her rights maintained? . . . [W]oman [is] . . . the drudge and slave of those who prate about her beauty and their chivalry."[13]

After ten years of involving themselves in the predicament of the impoverished woman, the members of the society postulated a causal relationship between poverty and prostitution. "In every large community and especially in cities there are multitudes of the young who . . . are thrown on their own resources and obliged to earn a subsistence . . . or become prey to the tempter. . . . Shame on . . . men who, by oppressing the hireling in her wages, . . . drive the young and unfriended to dens of shame, while they fill their coffers with the avails of unrequited toil."[14]

The members of moral reform societies throughout the nation agreed that, "[with] respect [to] the *low rate of wages*, the customs of society are cruelly oppressive to females." At the tenth annual meeting they adopted resolutions committing themselves to alleviate the suffering of working woman. Consequently the volunteers began filling their publications with "accounts of the great destitution" due to the "lowness of [women's] wages."[15]

Year after year the women protested the "low estimate of female labor" and told of efforts in other cities to remedy the plight of the female worker. From Oregon came the proclamation that "females must be better paid for their labor," and the society's London correspondent reported on the establishment of "societies for the relief of the Governess, the Dressmaker and the Seamstress." The members of the New York chapter—in an endeavor to assist the "50,000 women in [their] city who sustain themselves and their families"—announced their belief that thousands of the sex might be helped if "the avenues of business, now closed to them . . . were opened." The executive board of the society related their "experiment . . . to dispense with the services of men in their office and employ women exclusively. . . . [T]he business of folding, mailing, book-keeping, publishing, book selling, etc., has been done by females, and so far as [the board] can learn, entire satisfaction has been given."[16]

The pleas for the poor female worker continued. Yet the request that she be justly compensated for her labor slowly evolved into the insistence that any capable female be allowed to enter the traditionally masculine occupations and professions. This argument reflected the upper- and middle-class woman's increasing sense of herself as a capable human being. It found expression in the activities and publications of numerous female benevolent organizations, but the demand first appeared in the literature of the Moral Reform Society in the mid-1840s. An article published in 1846 examined woman's employment opportunities:

> Men have monopolized almost every field of labor. They have taken the learned professions, they have entered every department which commerce opens, and, indeed, almost every place where skill and talent is required, they have excluded women . . . and have only left to them the unmolested possession of the nursery. Women are thus limited to a few employments, hence these are overstocked with laborers. . . . It will avail little merely to denounce the oppression. . . . The great work to be accomplished is to increase the number of employments which shall be accessible to women and then to encourage the daughters of the land to undertake them. Does anyone ask 'Would you have them plead at the bar, or follow the plough?' I frankly answer 'Yes.'[17]

Declaring that "it is an honor to have it said that [a woman] can support herself," the members of the Moral Reform Society implored even wealthy females to "take in work; do anything but live a lazy and fashionable life." "Make every woman independent," they entreated. "Qualify her to do something whereby she can get her own living. No matter if her father is rich. . . . Let women be educated so that they can compete with men in those branches of business where they can do just as well as men."[18]

At a meeting of the association in 1843, Mrs. Bates of Westfield, Massachusetts, recommended that "females of requisite abilities be encouraged and assisted to qualify themselves to practice obstetrics." Other members evidently agreed. They agitated to open the medical profession to women. Applauding Elizabeth Blackwell's resolve to "take an independent course and act according to her conviction of right," the journalists declared: "We shall expect to see her sustained in her chosen path by the wise and reflecting . . . and that . . . her example will be an agency for good to her sex."[19]

The conviction that "the energies of woman should be fully developed . . . in mental and physical labor of all kinds" urged on the crusade to broaden the scope of feminine employment. Moreover, the realization and assertion that economic deprivation forced women into prostitution pierced another of the myths of nineteenth-century womanhood. This awareness affirmed that the harlot was not the depraved creature pictured by John McDowall and others. She was simply a poor woman, victimized by a discriminatory system. With the demand that more jobs be made available to women, the volunteers hoped to satisfy the needs of females in differing classes. Feminine labor would command a higher wage, and all females would have an increasing number of alternatives. With economic security, women could begin to exercise control over their own lives.[20]

Concurrent with their attack on limited employment opportunities, arguments for a more equitable method of educating females were advanced. Without knowledge or skills, women could never hope to become self-sufficient. In an article entitled "Intellectual Training," the author refuted anticipated criticism to her plan: "Does the delicate mother fear that I would make her daughters masculine? What does she mean by masculine? Gross, brawling, reckless . . . thoughtless. . . . For the world I would not do it, and should be just as unwilling to have your sons such. Does she mean by masculine—thoughtful, judicious, wise, learned, independent, self-respecting—I plead guilty."[21]

In the same context as these attacks, women explored the causes of their subordination. They invariably blamed the other sex: "Our brother man has evinced too little generosity towards us. . . . [A]s if fearing our equality with him, has he not done much to perpetuate our inferiority and check the development of intellectual energy? He . . . has, by obsequious admiration, stimulated his sister to that pursuit of trifles for which in his heart he condemns her. . . . [A]nd having thus debased his own endowments, to assist in degrading hers, he has disingenuously exulted in the superiority of his talents and acquirements."[22]

In "The Ladies of the Present Age," a student at Mrs. Atkinson's Seminary asserted: "What the ladies of our land are, the influence of our leading men has made them. . . . [T]hey form the standard of female excellence. . . . It [is] a pity indeed that the noble lords of creation . . . should object to a standard of their own formation. . . . The gentlemen think not that the female mind is able to keep pace . . . with theirs—[but] where the spirit of man has braved its glorious way, there the spirit of woman is capable of soaring."[23]

Protesting the "assumption of superiority in [their] brethren," women concluded that "[it] is the want of a proper education which . . . reduced them as a class to one uniform and inferior standard." The contributors declared that "in the earliest childhood . . . girls are [not] in any measure inferior to boys . . . [and that in] school . . . where girls and boys are assembled together in classes and instructed in classical literature girls are almost invariably more intelligent." One writer ridiculed the "common phrases" that the "true theater for a woman is the sick chamber" and there is "nothing so honorable to a woman as not to be spoken of at all" as "the "delight of Noodledom." Another protested: "So completely have the talents of women been kept down that there is scarcely a single work, either of reason or imagination, written by a woman which is in general circulation."[24]

Not only did women fail to achieve recognition in the world of arts and scholarship, but "few women [were even] capable of transacting the most ordinary business. They [were] consequently obliged to entrust all their affairs to their relations or to hire agents, by both of whom they [were] constantly defrauded and plundered." "How can girls . . . have judgment and decision when others always think for them?" the essayists queried. They cautiously proposed changing the methods of instructing women and began to argue for publicly supported colleges for their education.[25]

The increasing number of theorists opposed to the traditional manner of educating women's minds also criticized the prevailing ideas of feminine physical instruction. Denying that woman's inherent nature made her weak and infirm, articles appeared attributing female fragility to tight corseting, "breathing . . . impure air," and lack of exercise. It is "just as healthy for the girl" as for the boy to "run out of doors," one female declared. "I would have your daughters play out of doors just as many hours as your sons, and no one should call them girl-boys."[26]

In a piece entitled "Doctors vs. Ladies," an author castigated the medical profession for its indifference toward women. The *Advocate* hoped to counterattack the deleterious effects of custom on feminine health by discussing such topics as "Tight Lacing" and the "Consequences of Compression." These articles focused on the ramifications of years of indoctrination in feminine idleness and delicacy. At the same time they reminded women of the social conventions keeping their sex dependent and subservient.[27]

Throughout the third and fourth decades of the nineteenth century, members of moral reform societies attacked custom, men, and the educational and employment systems as responsible for women's degradation. Simultaneously, they unleashed an assault upon the legal codes that they found prejudicial. Their experiences with impoverished females, forced to support themselves by prostitution or face starvation, impressed the volunteers with the callousness of antebellum laws. They began to criticize the discriminatory ordinances: "Women have so long been called 'angels' that men seem to have come to the conclusion that they have no persons to protect; and as for property, they say women do not know enough to take care of it, and therefore the laws and customs of society virtually say they shall have none to protect. . . . The law in its kind care for woman . . . takes every cent from her. This is not exactly burning a woman on the funeral pile of her husband, but is rather a refinement on the Asiatic cruelty."[28]

Although members of the Female Moral Reform Society opposed all edicts biased against women, they naturally gravitated toward a particular kind of reform. For years they had tried to end the double standard and male profligacy by changing public opinion. Their experiences had revealed the weakness and insensitivity of laws allegedly protecting females from masculine sexual abuse. A drive for adequate legislation, therefore, grew out of their perceptions of the unjust decrees.

When Joseph Farryal, a notorious procurer, abducted and assaulted a young woman, the editors of the *Advocate* expressed their indignation. They were angered at the "prostration of the majesty of law, by the *form* under which the action [against Farryal] was brought—an action to recover damages for loss of services! A young and innocent girl insulted under aggravated circumstances, her health injured—her life endangered—and the offender can be brought to justice only by the contemptible plea of loss of services!"[29]

The stabbing of a licentious male by one of his victims elicited a response in the *Advocate* from many women, including reformer Lydia Maria Child. Defending the actions of the wronged young woman, Miss Child criticized the laws, which considered "woman a chattel or a plaything." She was outraged that "woman must acknowledge herself the *servant* of somebody, who may claim *wages* for her lost time! . . . It is a standing insult to womankind; and had we not become the slaves we are deemed in law, we should rise en masse . . . and sweep that contemptible insult from the statute-book." The inequities in the legal system incensed readers and contributors alike. A woman wrote to the *Advocate:* "One deep and strong impression of opinion should be heard through the *ballot box* on this subject to which our lawmakers should be compelled to listen, to which their action should be made to respond."[30]

The volunteers despaired of effecting a substantial change in the lawmakers' attitude through articles in the *Advocate.* This frustration mingled with their awareness of both woman's oppression and her capabilities to stimulate an audacious enterprise. "O that we women had the handling of such matters!" lamented one female contemplating the American legal system, while thousands of others responded to the initiative of the Moral Reform Society. The members believed that sexual acts under force or false premises not only violated a female's physical integrity but also her freedom and self-determination. The general indifference to these matters at once admitted society's denigration of woman and her powerlessness to control her own life.[31]

In 1838 they began a campaign that continued with increasing intensity for the next ten years. Women affiliated with the Female Moral Reform Society urged their "sisters [to] pour in petitions to the Several State Legislatures . . . praying that this foul stain on honor and justice may be washed away by enactments making the crime . . . an offense punishable with imprisonment." Month after month the *Advocate* carried a copy of the association's petition demanding that seduction and adultery be punished as crimes.[32]

The petition drive emphasized the common interests of women. It infused them with a sense of important mission while demonstrating woman's potential to effect social change through organization. Inviting "Boston, Philadelphia, Albany, Troy, Utica, Rochester [and] Buffalo" to join them, the New York chapter published news of its campaign. The petition-gatherers were met with the "usual objections such as 'women have nothing to do with the subject'—'it is out of her sphere'—'it is a necessary evil.' " They replied: "When women suffer wrong, it [is] 'lady-like,' it [is] 'her appropriate sphere' to petition for a redress of those wrongs." In 1840 the New York branch noted that it had sent approximately 20,000 petitions to the legislature. The Ohio chapter had done almost as well.[33]

Petitioning served to attract attention both to the project and to the feminine resolution responsible for it. In 1844 the Honorable Frederick Starr, former member of the New York Legislature, addressed a semiannual meeting held in Rochester, New York, and assured the assembled women that their "course is right." The New York *Tribune* "endorsed the petition of many thousands of the virtuous mothers and daughters of our State [that was] presented at Albany." And a lengthy piece carried by the Philadelphia *Public Ledger* also vigorously supported the effort: "Moral Reform societies, consisting . . . of women, have been founded in most of our cities." It confirmed that woman's "proper province" surely included "the protection of [her] . . . own rights."[34]

Women's growing perception of their own capabilities enabled them to persist in the face of opposition and to devise new strategies. The editors complained that the legislators treated "with civil contempt or indecent humor the applications of honest and honorable women for legislative attention to their own rights and to the crimes especially affecting the sex." They encouraged "every society . . . to appoint a committee of the most intelligent women belonging to it to wait upon the . . . [legislative] members for that county to endeavor to interest them personally in the subject before they come together."[35]

In the spring of 1845 a delegation of women from New York City joined with a group from Albany to attend the legislative debates on a proposal to make seduction "a State Prison Offence." The bill had been introduced in response to their appeal, and during the next three years the women exerted relentless pressure on the lawmakers. "Let our legislators know that the female portion of their constituents have some claims upon them," wrote the volunteers. And in 1848, just before the passage of their bill, the editors published the names of those who had previously voted against the measure and stated that if these men were reelected, they owed their success to "the libertine and his associates."[36]

The Act to Punish Seduction as a Crime stipulated that "any man who shall under promise of marriage seduce and have illicit connection with any unmarried female of previous chaste character shall be guilty of a misdemeanor, and upon conviction shall be punished by imprisonment." The victory called forth exuberant praise for the women. It represented both the successful completion of a long and arduous campaign and the culmination of the American Female Moral Reform Society's intense involvement with licentious conduct and moral reform. After 1848 the association, renamed the American Female Guardian Society and Home for the Friendless, directed its attention to the care of friendless women and children in the nation's cities. But it continued to fight for the liberation of women from society's bonds.[37]

In the period between 1834 and 1848, the first fourteen years of the organization's existence, important steps had been taken towards female emancipation. The society had been forced to defend its programs by asserting that women had the right to independent conscience and judgment as morally accountable autonomous beings with natures identical to males. Woman's new sense of self incited efforts to transform the social milieu into an environment where woman, free from sex-linked roles, could better control her destiny. The members of moral reform societies continued to expand woman's domain by circulating petitions, working with lawmakers, criticizing men's conduct, and forcing public policy to be more responsive to the needs of their sex. But they did not forget the deviant woman whose plight had been indirectly responsible for so many of their ideas and actions.

Concern with the fate of prostitutes after they had been arrested led members of the society to visit regularly the city prison and the penitentiary on Blackwell's Island. Appalled at the conditions that existed in these institutions, the women reported their findings in the *Advocate.* The female prisoners were "unable to read or write, and [were] herded together like wild beasts with nothing to interest or employ them. What wonder if new lessons are taken in iniquity, and sentiments of hatred and revenge against all whom they consider more fortunate, are nourished, until they become part of the very being?"[38]

On one occasion the visiting committee recalled that the sight of female prisoners "led [them] involuntarily to exclaim, 'O that we could speak in the ear of every sister in our land, we would beseech them to cultivate . . . sympathy and benevolence' for these women." The volunteers expressed "surprise and astonishment" that "not a single matron or nurse is provided for the female department [of the Tombs]; . . . this department being under the sole charge of the male keepers, and at night watched by male guards." From the courtrooms where they witnessed countless unfortunate females being tried and convicted, the volunteers wrote: "There seemed to be no more sympathy with these wretched beings, in officers, accusers, or judge than in the gigantic columns which supported the vaulted dome above them."[39]

Women of moral reform societies thus become impressed with the importance of assisting these outcasts of their sex. In 1840 a committee met with the mayor and the common council, urging the appointment of a matron to the female division of Bellevue. To substantiate their request, Mrs. Hawkins visited the state prison at Sing Sing "to observe what the appointment of a Matron had done for the women there." She reported that the matron "appeared uniformly kind and affectionate to those under her care; and thus affection and kindness has led them to respect and confide in her."[40]

In the early 1840s, while also working on the petition campaign, the society agitated to improve the conditions of female prisoners, the majority of whom were prostitutes and many of whom were diseased. Drawing on the experiences of earlier activists—Elizabeth Fry, the famous British prison reformer; Dorothea Dix, Fry's American counterpart; and Eliza Farnham, the first female matron appointed to a state prison—the members urged the formation of a separate association specifically devoted to helping female convicts. Decrying the "cruelty, injustice and woe experienced by the miserable inmates of [the] prisons," they hoped to "enlist all in favor of giving [the] direction [of women prisoners] to a portion of female energy and benevolence." In answer to their pleas, the New York Prison Association, formed in 1844, created a Female Department, which enabled women to supervise and regulate the care given to imprisoned members of their sex. But like so many new women's associations, the Female Department had first to contend with male opposition before it could commence its activities.[41]

Catharine Sedgwick, the noted author, served as the "first directress" of the organization from 1848 to 1863. On 2 March 1845 she wrote to a friend: "I went to a meeting of the Ladies' Prison . . . Society, where a committee from the men's society appeared to remind the women that they were but a department, that a report they had printed and which was just ready for publication would knock up all the magnificent plans of the House of Lords [that is, the men] . . . Some of [the ladies] were disposed to stand upon their reserved rights; some modestly hinted they had privileges as well as responsibilities, and it finally ended in an agreement for a meeting."[42]

The women's unit won a full measure of autonomy; it functioned effectively and energetically, building upon the precedents established by the Female Benevolent Society and the Female Moral Reform Society in their programs to help prostitutes. Its first report stated: "It is only a few years that those who have been cut off from society for their misdeeds, have been deemed worthy of attention." The publication detailed the abhorrent situation of women in the city prison and continued the agitation for the appointment of matrons. Yet, when municipal officials finally acceded in the demand, the victory proved to be ephemeral: "Before the experiment could be fairly tried, an alteration was made, and the matrons were mostly withdrawn."[43]

"To carry out the objects of our Society in reference to this class of prisoners will require of us, as a duty, to counterattack and remedy the ills which our city authorities inflict upon them with so unsparing a hand," wrote the women in their second annual report (1846). They proclaimed that there "are a thousand avenues to the female heart, which females alone can find; and they must be found and traveled." While the members tried to compensate for the lack of female supervisors in the prisons by visiting with, reading to, and counseling inmates of their own sex, they also became drawn to the plight of the ex-offender. "When a woman is discharged, penniless, . . . her almost inevitable fate is a return to vice. . . . [A] discharged *female* convict is necessarily an outcast from society." The volunteers knew that the options facing the former woman prisoner were hideous indeed. "She may starve—she may beg—she may return to vice, or she may put an end to her hateful life."[44]

As members of the Female Department of the New York Prison Association became convinced that "nobody feels the blame" for the fate of the discharged female convict, they resolved to work in her behalf. Many of the women took former convicts into their homes for months at a time. "But the number proved too great for this." And "it became evident to all that the Female Department could do nothing materially to benefit this almost hopeless class of unfortunates without a *house* in which to receive and keep them."[45]

After strenuous fund-raising drives, an asylum for these women opened in the late 1840s. Located at 191 Tenth Avenue, it was eventually called the Isaac T. Hopper Home and housed over one hundred women a year. Numerous women lent their skill and energy to making the enterprise thrive. Abby Hopper Gibbons, a participant in temperance reform, aid to the poor, and abolition, became active in the new project, as did Sarah Platt Doremus, who later achieved recognition for her roles in the establishment of the Nursery and Children's Hospital and especially in the founding of the Woman's Hospital in 1855. Sarah Martyn, long associated with the American Female Guardian Society, and Caroline Matilda Kirkland, noted author of stories depicting life on the American frontier, served as officers for the association.[46]

The members' collective experiences convinced them that the high rate of female recidivism had been created by the combined effects of the lack of self-esteem, the contemptuous treatment by society, and the inability to find employment. The attitudes and policies of the home attempted to remedy these deleterious influences. In *The Helping Hand,* a book publicizing the home, Kirkland wrote that the volunteers taught the inmates practical information. They believed that the "possession of a good business [skill] . . . would have saved some of [the] poor patients from degradation" and hoped that knowledge of a trade would prevent the need to return to a life of crime upon leaving the asylum.[47]

Discharged prisoners entered the home voluntarily and generally stayed at least three months. Members of the association either tried to place them with a private family or recommended them for employment after their departure. Those who ran the Hopper Home attempted to give the inmates more than proficiency in a trade.

They wanted the refuge to be a "place that shall offer the . . . kindness . . . of home." "She [who] remains at the Asylum," wrote Kirkland, "[is] treated not with a supercilious, a cold, a spurious kindness, but as a *woman* and a *sister.*" Guided by the conviction that "there is no heart so callous or obdurate that the voice of kindness and sympathy may not reach it," the members of the Female Department extended compassion to females both in and out of prison. Their belief that "women could work best independently for the redemption of their own sex" led them to sever connections with the male prison association in 1854 and operate as a separate society: the Women's Prison Association and Home.[48]

Convinced that they must "approach the most unhappy of [their] sex in the character of a . . . sister," the women filled publications with their progress, attitudes, and impressions. "Not infrequently is the kind word met with an irrepressible tear, the encouraging smile with a quick blush of animated hope," reported the fifth annual report. In the next year, the members responded to the query, "Did the women criminals choose freely to err?" They asserted: "Our experience . . . has shown us conclusively that in nine cases out of ten, no choice was ever made, for none was offered." Indeed, the volunteers reiterated that the inmates had been "driven" to commit the crimes for which they were being punished.[49]

Year after year the middle- and upper-class women who formed the Women's Prison Association wrote of their charges with sympathy. "In the case of very many female convicts, the heart has been crushed, the affections chilled and the sensibilities destroyed, by a long course of neglect, unkindness or oppression which might drive a wise man mad," they wrote in one account. In another, they described those "innocent" women who had "fallen into misfortune by no fault of their own." In a third they told of females whose "misfortunes are to be traced . . . to their ignorance and helplessness."[50]

The sentiments expressed in the Women's Prison Association's publications were similar to those articulated by members of the moral reform societies, and they had a very special significance. While the concern and compassion of the women for their wards between 1800 and 1830 was noteworthy indeed, the identification of the volunteers with deviant females after 1830 may be considered truly remarkable. Its importance derived both from the function of deviance in social conformity and cohesion and from the implications of woman's belief in the essential oneness of her sex.

By its very definition, deviant behavior implies a departure from some established norm, a violation of acceptable action and conduct. As such, it enables a society to acknowledge and reaffirm its unifying values by delineating what it will and will not permit. Ironically, the deviant person and the punishment or ostracism that his or her actions call forth have an integrative rather than a disruptive effect on the society. They allow a community to erect a symbolic boundary around itself, to define itself and its members through those acts and ideas that it cannot tolerate.

The prostitute and criminal, unanimously treated as social outcasts, thus had an importance in solidifying thought and giving a glimmer of stability to antebellum cities. By heaping abuse upon the erring female as a degraded, tainted creature who had none of the attributes of the true woman, society found another means of delimiting those qualities worthy of womanhood. Moreover, the traditional position presumably would be strengthened through the outrage that the nondeviant female population was expected to feel and to express toward the aberrant women.[51]

Nevertheless, as members of the Female Benevolent Society, the American Female Moral Reform Society, and the Women's Prison Association came to know deviant females "from the most intimate acquaintance of year after year," they perceived and articulated a likeness between themselves and the social outcasts with whom they worked. They did *not* emphasize differences between the prostitutes, the criminals, and themselves and thereby use their experiences to bolster and affirm their own place in society. Rather, the volunteers stressed the similitude of all women. And as they labored to restore their beneficiaries to social acceptability, they simultaneously implied their dissatisfaction with the conventional feminine role.

"We call them outcasts, but when we call them so, do we think of the fearful import of the word? To be an outcast, is to have lost that which is every human being's birthright," declared the eighth annual report of the Women's Prison Association. The members of the organization attempted to prove that a criminal act did not stem from a debased, defective nature and should not be treated as such. "It is the habit of the careless world to award praise or blame too much according to circumstances; giving disproportioned credit for virtues which cost no effort or sacrifice, and condemning, with a no less unjust severity, transgressions which have all the apology of ignorance," wrote the women in 1850. They called upon all to "soften . . . indignation," for "under certain imaginable circumstances we might have been no better than the wretch."[52]

"These poor . . . [inmates] of ours," noted Caroline Kirkland, "compare not unfavorably with more fortunate sisters of the human family. . . . In short, we are obliged to own that the faults of these degraded ones are our own, carried out to their legitimate consequences, and that of what we consider our superior virtues, they are often found to retain . . . [in] a number and amount which could hardly be expected under the circumstances." Lydia Maria Child, who during her long stay in New York spent considerable time with both the benefactors and beneficiaries of the Women's Prison Association, condemned those who "treat[ed] the inmates of penitentiaries and prisons as if they were altogether unlike ourselves—as if they belonged to another race." She emphasized the similarities of all women, each within "a hair's breadth" of being the other.[53]

As the volunteers urged that women who had committed misdeeds be accepted by society, they blurred the distinction between themselves and deviant females. In doing so, they postulated a mutual interest, intent, and need among all women. The Female Benevolent Society fought "to bring back the [feminine] wanderer to the path of virtue" and wanted "assurances given that she [could] be . . . restored to the confidence and esteem of her sex. Until females will thus arise and *assert the rights of their sex*, . . . nothing can be done." Indeed, they viewed the horrible treatment of prostitutes as related to the general oppression of women. The American Female Moral Reform Society dedicated itself to assisting the "many—sisters in the *common tie of humanity*, who are . . . fallen—treated as outcasts." They declared: "In seeking to promote . . . the elevation of our own sex . . . we recognize no distinction of station, or clime or color." The members repeatedly expressed their sense of unity with the "poor squaw" as well as with the "slave woman," whom they called "our sisters in bonds."[54]

The members of these societies believed that the "strong cords of friendship as well as of consanguinity" bound women together. No matter how vast appeared the social, economic, or intellectual chasm separating the virtuous from the erring women, the volunteers forcefully asserted that "our own nature is . . . distinguishable in the criminal." Harlots, vagrants, inebriates, thieves—"the fallen and the falling . . . are our sisters by the ties of a common humanity," proclaimed the Moral Reform Society. As participants in a humanity that they shared with the women who formed the societies, the deviant females had claim to natural rights, including "the natural right of women to the sympathy, counsel, and care of . . . their own sex.[55]

"Woman is the natural . . . aid of woman in her needs; the woman that feels this not has yet to learn her mission aright," stated the Women's Prison Association. "Among the most precious of woman's rights, is the right to do good to her own sex. . . . Every woman in misfortune or disgrace is the proper object of care to the happier and safer part of her sex. Not to stretch forth her helping hand, . . . not to defend her against wrong . . . is to consent to her degradation and to become in some sense party to her ruin. Because from the very nature of the case, if women deny her cause, she has no natural friend."[56]

The volunteers thus defied a society that demanded they regard prostitutes and criminals as outcasts who had forever forfeited all claim to humanity. They reached out to deviant females from the sense that all human beings had the same moral nature as well as from the awareness of the subtle and blatant oppression uniting the entire sex.

> It is time that women . . . should consider themselves as a community, having special needs and common obligations.

As they came to believe that women formed a distinct group, they transcended the boundary separating the aberrant female from the virtuous lady. And, in so doing, they implicitly rejected the stability, conformity, and adherence to the norms of the woman-belle ideal that the boundary was supposed to insure. For those who formed and joined philanthropic associations recognized the ties that bound them to the unfortunate women they called their sisters.[57]

The members had long experienced the agonies created by the imposition of boundaries and knew all too well the torment of being barricaded in and viewed as an inferior and flawed class that could never compensate for its damaged nature. The women who extended a "helping hand" to deviant females had known isolation. They understood the pain of being denied participation in society, the anguish of being "the object." Therefore, when they asserted a oneness of all females, they did so with a full realization of the injustices and inequalities that assumed different forms but affected every woman. Moreover, tens of thousands of women across the nation had gained a sense of themselves as autonomous beings with the right to independent judgment and conscience. This awareness had convinced them that a female, like a male, could step outside the rules of society and still retain her essential humanity.

Yet the identification of the volunteers with the deviant female implied more than the recognition and acknowledgment of a common nature and a shared oppression. Before the philanthropists came to empathize with the female outcasts, they themselves had felt disaffected from society. Their estrangement from the social milieu found expression in their attack on the men, customs, and laws that had shaped and limited their lives. This perception of the origins of woman's inferior position aggravated the volunteers' alienation from society. And, as they measured their attitudes, abilities, needs, and drives against those insisted upon by the yardstick of antebellum feminine normalcy, the woman-belle ideal, they understood that *they too were deviant women.*

10

In Want of the Splendid City

> There is no insurmountable solitude. All paths lead to the same goal: to convey to others what we are. And we must pass through solitude and difficulty, isolation and silence, in order to reach forth to the enchanted place where we can dance our clumsy dance and sing our sorrowful song—but in this dance or in this song there are fulfilled the most ancient rites of our conscience in the awareness of being human and of believing in a common destiny.
>
> —Pablo Neruda, *Toward the Splendid City,* Nobel Lecture

Women in female voluntary societies slowly recognized their anomalous position in American society. Their shared activities and observations had convinced them that they would find neither fulfillment nor emancipation by trying to fit their attitudes and behavior into the rigid stereotype of nineteenth-century womanhood. And, as a result, they drew new thoughts and policies out of their collective experiences. The volunteers pieced these together in an attempt to create a new environment for woman. First through associations but later through a variety of other endeavors, they tried to transform the social milieu into one where woman would be liberated from the chains of poverty, ignorance, and tradition.

The volunteers' efforts to reshape society in their own terms reveal much about their basic assumptions. The majority of these women appeared to accept the antebellum economic system. Some espoused socialist doctrines; most did not. While they fought to improve wages of factory operatives, few protested the factory system itself. They defended the worth of society's nonproductive members but stopped short of demanding quality public support for these groups. They urged the better treatment of domestics yet generally did not question their own right to household help. Repudiating woman's traditional role, they argued for a more equitable division of labor in the family, founded the first day care centers, but never endorsed anything approaching communal living. They were reformers, not radicals. However, the implications of some of their demands were revolutionary indeed.

Their goal was a sisterhood of women, not as an abstract idea, but as a reality. They hoped to achieve this unity by translating pervasive feelings of alienation into positive social action. Out of estrangement, then, came an attempt to change society. Woman's imaginative plans blended with a malleable urban atmosphere to produce a wealth of valuable institutions.

The number of charitable associations multiplied dramatically in the years after 1830. Most of the pioneer societies continued, even enlarging their scope of operations, and many new ones appeared. They performed those functions once considered a form of feminine heresy but now, in the second thirty years of benevolence, generally accepted as traditional. In addition to the "conventional" associations and to the moral reform and prison societies, two other types of organizations emerged after 1830. One kind was dedicated to helping women become economically self-sufficient; the other devoted its efforts to treating women's diseases and to enabling females to be cared for by physicians and nurses of their own sex. These reflected the increasingly feminist concerns of their members and added new dimensions to the progress already made.

The records of urban female voluntary associations in the years following 1830 reveal an augmentation of the ideas and activities initiated by the early benevolent organizations. The literature portrays woman's increasing confidence as she carried unpopular projects to successful completion and community acceptance. It also demonstrates her heightened belief in the unity of all women, overarching her sense of the individuality and diversity of her sex.

The history of the Association for the Benefit of the Colored Orphan discloses many of the trends inaugurated by the earlier societies. The association originated in 1836 through the efforts of "two Quaker ladies, Miss Anna M. Shotwell and her niece Miss May Murray," when they "found two wistful little Negro [orphans] . . . sitting on the steps of an old house in lower New York." After learning that none of the existing nurseries would accept Black children, the women became determined to establish a separate orphan asylum for them. Yet this task was fraught with difficulty. As the eighteenth annual report of the association recounted, "[The] feeble band who first went forth as pioneers [entered] into the haunts of the outcasts and the victims of cruel prejudice . . . among the diseased and degraded." No house could be found for the children because of "the existing prejudice against color, owners resolutely refusing the use of their property on any consideration the Managers could offer."[1]

Undaunted, the women selected an old double frame cottage on West Twelfth Street near Sixth Avenue for their home. But they immediately petitioned the common council for a grant of land on which to erect a new building. Finally the fifth annual report (1841) acknowledged the "appropriation by the Corporation of the City of twenty lots of ground on 5th Avenue between 43rd and 44th Streets." The asylum, "the first . . . institution of its kind in the country," prospered under the indefatigable efforts of its managers. Starting with twelve pensioners, the average number cared for by the institution reached eight hundred within a few years.[2]

Inevitably drawn to the plight of the Black woman, the members created a lying-in department and attempted to find employment for other women in the area. The work of the association attracted notice. In 1844 the volunteers reported that the asylum "had been visited and inspected by the Mayor and Common Council," who granted the institution "20 additional lots of ground adjoining their premises." The progress of their organization, especially when contrasted with its inauspicious beginnings, supported the members' proclamation that "their toil and skill and patient perseverance" had assured the "success and permanence" of their "benevolent effort."

Heartened by the attainments of the Colored Orphan Asylum, other orphanages dedicated to helping specific groups of children appeared and prospered. Located on Prince Street, the Female Orphan Asylum of the Roman Catholic Benevolent Society sheltered hundreds of girls raised in the Catholic faith. The Orphan's Home and Asylum of the Protestant Episcopal Church, situated on the southwest corner of Forty-ninth Street and Lexington Avenue and governed "by a Board of Lady Managers," housed orphaned or abandoned Protestant children. St. Joseph's Orphan Asylum, organized in 1858 for "the maintenance of orphan, half orphan, homeless and neglected children, especially those of German origin," added to the increasing number of children's refuges founded in the Empire City after 1830. These institutions, established in New York through women's actions, had counterparts in cities and towns across the nation.[3]

In addition to assisting orphans, the volunteers reached out to other segments of the urban female population. The Ladies' Christian Union of the City of New York began an association in 1858 to promote the "welfare of women, particularly the young and unprotected employed in stores and manufactories." Similar organizations founded in Boston, Philadelphia, Baltimore, and Chicago secured homes with private families and obtained employment for young women. The House of Mercy in New York City, emulating the programs of the Female Benevolent Society and the Women's Prison Association, provided a refuge for "fallen females."[4]

Other urban women formed associations to relieve the needs of impoverished and sick elderly women. The Ladies' Union Aid Society was established in 1850 "through the persevering energy of Mrs. E. A. Farr, Mrs. M. W. Mason, Mrs. B. F. Howe, and the other ladies associated with them." The Church Charity Foundation "[owed] its origin to a private enterprise which had been undertaken by a few noble-minded and generous ladies." The Brooklyn Home for Aged Indigent Women began to function in 1851, while the St. Luke's Home, situated at 543 Hudson Street and dedicated to assisting "indigent Christian females," opened the following year.[5]

While many female voluntary societies directed their attention to a specific group dispersed throughout the urban population, others devoted their energies to a particular geographic area. Few of the latter received more disparagement for their plans and ultimately more publicity for their accomplishments than the Ladies' Home Missionary Society of the Methodist Episcopal Church. The society embarked upon an audacious scheme: it wanted to bring philanthropy to the Five Points.

The region that lay to the south of Canal Street had become a mecca for the poor, the desperate, and the derelict of the city. Residents viewed it as a "great moral ulcer located in the very heart of the city, being only a few hundred yards from the City Hall and Park, and within 3 minutes walk, and in plain view of Broadway." Fredrika Bremer, who accompanied prison reformer Abby Hopper Gibbons through the area, found "every grade of moral corruption, festering and fermenting [there]." For precisely these reasons the Ladies' Home Missionary Society chose this site for their work.[6]

The society, established "to perform . . . acts of charity and benevolence," already sponsored seven missions in the city's destitute neighborhoods. Yet in 1848, when the organization first considered extending its field of operations to the Five Points area, the plan evoked adamant opposition. One contemporary reported that the "proposition met with hearty laughter, so chimerical did the idea appear." Nevertheless the women "expressed their determination to send a missionary there [and] . . . they did in 1850." In the narrative of their efforts, *The Old Brewery and the New Mission House at the Five Points* (1854), the members recalled that at first "it was thought extremely hazardous for the ladies to visit families in that neighborhood and to gather in children for the schools." But the women would not be deterred. And "even the Old Brewery with its numerous cellars, dark passages and attics became familiar to a few who had moral and physical courage enough to bear the sight, inhale the air and hear the sounds."[7]

The volunteers—including Phoebe Palmer, revivalist, author of *The Way of Holiness* (1845), and dedicated worker in New York City charities—rented a room, formerly a liquor store. The accounts of their labors in the Five Points disclosed the desperate condition of the women living there. Of one widow they wrote: "Alone, unaided, she began the struggle of life, with three helpless children dependent on her exertions." "A poor woman . . . almost frozen to death" and one "on a wretched pallet in the corner . . . [who was] dying of consumption [and had] no hand to smooth the tangled hair or wipe . . . her brow" were but two of many women whose anguished histories darkened the pages of the society's book. These experiences persuaded the members to organize a house where they could employ their beneficiaries and also to begin an informal employment agency.[8]

As the volunteers' struggles in the Five Points became successful, they aroused the attention of substantial portions of the community. The women met with New York's most affluent men, including Anson G. Phelps, William B. Skidmore, and Daniel Drew. To this group they divulged their plan to purchase and renovate the Old Brewery and establish a permanent settlement house. The gathering, held in 1853, only five years after the members first announced their aim in the Five Points, demonstrated the magnitude of their triumph. Now, instead of being met with ridicule, their proposal received strong support. The common council agreed to appropriate $1,000 and within a short period the women obtained pledges for an additional $5,000.[9]

After purchasing and demolishing the dilapidated building, the society erected a structure containing a chapel, schoolrooms, baths, and twenty apartments designed to be furnished without charge to families residing in the area. The project quickly caught the public imagination; prominent citizens bestowed exuberant praise on the women.

R. A. West, a New York attorney, proclaimed: "What no legal enactment could accomplish—what no machinery of municipal government could effect . . . women have brought about, quietly but thoroughly and triumphantly. . . . The great problem of how to renovate the Five Points had engaged the attention of both the legislative and executive branches of the city government, and both had abandoned the task in despair. . . . [I]t will be an imperishable honor to the Ladies' Home Missionary Society . . . that with them the idea originated, and by them has so successfully been carried out." The achievements in the Five Points paved the way for settlement work in other cities. The triumph reinforced woman's belief that she could make significant contributions in the community and provide essential social services for her sex.[10]

This heightened confidence is also found in the records of those early societies that continued to operate successfully throughout the century. The New York Female Assistance Society boasted in 1836 that it would "relieve the suffering of hundreds of sick poor who might else suffer extreme distress or perish as too many have done in the abodes of poverty and want in this great city." In 1844 the Society for the Relief of Poor Widows with Small Children felt "constrained to say . . . that the institutions in this city under [woman's] direction" have been unquestionably the most successful.[11]

As they received the acclaim of other city dwellers, the members of those female voluntary societies founded before 1830 felt more secure in the value of their achievements. This self-assurance led them to defend more forcefully the recipients of their aid as victims of society's oppression of women. In 1844 the Society for the Relief of Poor Widows asserted that the "increasing rate of rent, the increasing price of articles of food, the insufficient pay, and limited sphere of labor . . . falls . . . crushingly upon the objects of this charity—women." And the Seamen's Aid Society of Boston criticized the opinion "not infrequently urged . . . that in our favored country all persons who enjoy health and will work and be prudent can support themselves and families comfortably." They strongly denounced this position as "not correct."[12]

As in its earlier years, the Seamen's Aid Society assumed an explicitly feminist stance. Formerly it had urged the creation of additional benevolent societies to alleviate the feminine poverty and deprivation its members encountered. But now the volunteers agitated for legal remedies. And, along with the women of moral reform societies, they became the first organization of females in America to argue for legislative enactments favorable to their sex. In 1837 the women attacked "the law which gives to the husband uncontrollable power over the personal property of his wife."[13]

Calling the decree "legalized plunder," they wrote: "It would be easy to show the flagrant injustice of this law in its operation on the rich; how, not infrequently, the property of the wife, inherited from her father, is squandered by her extravagant husband. . . . Though she possessed a million dollars before she marries, she cannot, after she is a wife, dispose of a dollar in her own right, she must go to her husband to beg money for her charities." The statute threatened and affected their own lives. But the women insisted that they were "pleading the cause of the poor [female] to whom this law, which subjects the property earned by the wife, even when separated from her husband, supporting herself, and . . . [maybe] a family of young children, by the labor of her own hands, to seizure for his debts, is as cruel as those of Draco! Though it be not written in blood, it has wrung seas of bitter tears from the broken-hearted wife."[14]

In their efforts on behalf of the impoverished females of Boston, the members had met many a woman whose "husband, after spending all his living, is gone for months, or years, contributing nothing to his family; the wife . . . labors and saves . . . [but if] the [h]usband returns . . . he can take all her furniture, even her clothing and that of her children, and sell them, legally for rum. . . . [T]here is no remedy while the law gives to the husband the uncontrolled right over his wife's earnings," the women continued. "And although the . . . ladies, who constitute the Seamen's Aid Society, may not one of them suffer in consequence of the statute; yet, they should feel none the less for those who are subjected to its demoralizing and soul-withering influences." They proclaimed:

> The sympathies of woman should always be awakened by the woes of woman for the *lot of all is, in the main, the same*—Yes, let us pray not each one for herself, but for our sex . . . till the oppressions . . . are removed.[15]

As the members of the Seamen's Aid Society worked to extricate females from their legal bondage, the women of other associations strove to emancipate their sex from another form of slavery. After 1830, urban women developed countless institutions dedicated to helping those they called "their toiling sisters 'who rise early and late take rest.' " The volunteers established homes for the friendless, houses of industry, and industrial schools in cities throughout America. Their common program—to shelter, train and employ needy females—grew from their past experiences in benevolent societies.

The American Female Moral Reform Society, now renamed the American Female Guardian Society and Home for the Friendless, stated its reasons for initiating a house of industry: "The first idea of a . . . [home] originated in the Publication Office where poor women flocked for aid and comfort." The society's "Register of Direction for . . . females needing employment . . . [gave the members] abundant opportunity . . . to become personally acquainted with the . . . *wants* and *exposures* of the destitute and friendless." "The *alms-house, watch-house* or *Tombs*, are the only shelter afforded the friendless- unprotected female whose only crime is poverty and the need of employment." Hoping to achieve the "self-preservation and self-elevation" of their sex, the volunteers rented a small house on First Avenue and Second Street as a temporary lodging for their new project.[16]

Members soon reported that "the building was overcrowded and there was considerable illness among the inmates and those in charge." The board, adopting the policy of accepting all women who desired admission, had received over six hundred females in less than a year. A larger accommodation became mandatory, and the volunteers began a fund-raising drive. So earnestly did the women plead the cause of impoverished females that contributions to the Home Building Fund poured in from such outstanding New Yorkers as Horace Greeley, Lewis Tappan, James Lenox, and Abraham Schermerhorn. The cornerstone was laid on 5 May 1849, just two years after the women had commenced their venture.[17]

The completion of the Home for the Friendless and House of Industry, symbolizing woman's efforts on behalf of the less fortunate of her sex, elicited enthusiastic applause. One speaker at the dedication declared:

> We have seen . . . ladies willing to encounter every difficulty, and even contumely, in pursuit of the means where with to erect an institution for the reception of the poor and friendless, and with a spirit that nothing could discourage or repress. . . . Too much praise cannot be accorded to those who in the midst of every discouragement were determined to prosecute with every energy.

E. W. Chester, a New York attorney, asserted that the building would "stand as a monument to . . . [women's] charity, their perseverance, and their warm-hearted philanthropy." The women gloried in these tributes and proclaimed: "Not only . . . [is] ours the first Home for the Friendless, but one of the first enterprises of any magnitude in our city and country exclusively under the guidance of women."[18]

To be sure, the members enjoyed the profuse praise their work called for; yet the women found a more compelling purpose in their efforts. Sarah Bennett, editor of the *Advocate*, wrote: "This association has bridged the amazing chasm which separates the extremes of society. . . . Those who have crossed the bridge have learned lessons in the abode of penury, . . . and at the pauper's death-bed, that cannot be forgotten amid the comforts and enjoyments of home. The *same* is emphatically true of each and . . . [every] sister association." The poem "A City Street," which appeared in the *Advocate*, expressed similar sentiments. Finding that "life's severest contrasts meet,/ Forever in the city street," author Mary Howitt rhymed:

Hence it is that a city street
Can deepest thought impart
For all its people, high and low
Are kindred to my heart,
And with a yearning love I share
In all their joy, their pain, their care.

Catharine Sedgwick, first directress of the Women's Prison Association and intimate friend of members of the Female Guardian Society, also believed female organizations could help to transcend social and economic differences. "I have just come from the House of Industry," recorded Miss Sedgwick, "from the infinite complicity of . . . committee[s]. . . . I received about 200 registered names, etc. poor women eagerly seeking work. . . . The best of it all is to see the ladies . . . in close contact with these exuberant daughters of Erin, earnestly devoting themselves to the relief of their wants. It will be a noble institution."[19]

The Home for the Friendless and House of Industry attempted to offer poor women an alternative to a life of poverty or crime or to a marriage based on economic considerations. It gave destitute females emotional and financial support while helping them to earn a livelihood. The *Advocate of Moral Reform* (now called the *Advocate and Family Guardian*) and many other newspapers carried the story of this successful enterprise. Philadelphia, Poughkeepsie, Rochester, and Syracuse soon established similar institutions, which ultimately appeared in most American cities. And within the Empire City still more organizations arose to assist impoverished women.

The Mariners' Family Industrial Society of the Port of New York, the Woman's Benevolent Society of the Calvary Church, and the New York House of Industry and School shared a similar purpose. Each hoped to assist destitute women and to give their sex "a spirit of independence." The Ladies' Helping Hand Association taught women sewing and needlework, while the New York Working Woman's Protective Union, established in 1863, dedicated itself to ameliorating the condition of the factory worker. Comparable associations quickly appeared in Boston, Philadelphia, Chicago, and St. Louis.[20]

Efforts to alleviate the plight of females dependent upon their own wages for existence assumed many forms. One of the most popular was the industrial school, which proliferated in the middle of the century. One member explained why the American Female Guardian Society established many such schools: "These children are too poor to avail themselves of the . . . generous provision of the public." "Lack of suitable clothing" and "the necessity which often require[d] their assistance at home" combined to prevent numerous youngsters from attending public schools. Women, therefore, founded institutions where girls could receive an education like that given in the city schools, while simultaneously learning to support themselves. The industrial schools taught sewing and other skills, provided a free lunch that the children helped to make, and willingly "waived" certain regulations "for the good of the children."[21]

The Female Guardian Society sponsored more than twenty schools and viewed each as a base for social service work in its desolate surroundings. Other voluntary organizations throughout the city and state founded scores of analogous institutions. The German Industrial School in Manhattan reported that most of the girls who attended had formerly tried to earn a few pennies on the city streets. The Wilson Industrial School for Girls, located at 125 St. Mark's Place, similarly recorded that before its opening in 1853 its students had "passed their time in the street as beggars [and] rag pickers." Taking the name of its founder, Mrs. James Wilson, this school advised the public of the "possibility of establishing self-sustaining trade-classes."[22]

Older girls received an education as well as payment for their services, "and thus the feeling of independence [was] cultivated." "Girls have left the Tailoring Department, and now maintain themselves by that trade," stated one report. Another noted that some of their graduates could command from "five to seven dollars for their dressmaking skills," while other students had become qualified to work as private tutors. "Corporal punishment, the use of scolding and of loud and angry tones in speaking on the part of the teachers is entirely dispensed with," wrote the women. Indeed, they attributed their successes to a sincere interest in the students' physical and emotional welfare.[23]

The Brooklyn Industrial School Association, organized in 1854 by "two philanthropic women, Mrs. Sharp and Mrs. King," established several schools in different parts of Brooklyn. These shared in the general features of industrial schools, but also instituted two novel programs. "Mothers' Meetings," held periodically at each school "to assist and encourage the burden bearing, often disheartened, mothers," gave poor women an opportunity to share their problems and thoughts with one another. Each school also had a nursery, which accepted the children of working women and placed them under the care of nurses. As a report noted: "This is a great relief to indigent women, who are thus enabled to go out to service."[24]

The imaginative plan filled an important need, for working mothers could not afford to pay someone to watch their children and usually had no alternative but to leave them unattended. The *Advocate* reported frequent fires "in consequence of mothers being obliged to lock up their little ones while they go out to obtain the mere necessaries of life." Mothers who resisted locking their youngsters in an unsafe dwelling unwittingly created the phenomenon of "street children." These youths passed long days and nights on the city's avenues and boulevards, forming a visible sign of urban poverty and suffering.[25]

The special needs of another group of working women awakened the sympathies of Mrs. Thomas Addis Emmet, a manager of the Marion Street Lying-in Asylum, and of Mrs. Cornelius Du Bois. They were struck by the "miseries of infants . . . and the suffering of mothers whose poverty forced them to give the nourishment intended for their own infants to the children of the rich." Pooling their energies and resources, they organized an asylum "for the maintenance and care of the children of wet nurses, and the daily charge of infants whose parents labor away from home." Thus emerged the first institution in the city, and probably in the nation, *primarily* devoted to day care.[26]

Called the Nursery for the Children of Poor Women, at its formation in 1854 the establishment was located on the corner of Lexington Avenue and Fifty-first Street. It included among its managers Sarah Doremus, who had succeeded Catharine Sedgwick as first directress of the Women's Prison Association. Dedicated to relieving the "sorrows and wants of destitute mothers," the organization sheltered their young children and provided infants with special attention. The widespread illness among the youngsters forced the volunteers to expand their facilities, and in 1856 they organized the Children's Hospital. The institution, which ultimately included a lying-in hospital, also admitted illegitimate children to prevent "suicides of erring mothers." It attempted to meet several specific needs of poverty-stricken women, becoming another tangible expression of women's efforts to help one another.[27]

Similarly, the upper- and middle-class women who struggled to found the Woman's Hospital regarded their institution as "the work of woman for the benefit of woman." The members of the Woman's Hospital Association declared their "object and business . . . [to be the provision of] a hospital intended for the treatment of diseases peculiar to woman." Further, they "knew that many women were passing weary days and nights of agony, debarred by poverty from seeking medical aid, and for whom no shelter was provided." This attempt to relieve "suffering that no mere man [could] . . . possibly understand" found support among many women, including Sarah Doremus, who ultimately became the president of the board of the new hospital. Her widespread contact with women prisoners and with other destitute females, many of whom suffered from gynecological diseases and disorders, had unveiled the physical anguish of women prevented by poverty and ignorance from getting help. She resolved to make medical assistance more accessible to the poor.[28]

Urging "every woman . . . to aid in healing her suffering sisters," Doremus was joined by other members of the organization to raise money for the proposed health center. They campaigned vigorously, boldly ignoring the prohibitions upon their sex discussing the reproductive organs. By 1855 the women had adequate funds to purchase a private home on Madison Avenue. Equipped with forty beds and medical facilities, the Woman's Hospital began admitting patients. The constitution stipulated that the "surgeon's assistant must be a woman," and its reports declared that, "[to] the poor, its wards and all that it can offer are free." Under the auspices of women managers and visiting committees who administered the facility, the hospital quickly won the enthusiastic support of the citizens of New York.[29]

At the first anniversary celebration of the establishment of the Woman's Hospital, doctors and other men of note heralded the "formidable . . . task" achieved by the founders. Dr. John W. Francis credited the women with making the city aware of the "claims" of the "particular class of diseases to which the . . . Woman's Hospital is devoted." "To the brave and intelligent labors of a society of New York ladies . . . [the hospital] owes its existence." The women, "their union strong . . . , put all on trial. . . . [T]hey coalesced as one power in the promotion of their design, and their courageous and determined actions, like those of Mrs. [Joanna] Bethune, . . . Miss Dix . . . and Florence Nightingale, vindicate the true character of their sex beyond dispute."[30]

The Woman's Hospital, which grew in size and importance, greatly expanded the medical facilities available to New York women, particularly of the poorer classes. Yet it never achieved the fame of the New York Infirmary for Women and Children, organized in 1853 under the direction of Dr. Elizabeth Blackwell. Gaining distinction throughout the nation as the "first medical charity established by female physicians, . . . [it represented] the first hospital organized for the instruction of women in practical medicine."[31]

The New York Infirmary began in 1853. With the aid of sympathetic women, "a small room was engaged in a poor quarter of the town near Tompkins Square." The act of incorporation stated that the purpose of the institution was "to afford poor women the opportunity of consulting physicians of their own sex." Blackwell recalled that the infirmary was met with vehement hostility by many males, who told her that a "[woman] doctor would be looked upon with so much suspicion that the police would interfere [and] that if deaths occurred their death certificates would not be recognized." The female population, however, now long accustomed to receiving support and assistance from members of their own sex, obviously believed that women could indeed practice medicine with skill and intelligence. They flocked to the new infirmary.[32]

An early report of the clinic recorded that "over 200 poor women have received medical aid. All these women have gratefully acknowledged the help afforded them." A later publication noted:

> [The] rapid increase of the patients of the Infirmary, the number treated this year being more than double that of [the last], shows how highly poor women appreciate the advantage of being able to consult physicians of their own sex. The same thing is proved by the fact that the patients of the Institution have come from all parts of the city, from Brooklyn, Williamsburgh, Long Island and occasionally from New Jersey and New England. Many instances might be mentioned in which patients have sought relief after suffering for years without being willing to apply to any other public charity.[33]

"The medical service is conducted entirely by women," proclaimed a memorandum of the infirmary, which detailed the special services supplied by the institution: "Poor women are attended at their own homes, by the junior physicians. . . . Night after night is spent . . . in these dens of misery, ministering to the wants of the sick." A free outpatient dispensary was open every morning to all women, and limited inpatient hospital facilities were also available. One staff member, called the "sanitary visitor," was responsible for giving "simple, practical instruction to poor mothers on the management of infants and the preservation of the health of the families." The doctors also helped women to find suitable employment, suggested appropriate charities, and even rendered financial assistance.[34]

"The essential feature of this Institution is that it is an effort of women to help themselves by the steady and earnest cultivation of a valuable field of industry," declared an annual report of the infirmary. Dismayed by woman's ignorance of her own body, Elizabeth urged her sister and co-worker, Dr. Emily Blackwell, "to collect all [available] information . . . about maternity, the rational of the sexes, and kindred subjects." She added: "We have a vast field to work in this direction. . . . I feel as if it were peculiarly our duty to meet this want."[35]

Shortly after Emily's arrival in New York, Dr. Marie E. Zackrzewska, a young woman who had been sent to Elizabeth for encouragement by the House of Industry, decided to work with the sisters. Together, the three women strove to establish a separate, complete teaching hospital. Up until this time, although some women could receive college medical instruction, "no hospital was anywhere available either for practical instruction or the exercise of the woman-physician's skill. To supply the need had become a matter of great urgency," and Elizabeth Blackwell exhorted women to create institutions "to meet their own needs."[36]

The establishment of a hospital by women physicians excited strong resistance, but the doctors were determined. They resolved to "provide treatment for poor women and [female] children by physicians of their own sex, to form a center for the work of women physicians and to give practical instruction to women medical students [and nurses]." Most important, the hospital would alleviate "a vast amount of suffering—often the cause of death could . . . [be] averted—[now] that woman's heart has been moved to claim as her rightful prerogative the privileges of an education that will qualify her to administer to the relief of the suffering of her sex."[37]

Finally, this institution would "gain the attention and respect of the community, and win that confidence from the profession which would induce them to receive its students to their wider opportunities." The project eventually won the support of Horace Greeley and his New York *Tribune.* Henry J. Raymond, founder of the *New York Times,* as well as innumerable male physicians, endorsed the venture. And in 1868 Elizabeth Blackwell's plans for adding a women's medical college to the New York Infirmary came to fruition. The institution, which admitted students from all over the nation, stood as a monument to woman's initiative, courage, and dedication to the advancement of her sex.[38]

Guaranteeing that "women . . . receive the blessings of a medical attendance from skillful physicians of their own sex," the New York Infirmary for Women and Children and the Woman's Medical College were the natural offspring of woman's labors in hundreds of female voluntary societies over a period of fifty years. The woman doctor insisted upon her right as a fully equal individual to enter a male bastion of privilege and authority and extended free medical treatment and advice to others of her sex. This help, coming as it did from a female physician, had a significance even beyond the undeniable importance of making such assistance available to prisoners of poverty, inhibition, and ignorance.[39]

The woman doctor gave instruction in hygiene and health care. She treated the whole person rather than only the specific symptom, and she recognized the social context of illness. Moreover, by demonstrating interest in feminine diseases, particularly those involving the reproductive organs, the female physician helped her patients to overcome years of embarrassment, fear, and alienation from their bodies. Thus she broke through the barrier that prohibited women from pursuing a professional life and challenged the concept of sex-linked roles. At the same time she helped other females to feel more comfortable with and to exercise greater control over their bodies and, consequently, their lives.

Woman's benevolent involvement in the years after 1830, then, demonstrated both her estrangement from nineteenth-century society and the beginning of her attempt to transform the social milieu into one responsive to the plight of her sex. These efforts contrasted with the ethos of the woman-belle ideal, which spoke in the singular and dictated a monolithic code for the entire sex. For the vivid experiences of members of the female voluntary societies had taught them that all women did not have the same needs. Although the social and economic backgrounds of the volunteers necessarily limited their perceptions, they formed societies they earnestly believed would ameliorate the conditions of impoverished females and help them toward self-fulfillment.

The associations of the first three decades of organized philanthropy agitated for numerous reforms and had crucial significance for the development of feminism. Yet generally they did not establish lasting institutions. The organizations developed during the years from 1830 to 1860 founded day care centers, schools, training and employment facilities, and hospitals. These varied establishments expressed women's sense of themselves as individuals having different needs, yet bound together by special interests and obligations as well as by the burden of oppression. And they revealed women's refusal to continue to allow men, the traditional authority figures, to dictate and define their needs. Disclosing the importance of freeing women from the tyrannies of deprivation, prejudice, and sex-related roles, the organizations worked to help the members of their sex begin to claim possession of their own lives.

Ironically the myriad of institutions formed by woman in the antebellum period—shaped out of her alienation from society—greatly enriched the quality of urban life. They brought humanity to the frantic, impersonal nineteenth-century cities and provided a wealth of vital social services. Anticipating the creation of municipal agencies, these organizations demonstrated flexibility and sensitivity to the needs of females in urban America. The activities of the nineteenth-century woman, coming from within the still narrow confines of her existence, may be seen not only as helping to advance the interests of her sex, but also as working toward a better life and, perhaps one day, "Splendid City."

Yet, predictably, as governmental officials and other prominent citizens praised woman's talents and acknowledged the value of her accomplishments, her anger at being denied full participation in her community increased dramatically. Allowed to contribute her time and skills on a voluntary basis only, she was still barred from most forms of remunerative and rewarding employment. And as women absorbed the meanings of their cumulative experiences, they began to understand the limits of voluntarism both for themselves and as a vehicle for effective change. Throughout the 1850s they not only demanded broader opportunities and rights for their sex but insisted that the public assume responsibility for their oppression.

11

When Lions Are Painters

A painter once exhibited to a lion, a splendid picture in which Hercules was represented conquering the Nemean lion, who lay prostrate and bleeding at his feet. After examining it steadfastly for some time, the king of beasts exclaimed haughtily—"This is all very well, but if lions were painters, we should see the other side of the picture."

—*Aesop's Fables*

The history of woman's involvement in female benevolent societies emerged as a denial of the prevailing nineteenth-century conception of female nature. Yet while woman donated her energy and talents to a community made better by these varied contributions, her basic position remained unaltered. A widening gap developed between woman's awareness of the worth and dignity of her sex and society's denigrating treatment of its female population. Not surprisingly, this dichotomy produced an unremitting tension as women became increasingly frustrated over the nation's reluctance to alter its theories and attitudes.

As woman absorbed the lessons of almost a half century of organized charitable activity, her discordant relationship with society became intensified. At the same time it became understood in a new way. No longer would she confide her yearning for fulfillment to locked diaries. No more would she express her faith in feminine potential through fictitious heroines. The shared experiences of voluntary associations throughout America had impelled the formation of a feminist ideology, enabling women, forcefully and directly, to claim increased rights for their sex.

Females whose thinking had been shaped by organized benevolence produced countless articles urging woman's emancipation. Some wrote in their capacity as managers or members of particular societies; others wrote as private individuals. But all expressed ideas nurtured by philanthropic involvement. Confident that their past activities guaranteed them at least society's attention, women agitated for expanded employment and educational opportunities, legal rights, and the end of sex-determined roles.

From the beginning, feminine voluntary associations had argued, implicitly and explicitly, for greater freedom. Members' dim perceptions of their autonomous identity had fostered pleas for fairer treatment. But as the century approached its middle years, women recognized that they possessed the same human nature as man. They ultimately concluded that woman had the same abilities, duties, and responsibilities and, therefore, merited identical rights.

The volunteers generally refrained from polemical refutations of woman's alleged inferiority. They believed that the rich history of female organized philanthropy had demonstrated equality beyond question. Now they claimed prerogatives that years of charitable endeavor assured them all women deserved. As the members argued for woman's liberation, they articulated a variety of views. They were eclectic, often inconsistent. Yet the profound conviction that woman had value as an independent being whose essential dignity emanated from her humanity joined the disparate writings together and gave them unity.

Assertion of woman's worth beyond the possible relations of her life as mother, wife, sister, and daughter formed a dominant theme. Numerous essays urged that woman be trained for independence so that she could assume responsibility for her own life. The *Advocate and Family Guardian* by the late 1840s had become an expressly feminist publication. Concentrating its energies on the various phases of woman's emancipation rather than on the specific activities of the American Female Guardian Society, the periodical declared that woman is "possessed of . . . common humanity, having personal responsibilities for which she alone is responsible." It continued:

> It is manifest that whatever will increase her power, whatever will command the respect of others, in brief whatever will enable her more successfully to accomplish life's greatest purposes is rightfully hers on the plainest principles of common justice.[1]

An article entitled "The Wrongs of Woman," appearing in an 1854 issue of the *Advocate,* stated that there is "no feeling more universal among . . . human beings than the desire to be independent, to take care of themselves. . . . [I]t's lamentable that there should be so large a portion of the human race so educated that they must depend on others." The author concluded by mocking male objections: " 'Oh you deprive woman of all her charms, if you make her self-reliant and give her independence,' exclaim very many who are so fearful of the encroachments of females upon their privileges and prerogatives."[2]

Entreating mothers to "educate their daughters to far greater self-reliance," the *Advocate* thought that "no woman of health and sound mind should allow herself to feel dependent on any body." A woman from New England believed it "necessary" for "young women in this country . . . to acquire a knowledge of several trades." She urged that the wages be sufficient "[to] enable [young women] . . . to be . . . independent." And Mrs. C. F. Fonda from Wheaton, Illinois, looked forward to the day "when woman comes to occupy her true position . . . and is allowed to qualify herself for self-support."[3]

To dramatize the demand that women be allowed to control their own lives, the *Advocate* printed the "true" story of M- L-, a young mother whose husband died after squandering all their money. Although told that redress was possible, she had been "educated to regard it as 'unladylike for a female to journey without an attendant, . . . not appropriate for her sphere to appear in the marts of business or to seem to *know* right from wrong in what might pertain to legal transactions.' " Yet M- L- decided that "she must brave a false public sentiment and adopt the *true idea that woman can do with propriety whatever . . . she may have the strength and wisdom to perform.* . . . She sought advice, made herself familiar with the laws of her state [and] . . . employed counsel in whose hands she placed the data necessary [for recovery]." As the editors related the happy ending of their tale, they declared that the "struggles of the past few years have made M- L- a truly energetic, self-reliant woman . . . [who] has become conscious of her own powers."[4]

Sarah Martyn, a former manager of the Female Guardian Society, similarly exhorted women to independence. In the *Ladies' Wreath,* a feminist periodical which she organized and edited, Martyn wrote that "every healthy young woman ought to be so trained as to be able to make her own way through the world, without the necessity of dependence on any other. No matter what her rank or station may be, she ought . . . to be able to support herself through life." Eliza Farnham, first female matron of a state prison and co-worker with the members of both the Female Guardian Society and the Women's Prison Association, shared Martyn's views. She boldly proclaimed: "All women sacrifice more or less to man for what their . . . necessities imperiously demand, and this sacrifice has only to be continued by imperceptible degrees to make *all women* in the course of time *prostitutes.*"[5]

Few women in the nineteenth century would have publicly dared to articulate Farnham's views. But countless females denounced the decree that "to get married is absolutely necessary to . . . [women's] respectability and support." Melva, whose *Home Whispers* appeared as a serial in the *Advocate* and also as a separate book published by the Female Guardian Society, joined the tirade. There are many husbands, she wrote, "who practically ignore woman's equality with man—who have been educated to believe that she was created a necessary and convenient auxiliary to him, and that she best fulfills the primary ends of her being, when she unquestioningly does the bidding, and in all possible ways, promotes the wishes and comforts of the 'lords of creation.' "[6]

"O it's not the worst thing in the world . . . to be an 'old maid.' Not half so bad as to be the disappointed, wretched wife of something that would disgrace a brute," declared the *Advocate.* And Sarah Martyn believed that among the "false sentiments" of the era "there are none more pernicious than those which represent love and marriage not only as essential to the happiness of our sex, but in reality the only end and aim of our existence." Catharine Sedgwick hoped to "persuade . . . [her] young countrywomen so to reverence herself . . . that she will not give her hand without her heart, nor her heart till she is quite sure of his good desert who seeks it." In the preface to *Married or Single,* written in the late 1850s, Sedgwick enunciated her wish that all women would "raise . . . [their] voice with all . . . [their] might against the miserable cant that matrimony is essential to the [female] sex—that a woman's single life must be useless or undignified—that she is but an adjunct of man—in her best estate a helm merely to guide the nobler vessel. . . . [W]e believe she has an *independent power to shape her own course,* and to force her separate sovereign way."[7]

The demand that marriage be viewed as *one of many* alternatives open to women emerged from the experiences of females in benevolent societies. Understanding the numerous and varied ways in which women could find fulfillment, the volunteers insisted that "[woman's] sphere is unquestionably as extended as human interests, and her appropriate labor whatever she has ability to do well." Women must be "taught that to be happy they must be useful in *whatever sphere* they might move . . . [and] impressed that life had *many missions* of which marriage was but one." "Woman's Rights, and her sphere of duty and employment are properly attracting public notice and exciting discussion," claimed the *Advocate* in

1858. The editors emphasized that "different individuals have different tastes and capacities, adapted to perform . . . various acts." Sedgwick sarcastically applauded the "discovery . . . made that a woman is capable of something besides praying, loving, sewing and spinning," while Sarah Martyn satirized those who decreed "that WOMAN'S appropriate sphere is limited to her own family circle." *Golden Keepsake* (1851), a gift book concerned with woman's emancipation and edited by Martyn, inquired if the "denunciation" of women who left "her appointed bounds . . . brought into disrepute the names of Miriam, Deborah, and Hannah."[8]

The staff of the *Advocate* wrote that they "must beg to dissent" from the "position" that "the duties of the family should be performed by [woman] . . . and [that] this is her 'appropriate sphere.'" "Look at the voluntary benevolent associations and institutions under our country whose origin and continuance may be traced to woman's agency," they directed. "Thousands and tens of thousands of the ignorant, destitute and helpless, [are] now being . . . [helped] who, had woman's mission begun and *ended* at home, would have met a dark destiny. . . . [T]he magnitude of woman's mission enlarges, the longer we contemplate the picture." "Many a woman is lost to society after she becomes [a mother]. . . . But this should not be," declared the *Advocate* in 1852.[9]

The Female Guardian Society strenuously urged philanthropic organizations as an initial step to expanding woman's place in the world. A member acknowledged the possible obstacles, yet added: "Still, if you are not sure that your duty lies at home, you will be a gainer by the sacrifice; . . . a worthy example set to others." "To every woman, whatever occupation she may occupy, life is a fact, stubborn, earnest, real, to be shaped and moulded by her own efforts, or to be borne and endured by her own fortitude," wrote those women engaged in the struggle to control their own lives.[10]

The idea of an undefined, dynamic sphere for women had important implications. If woman could select her own realm according to individual interests and needs, then she could enter any trade or profession and compete with man in all phases of his life. There would, in fact, be no *woman's* sphere and no *man's* sphere, either. This concept admitted no difference between male and female natures, duties, responsibilities, and rights. Undoubtedly the idea proved threatening to nineteenth-century males, as well as to some females. Yet many women apparently accepted this new notion. And they forcefully argued for the end of "woman's sphere."[11]

"I would not live in a house that had to be scrubbed. It is senseless, useless drudgery . . . invented to kill [women] and Old Man Time," declared Jane Grey Swisshelm. A leader in the movement to reform the legal status of women, Swisshelm's *Letters to Country Girls* was excerpted in the *Advocate* and repeatedly recommended. "What I object to in housekeeping, is keeping houses and making them the centre around which things celestial and terrestrial must revolve. I do not believe . . . the chief end of woman [is] to keep *them.*" Swisshelm thought that man relegated woman to the domestic domain because he was totally indifferent to her needs.

> [Males] see no paper but a religious or political one. The former never speaks about woman, except to lecture her about her *duties,* her obligation to obey her husband—her vocation to forget herself and live only for the welfare of her liege lord and some particular church. The latter never speaks about woman or her interests a bit more than if such a creature never existed. The laws and policy they are discussing set her down midway between men and monkeys. She has no vote to solicit, no offices to confer but is a kind of appendage to her master. Of course the ignorant boor gets a vast opinion of his own importance, as it is continually held up to view by church and state; and it cannot be wondered at that he practices what our divines, statesmen, philosophers and poets teach.[12]

Eliza Farnham focused on another facet of the problem: the female response to being restricted to the home. "To patter over the floors or carpets; to keep well cleansed, clothed and fed the bodies of her household; to mix and bake the bread of a family; to churn its butter . . . make its dessert and its beds, is certainly not an expanded circuit of action for any human soul. . . . Prison is prison despite . . . meek deportment therein. . . . Measured by man's stage, hers *is* a prison. . . . I wonder not that Woman protested against that imprisonment and solemnly affirmed that it could not, should not endure."[13]

If woman wished, both in fact and in theory, to be free from the domestic realm, man had to be educated to share in the household. Women from benevolent societies, already experienced in lecturing to men, now exhorted them to participate in the functions of home. The *Advocate* in 1854 declared the need "to educate boys to be sympathizing, active, home-helping husbands. . . . [For] boys who are taught that 'girl's work' or woman's work is degrading will not, when men, consider it honorable to ease a wife's burdens." The *Ladies' Wreath* argued similarly and frequently published articles refuting the notion that affection in a man toward his family was "a sign of weakness." Melva asserted that "man as well as woman needs to be educated for domestic life" instead of being taught to "look upon domestic life as a theater for the exercise of man's petty tyrannies."[14]

This critique of the traditional nineteenth-century home was closely allied to an assault on society's treatment of the female wage-earner. With few available jobs, each paying a paltry sum, the working woman's sphere was even more circumscribed than that of the woman chained to her household. Virtually no opportunities for self-fulfillment awaited the female operative. So after decades of involvement with these destitute women, the volunteers campaigned vigorously for female workers.

Contemporary scholars have claimed that "feminist propaganda rarely mentioned women's wages and conditions in industrial enterprises until . . . the turn of the century." In fact, however, the first body of feminist literature in America—that produced by the women of urban female voluntary societies—devoted more attention to the plight of the woman laborer than to any other single cause. "Are the [seamstresses] . . . to be left to starvation under the assurance that it is the natural consequence of trade?" asked the *Ladies' Wreath* in 1846. And it added: "While political economists are solving this difficult problem, society may go on taxing them for its luxuries; capitalists may double their gains from [women's] overwrought strength." In another article printed in 1846, the author pleaded for the "oppressed operative . . . who produce[s] property which thousands other of [her] sex only live to consume."[15]

The circumstances of their "suffering sisters" engaged the perpetual attention of those whose lives had been molded by female voluntarism. "Home Philanthropy," an essay written by Ann Stephens, long-time member of the Female Guardian Society, appeared in both the *Ladies' Wreath* and the *Golden Keepsake.* It urged that more employments be opened to the sex. But Stephens warned that if they "are to enter upon any of the trades now pursued by men, let it not be to reduce the wages of mechanics, which are already sufficiently low . . . and [consequently] enrich the capitalist."[16]

Generally, however, the early feminists ignored the condition of the *male* worker and made the "unequal . . . rate of compensation for the labor of the two sexes" the focus of their polemics. "A Plea for Female Operatives" criticized "those calling themselves gentlemen" who prefer to have "a garment made by a woman because she will do it for half price, and it will be quite as well done." "It seems to us," wrote the staff of the *Ladies' Wreath,* "that while there are so many paths of profitable industry open to man and comparatively so few to woman, every principle of honor and justice demands that where the labor of the latter is equally productive it should be to herself equally available. Monopolies are . . . always . . . oppressive, and the fact that man has enjoyed a monopoly of profit so long, does not change the nature of the case or furnish a reason for its continuance."[17]

Predictably, the realization of the blatant inequalities bearing down on the female worker aggravated woman's frustration with her inability to effect significant change.

> When the manufacturing interests of a country suffer, when the commercial interests are threatened . . . [i]t becomes a subject of general interest, often serious legislation, because men have the power and will to clamor at the halls of legislation, and make their wants felt at the strongholds of power. We can only plead, where they de-

> mand—expostulate where they threaten and expose, and oppose female helplessness, shackled down by a thousand restraining influences, where they stand forward in their own behalf and wrestle for their own rights.

Both the *Ladies' Wreath* and the *Golden Keepsake* supported those "female operatives . . . who came together as sisters . . . to claim the acknowledged human right of receiving food, shelter, and raiment for the labor of their hands." The magazines asserted that "those of our own sex who are suffering under this grinding system of [economic] oppression and injustice, have a right to expect from us whose lot is differently cast both feeling and action in their behalf."[18]

In the course of their campaign for female workers, the editors of the *Advocate* could not resist noting their own contributions to the cause. Their "Home Printing Office" had opened "a new field of remunerative labor for women," and the "training received [there] . . . may fit woman as well as man to use that mighty power—the press." Moreover, they believed "the *Advocate* may be cited as a noble instance of widely-extended influence of more desirable character, exerted by a periodical wholly conducted by women—a paper that, by its own merits, has attained a circulation only reached by few of its contemporaries."[19]

As in its earlier years, this magazine printed the members' account of their visits in order to bolster the organization's campaigns. Deploring the dearth of jobs, the Female Guardian Society's home visiting committee reported: "A. wants to get work to do, house cleaning, washing, sewing—anything she can do. Has an aged mother. B. has a babe of 14 months in her arms, has three older children, needs clothing and everything. Her husband went away last September to seek for work, since which has not heard from him." And so the long list continued, as the women used every opportunity to detail the misery and poverty of their "struggling sisters."[20]

Along with frequent catalogues of feminine woe, the *Advocate* diligently publicized any effort to help the destitute of the sex. The editors had exuberant praise for "Mr. Stimson, the proprietor of the Day Book, in his experiment of teaching girls to set type" and heartily endorsed the "opening of Clerkship positions in Philadelphia to women." They urged "New York and other . . . cities [to] follow the excellent example of the 'City of brotherly love.' " "Is it not time to remember that women cannot live on air, or even on compliments[?]" they asked. "Both justice and policy demand . . . [women's] admission into walks of usefulness suited to their powers and yielding the means of decent livelihood."[21]

Jane Swisshelm satirized the masculine response to woman's entering the traditional male fields of endeavor: "Let her aspire to turn editor, public speaker, doctor, lawyer—take up any profession or avocation which is deemed honorable and requires talent and O! bring the Cologne, get a Cambric Kerchief and a feather fan. . . . What a fainting fit Mr. Propriety has taken! Just to think that 'one of the dear creatures,' the heavenly angels, should forsake the . . . woman's sphere to mix with the wicked strife of this wicked world! What rhapsodies we have . . . about soiled plumage on angels' wings; while stern matter-of-fact tyrants crack their whips and shout 'Back to thy punishment false slave!' "[22]

Caroline Kirkland, who as a member of the Women's Prison Association had eloquently defended the humanity of female convicts, blended wit with anger to produce a delightful essay on women writers. Because "lordship [is] so much an object of desire among the stronger part of the creation . . . , we shall take care to deal with the subject after the desultory, unsystematic and feminine manner," she began. "We repudiate learning, we disclaim accuracy, we abjure logic. We shall aim only at the pretty prattle which is conceded to our sex as a right and admired as a charm." She quipped "that some gentlemen would award a palm . . . to her who writes a Cook's Oracle, where a rod or a fool's cap would be the doom of a lady who should presume to touch political economy. The novel of fashionable life, provided it have no suspicion of a moral, and make no pretension to teach anything whatever, may pass as feminine, . . . but a novel with the least bit of bone in it is 'mannish.' "[23]

Obviously departing from those male views effectively derided by

Caroline Kirkland, the *Advocate* strenuously campaigned for the admission of women to all professions and occupations. In the course of organized benevolence, females had demonstrated the requisite qualities and abilities to pursue every possible career. Moreover, they were able to appreciate the dismal consequences of monetary need. Experiences informed the volunteers' arguments and led to the demand that "every daughter, as well as every son, should have a profession." In issue after issue the *Advocate*'s editors propounded the same theme: "Every girl should have a trade, a business, a profession, or some honorable and useful way of gaining a livelihood—some employment in which her powers of body and mind may be amply developed. If she has not, she will be dependent upon somebody, and her dependence will degrade her."[24]

The members of the Female Guardian Society, always sensitive to the importance of their periodical in circulating information and ideas, devoted considerable space to a series of feminist lectures held in New York City in 1858. Woman had been "cramped in her action and forbidden to use the faculties which God had given her, to gain an honorable position in society or even to earn bread for herself and children," complained one speaker. "Let the thing regulate itself!" the lecturer urged. The editors reprinted most of the address and endorsed the closing remarks: "[The] principle which many of the advocates of women's rights contend for is simply this . . . that a woman is always in her sphere when she is doing what God has given her that faculty to do."[25]

The assumption that woman should define her own realm inevitably gave impetus to the insistence that she receive an education equal to man's. Like the pressure for greater employment opportunities, the drive for expanded education combined the *need* for woman's economic self-sufficiency with her *right* to self-determination. In 1855 the *Advocate* quoted from an article, "The Education of Females," appearing in a Buffalo newspaper: "There are certain of woman's rights which we are prompted to own and defend. . . . It is right that women as well as men should be furnished with the means of acquiring such knowledge as will be profitable to them."

Other essays articulated the opinion that "a good education is, to a woman . . . an independence."[26]

One writer for the *Advocate* asserted that "[daughters'] intellectual abilities must be cultivated and their minds richly stored with treasures of knowledge and wisdom." Another declared: "She obtains her enjoyments from the same sources [as man]. The world without was equally intended for her benefit. Earth with its ten thousand voices is . . . presenting its wonders for her to explore. And there is no argument from experience or from the word of God why the road to these rich and pure enjoyments should be laid open with so much care to the one . . . [sex] and so . . . shut to the other."[27]

Critical of all obstacles to woman's full physical and mental education, the Female Guardian Society condemned custom, which taught that "it is unladylike to run and romp and climb trees and skate." The prevailing codes "so educated [woman] that none of her powers, physical or mental, can ever attain a full and healthy action," protested an article reprinted by the *Advocate.* The editors also denounced the clergy's failure to promote the education of their sex. "They have not done it, nor do they intend to do it. . . . This state of things ill becomes a people that boast enlightened views on the subject of mental culture. It ill becomes the professors of . . . religion."[28]

Jane Swisshelm castigated parents for promoting women's inferior position. "If [they] would give their daughters the same mental training they do their sons, they could not be converted into slaves so handily." For as Swisshelm advised young women: "[You must] know . . . your own duties and do them. You should . . . act and judge for yourselves; to remember that you each have . . . a mind of your own. . . . When you once get these ideas fixed, and learn to act upon them, no man or set of men, no laws, customs, or combination of them can seriously oppress you. Ignorance, folly, and levity are . . . essential to the character of a slave. If women knew their rights . . . we would never hear of men [dominating them]."[29]

These early feminists agreed that their sex suffered under many varieties of slavery. Fashion was a subtle, yet nonetheless important, form of bondage. The contemporary mode of dress presented a tangible symbol of woman's utter uselessness as well as her submission to authoritarian custom. In their discussion of clothing, the contributors to the *Advocate* first criticized the current styles as injurious to female health. But by the 1850s they viewed dress as another mode of subjugation. Blaming men for their role in fostering uncomfortable and cumbersome feminine attire, the periodical urged "the women of America . . . to arouse to a consciousness of the responsibility resting upon THEM and firmly discountenance any [damaging] demand of fashion." They declared that "improvements [in fashion] should be the fore-runner of thorough revolution—our sex should rise above subserviency to fashion's despotic rule."[30]

Throughout their various campaigns, members of benevolent societies acknowledged the importance of association in effecting change. As in earlier years, they articulated a belief in the unity of women. "The duty of women to women has been deeply impressed upon my mind," wrote one female active in organized philanthropy. Others referred to the "bond of union" and to the "cementing link" that joined them together. A writer who signed her letter "AN OBSCURE COUNTRYWOMAN" disclosed sentiments felt and expressed by volunteers throughout the nation: "We WOMEN whether in thronged cities or quiet country spots should feel that we are one united sisterhood, bound together by one common interest."[31]

The "one common interest," the advancement of the female sex, assumed numerous forms; and deliberate display of woman's abilities was one of these. The *Ladies' Wreath* detailed in great length the achievements of those in voluntary organizations who "fought and nobly conquered many of the great moral evils of the day." The *Advocate*, never missing an opportunity to praise its own accomplishments, printed a letter in 1857 by a woman who "found it difficult to believe a work so great was undertaken by *females* alone." She confided: "I certainly never had a low conception of the energy or self-devotion of woman, but nothing has raised my ideas of her abilities so high as an acquaintance with the workings of the Home for the Friendless."[32]

The attainments of members of benevolent societies obviously furnished the volunteers with the most accessible role models through which to demonstrate feminine ability. But toward the middle of the century, these original feminists initiated an important and convincing method of proving woman's competence. Substituting individual interpretation for the prestigious weight of historical writings, the members searched the past for evidence of woman's important involvement. They demanded that the writing of history be revised to reflect woman's vital participation in bygone days. Eliza Farnham asserted that "history has been neglectful and cold towards women," while other females tried to compensate for this indifference.[33]

The *Ladies' Wreath* had a regular feature on eminent historical women, and their story of "Isabella of Castile" exemplified the purpose of these biographical sketches. "Not as the wife of Ferdinand . . . is Isabella the dearest historic name royalty ever gave. . . . [But] when the kings heard with cold incredulity, and learned prelates condemned with bitter sarcasm, the noble plans of Columbus, Isabella studied them with . . . patience, and believed . . . and resolved to prove that belief, though she might meet the sneers of rival royalties, and the urgent remonstrances of her own nobles at every step of the enterprise. Worst and hardest of all, she had to meet the disapproval of her . . . husband."[34]

One did not, however, have to look abroad to find examples of female courage. The "Pilgrim Mothers" provided the "new historians" with an important source of material. Martyn, in the *Golden Keepsake,* criticized those who consider "the graves of the pilgrim fathers as the proudest and most enduring monuments of national glory." She continued: "The voyagers of the Mayflower on the . . . errand of freedom came not alone. Standing by their side on the trackless ocean, or in the howling wilderness were . . . women who had freely given up all the elegancies and comforts of home, and all the endearments of kindred, to share their perils, their privations and sufferings." An article in the *Ladies' Wreath* similarly stated: "We present the Pilgrim mothers to our . . . readers . . . as lofty models of excellence intended for their imitation."[35]

"We hear enough about our forefathers. They were nice old fellows, no doubt. Perfect bricks in their way. Good to work, eat or fight," wrote the editors of the *Advocate* with uncharacteristic levity. "But where are their companions? Our foremothers. Who landed at James River and came over on the Mayflower and established the other early settlements? Were there any women among men? One would think not. . . . All hail to noble old boys, our forefathers say we. May the glory of their deeds never be less, but the good book tells us to 'render unto Caesar,' etc, and we wish to speak a word in season for women generally and especially for our noble . . . foremothers lest time and the one-sided page of history shall blot them forever from our memories." The members of the American Female Guardian Society agreed that the "history of every country should have as much to record of woman as of man; but this can never be until woman's field . . . is extended."[36]

In the course of their many activities to expand woman's sphere and rights, members of benevolent societies across the nation had challenged authority in its varied embodiments of custom, law, and philosophy. They had not shrunk from forays with the clerical, medical, educational, or historical professions. But with the exception of a few brief encounters with the Scriptures, they generally avoided direct confrontation with biblical decrees. Yet by the 1850s women felt sufficient confidence and conviction to use the Holy Book to support their claim of equality. The volunteers thereby refuted the most persistent and esteemed theories of woman's inferiority.

The essay "What Rights Have Women," published in an 1852 issue of the *Advocate,* set forth its intention to give "a connected view of *Bible* teaching in relation to . . . the question of 'Woman's Rights.'" Examining the contention that God assigned different spheres to men and women, the author asked: "What was the practice of those who knew and did God's will?" And a detailed reply followed: "Rebecca drew water for the camels of a passing stranger as an act of common courtesy. Gen. XXIV 14. Rachel kept her father's sheep, though it was one of the most arduous of out-door services. Gen. XXIV 9, 31, 40."[37]

After providing many examples of women who, departing from

the traditional feminine realm, "were an honor to their families," the article attacked the biblical doctrine of woman's subjugation to man. "Deborah was the wife of Lepedoth. How did she understand the law 'Thy husband shall rule over thee?' . . . As a prophetess she was governed wholly by the spirit of prophecy. As the Judge of Israel 'she ruled justly in the fear of God.' . . . She led her armed men into battle, and God gave her the victory. . . . No account of her husband is made in the history. . . . He did not prevent her from 'ruling over men.' "[38]

The exposition continued with lengthy quotes from the "portraiture of a virtuous woman," including the following descriptions: "She maketh fine linen and selleth it and delivereth girdles to the merchants. She girdeth her loins with strength and strengthened her arms." Drawing significant implications from the foregoing characterization, the essayist wrote: "Though a business woman, she was well educated, and kindness ruled her tongue like a law and what renders her course more remarkable is the fact that she had a husband well qualified to take charge of his own business, and able to support her in idleness. . . . Her virtue is represented as invulnerable, not merely in spite of her occupations, but as the fruit of them." "I would that all homes were as happy as hers," added the writer, before the concluding remarks of the long and well-documented piece.[39]

Of the six main points arrived at "from these teachings of God's book" and listed in the summary, the first and last were of most significance:

> 1. That the Creator has not assigned to the different sexes different spheres of action. But left to *each individual* . . . the choice of position and pursuit. So far as God is concerned, a man may be a *cook* and a woman an *artist.*
>
> . . . .
>
> 6. That we are not merely to tolerate, but actively and heartily encourage conformity to these Bible teachings and glorious examples. Were I required to gather up into a single sentence the

> purport of these teachings and examples, I would do it thus. *The rights and privileges of the sexes are equal—are the same.*

The author of the treatise ended by urging those engaged in benevolent activity to continue their work "to [grant] to *all* their birthrights." And the women who had pioneered in efforts on behalf of other females complied by aggressively promoting a potpourri of legal reform campaigns throughout the 1850s. Believing that women's "talents and virtues [should] place them on a footing of perfect equality with the other sex," the volunteers condemned "lawmakers . . . who have forgotten to legislate in behalf of the female sex and then have adduced the very disabilities they themselves have imposed as proof of . . . inferiority."[40]

Those involved in reform endeavors agitated for temperance laws. In 1855 they applauded the passage of a New York State Prohibitory Law by asserting: "Woman has suffered long enough to suffer no longer; endured enough to command the sympathy and united efforts of her sex, to free her and her helpless babes at once and for ever, from the galling yoke [of intemperance]." As in their earlier years, benevolent societies fought for the passage of laws "protect[ing] . . . the property and earnings of married women." Their experience had taught that "[there] are . . . hardworking wives in [New York] State, more especially in the large cities, whose unceasing efforts to support themselves in respectability and to provide decently for their children are perpetually thwarted by lazy, profligate and drunken husbands."[41]

The demand for equitable legislation inevitably led to the insistence that women participate in the decision-making process. The *Advocate* quoted from a lecture entitled "Subject of the Legal, Social and Industrial Position of Woman." The address focused on the "strange inconsistency that a woman, whatever her rank, position, or estate, or however large a revenue she might pay for the support of government, could not have the slightest voice or vote by which to influence its action." Critical of laws "which take from a woman the plainest natural rights," the American Female Guardian Society commended the views of the speaker, who "demand[ed] everything espoused by the most ardent advocates of Woman's Rights."[42]

Arguments for legal changes persisted. They flowed from the belief that woman's identity entitled her to full participation in the natural rights of humanity. "There can never be a question of Natural Rights in any living being, after we have learned to read correctly its whole natural constitution," wrote Eliza Farnham. "[Woman] is the natural possessor of every right which is [man's]."[43]

The appeal to basic human rights was compelling. Women would use it again and again in their quest for freedom. It began as a hope and became a conviction. It started with small groups of urban women in the early 1800s and grew with female voluntarism during the ensuing half-century. Thus, through their activities, doctrines, courage, and compassion, members of benevolent societies became America's first feminists. And their belief that woman is an autonomous being whose value and dignity stem from her common humanity is their legacy to the present. It is at once a rich heritage and an awesome responsibility, for this vital concept still exists only as an idea. It remains for the future to make it a reality.

Summary

> Through the unknown, remembered gate
> When the last of earth left to discover
> Is that which was the beginning
>
> T. S. Eliot, *Little Gidding*

Nineteenth-century woman's claim to natural rights was an integral part of her quest for complete freedom from the rigid theories of the woman-belle ideal, a stringent code that decreed her inferiority and denied her individuality. The process by which generations of women came first to perceive their subordinate position and later to demand the emancipation of their sex is deeply rooted in the tumultuous antebellum era. The decades after 1820 reverberated with transformations in politics, religion, immigration, social structure, and industry. Additionally, the advent of furious urbanization exaggerated the impact of these changes while it created new and unsettling problems.

Relentless city growth challenged inveterate and cherished beliefs about the future form of the nation and man's position in it. This threat to enshrined principles had important ramifications for the female population, at once heightening woman's oppression and setting the stage for her future efforts at emancipation. The movement for woman's independence did not develop naturally out of the liberal ideologies of the Age of Enlightenment; it had a heritage uniquely its own. It is, therefore, to the complicated transfigurations in nineteenth-century society and to the responses they called forth that one must look for an explanation of the origins of American feminism.

America's early years seemed rich in potential for women. A lively debate, pursued in earnest on both sides of the Atlantic, inquired into the female nature and ability. Clerical and secular leaders propounded theories of woman's aptitude, importance, and human dignity. These slowly gained acceptance, finding natural allies in the ideas of the eighteenth-century political and religious revolutions, which emphasized the substitution of individual conscience for authority. Moreover, the philosophies of woman's competence and importance maintained an intimate and genuine association with the reality of her life in the New World.

During the colonial era restrictions upon the activities of the allegedly inferior sex were abated by necessity. Women enjoyed access to most occupations. Lending skill and energy to the development of their communities, they commanded respect as effective participants in society. In frontier settlements and nascent cities, women labored alongside men and shared in the hardships, responsibilities, and advantages of life in America. Of course, colonial women rarely received treatment comparable to that accorded the other sex. Nonetheless, their position in American society appeared to be markedly and tenaciously advancing.

Yet as persistent urban expansion made a mockery of man's plans and hopes, he experienced a loss of identity, of control, and, perhaps even more important, of a coherent set of values around which to understand and organize his life. The ethos of agrarian America with its promises of a harmonious, stable, democratic society, unmarred by social strife and competition, and its images of abundant harvests and tranquil, lush verdancy loomed large. But it could no longer inspire and give meaning to the lives of growing numbers of

Americans. Indeed, rather than assuaging fears and anxieties, the pastoral legend intensified the insecurities of city dwellers throughout of the nation. They suffered unpalliable guilt at the realization that the rest of the nation viewed their way of life as an anathema to its most beloved traditions.

The old beliefs became less relevant to an ever growing part of the population. And Americans, particularly those living in cities, searched for a way to cling to the values of an idealized yesteryear while accommodating to the realities of the present. By the creation of a complicated philosophy, an urban-agrarianism, Americans admitted their yearning for stability, identity, security, and shared ideals. Through this troubled search they eventually realized that they could embrace the future with enthusiasm without relinquishing the best of an illusory, bucolic past. By transforming their conceptions of an agricultural paradise into a set of prevailing images and perceptions of womanhood, Americans could preserve the qualities they valued most, while enjoying the advantages and opportunities of a new era.

The woman, quietly tucked away at home, creating a haven of peace and order, provided a salubrious contrast to the shrill urban milieu. As the repository of all virtue and morality, woman became the substitute for a bountiful nature who nourished and nurtured, purified and sustained. Blissfully noncompetitive, she remained unsullied by a corrupt world. She emulated the serene garden, free from the rampant vying for money, power, and position so characteristic of industrial cities.

Thus man made woman the ballast on his unsteady journey into the future. He reached out for a sense of personal identity, which he found by insisting that woman's nature, totally unlike his own, was comprised of certain inferior, unchanging qualities. By attributing specific characteristics to the "weaker sex," man—no matter what his social position—could feel superior to someone over whom he could exercise substantial control. Moreover, the rigid differences he postulated between male and female recompensed for the fluidity of class lines that seemed to defy his domination. The composite traits of nineteenth-century womanhood merged into the implacable theory of the woman-belle ideal. It gave man a foil for his ambiguous identity but forced the pernicious effects of urbanization to fall with a particular harshness upon the already subjugated female population.

Whether she languished idly in her chamber or struggled to earn a pittance on the city streets, the urban woman collided with the destructive tenets of nineteenth-century womanhood. Indeed, all American women suffered under the harsh dictates of the monolithic creed. The prevalence of feminine invalidism, the content of private diaries, and the character portrayals and plots of their fiction arose as visible signs of feminine emotional distress. But lacking the context in which to understand their unhappiness, women berated themselves for their own "inadequacies" and remained alienated from themselves and isolated from others of their sex.

It remained, then, for the rich variety of urban life, with its blatant extremes and devastating poverty, to give shape to woman's anguished search for importance and companionship. She formed hundreds of associations dedicated to helping the aged, infirm, impoverished, and deviant female in cities across the nation. Woman's vaguely perceived needs, drives, and wishes found definition in the collage of the city. Her experiences forced a reevaluation of her own life through a growing awareness of society's actions and attitudes towards the female sex. The reality of her own oppression became inescapable. Slowly, she began to challenge and defy the theories of woman's inferiority. For the vivid and complex interactions of the city impelled generations of women to appreciate and respect the diversity of their sex. Simultaneously they recognized both the burden of oppression and the gift of humanity that bound them together. And from the subtle synthesis of urbanization and woman's quest for self-realization emerged the origins of American feminism.

Female benevolent societies in the years between 1800 and 1860 transformed the imprecise perceptions of women throughout America into a compelling feminist ideology. Woman's assertion of her independent status evolved gradually from the activities and ideas of urban women. Continually enlarging their sphere beyond the home, the members raised revenue, maintained extensive records, organized elaborate meetings, worked with civic leaders, and brought difficult programs from inception to completion. Through their varied activities, they demonstrated qualities traditionally associated with men, thereby disproving myths of feminine inadequacy. They inaugurated networks of social service agencies in scores of American cities and eventually recognized the value of their contributions to urban life. Volunteers dared both to criticize male conduct and to challenge the prestigious weight of authority in its many guises. While learning to trust their own ideas and achievements, the members found outlets for their varied personalities within the diversified structure of urban organizations. Their many involvements also brought them closer to other women.

A web of interdependency emerged, for this sense of individuality grew out of a belief in the sisterhood of women. Antebellum woman's growing self-awareness inevitably heightened her commitments to the rest of her sex. Not only did the volunteers rely upon the encouragement of their colleagues in their continuing efforts for self-determination; in a special and crucial way they were acutely dependent upon their wards for their own individual emancipation. The uncompromising pattern of nineteenth-century female perfection, the woman-belle ideal, foreclosed virtually all paths to feminine gratification. But the malleable urban milieu unwittingly provided women with one vehicle sufficiently flexible and durable to launch them on their arduous journey to freedom. By fostering the development of female voluntary societies, the American city determined the direction of women's quest for liberation.

The extent to which women of the upper and middle classes could disengage themselves from society's bonds related to the scope and nature of their activities on behalf of the poor and downtrodden of their sex. The wider and more audacious the schemes of benevolence, the greater would be the acceptance of woman's constantly enlarging sphere. The more daring the plans, the more splendid and significant would be the ultimate achievements that could be used to demonstrate woman's versatile abilities to a watching community. The more abundant their experiences with the various forms of woman's oppression, the easier it would be for the members to understand the meaning of their own existences. And, the broader their contacts with different females, the better they could clarify and refine their thinking about woman's position in society.

Yet, the attempts of economically secure women to achieve fulfillment through voluntary societies were neither consciously nor even largely self-serving. The era's rigid impositions on feminine behavior may have originally forced wealthier women to seek their liberation through work for impoverished females. But the deeply felt sympathy and concern soon developed a momentum and a rationale of its own.

The members postulated a community of women. They continually emphasized the similarities between themselves and Black, Indian, and immigrant women. All women, regardless of background or position, were basically the same: objectified by a society that denied their autonomy. Theirs, then, was a vertical, rather than a horizontal, dichotomy, largely shaped by the monolithic precepts of the woman-belle ideal. For the ethos had implicitly used the myths of fixed differences between the male and female to compensate for the instability and insecurity of the antebellum class structure. The perception of a people separated and stratified by sex, rather than class, intensified the members' belief in the unity of all women. It reinforced the many efforts to help their "struggling sisters" to a fuller existence and stimulated the growth of a feminist consciousness.

By a unique blend of circumstances, the development of feminism bound together the lives of different classes of urban women, making the freedom of the one a function of the emancipation of the other. Yet, it is also true that the proximity of urban life, necessitating the intense interactions of widely disparate female existences, forced woman to argue for independence from the most inclusive of all principles: woman's common humanity. In this way, the city dictated the development of nineteenth-century American feminism as a broadly based movement on behalf of all women.

Originating as it did in the experiences of members of female voluntary associations, nineteenth-century American feminism did not limit its perspective to any one specific right but embraced many different aspects of woman's emancipation. In 1860, the volunteers articulated their understanding of woman's freedom and the meaning they attached to their efforts:

> Agitation and discussion are the instruments of tillage of truth. Society must reap the fruits—it already does, however loath to acknowledge its indebtedness—fruits that are relieving it of its old stagnation . . . and emancipating woman . . . not solely or chiefly from the trammels of legal disabilities, but from subtler chains . . . from many fetters and . . . oppressive servitude.[1]

The ideology was as expansive as it was vibrant. Woman, a complete and independent person whose value and dignity emanated from her basic humanity, possessed a nature identical to man's. She had the same abilities and responsibilities as the other sex and hence deserved complete and equal rights. This belief in the individual integrity of each woman stimulated a wide variety of subsequent demands. The volunteers insisted that woman be given greater employment and educational opportunities and urged that she be permitted to select her own field of endeavor without reference to a traditionally defined "woman's sphere." They further importuned that woman, free from the restrictions society placed upon her sex, be allowed to participate fully in the prerogatives and privileges that were the natural birthright of each and every human being.

With autonomy the leitmotif of the many varied demands, the feminism that evolved from antebellum cities encompassed numerous phases of woman's freedom. Yet by the end of the nineteenth century, the suffrage campaign, one of many facets of woman's quest for emancipation, dominated all other issues and concerns. The argument for the franchise was based upon the philosophies of woman's nature and rights that arose from the experiences of women in American cities. But the drive for the vote attenuated and distorted the feminist thinking and vision that had infused it with ideological substance. As women came to see suffrage as the panacea for every problem, they invested all their energies into the crusade. The ballot took on an almost mystical importance. Enfranchisement became wrongly equated with the end of oppression, and suffragists would unknowingly sacrifice much to achieve it.

In their fight for the vote, women both ignored and compromised the principles of feminism. The complexities of American society at the turn of the century induced the suffragists to change the basis of their demand for the franchise. They had originally argued that it was the natural right of *every woman*, as well as every man, to participate in the legal system that would govern them. Now, however, the suffragists moderated their platform as massive immigration once again transformed the texture of life in the United States. Seeking wide support among other white middle-class Americans, the campaigners urged that women be given the vote to balance the impact of the foreign born.

Thus the suffrage rationale of the early twentieth century used the persuasion that native-born women outnumbered foreign-born men and women combined. Moreover, women advocated an educational qualification for voting that could prevent the "less desirable" members of the population from taking part in the electoral process. These two tenets of the later suffrage movement denied the basic human rights of lower-class women. They implied a distinction in the essential worth and dignity of women not found in antebellum feminism.

As the drive for the vote ruptured the idea of a community of women dedicated to helping one another, so too did it obscure and vitiate the philosophy that had produced the suffrage agitation. The ideology emerging from the cities had urged woman's freedom from sex-determined roles, her privilege to control her own life, her right to fulfill her autonomous identity. But in their efforts to secure the ballot, women dismissed or discounted these theories. The woman's movement that developed between the years 1800 and 1860 was a probing body of thought. It stood on the threshold of recognizing that the liberation of one class of women depended upon the freedom of all others. It has, indeed, been the misfortune of the twentieth century to have remembered only the suffrage campaign while forgetting the origins of American feminism.

Notes

INTRODUCTION

1. Elizabeth Cady Stanton, "The Solitude of Self," quoted in Aileen Kraditor, *The Ideas of the Woman Suffrage Movement 1890–1920* (New York: Columbia University Press, 1965), pp. 40–41.
2. Page Smith, *Daughters of the Promised Land* (Boston: Little, Brown & Co., 1970), p. 104 (emphasis added). Aileen Kraditor, *Up From the Pedestal: Selected Writings in the History of American Feminism* (Chicago: Quadrangle Books, 1968), pp. 13–14 (emphasis added).
3. For a discussion of women's rights and feminism, see Gerda Lerner, "Women's Rights and American Feminism," *American Scholar* (Spring, 1971), 40: 237.
4. Kraditor, *Up From the Pedestal,* p. 14. Eleanor Flexner, *Century of Struggle* (New York: Atheneum, 1970), p. 41.
5. Boston Female Anti-Slavery Society, First Annual Report (1835), p. 6. Also see Anna Hallowell, *James and Lucretia Mott: Life and Letters* (Boston: Houghton Mifflin Co., 1896), p. 10. Also see Keith Melder, "Ladies Bountiful: Organized Women's Benevolence in Early Nineteenth Century America," *New York History* Quarterly Journal of the New York Historical Association (July, 1967), pp. 231–254.

CHAPTER 1

1. Mario Schill, *La Fille d'Alliance de Montaigne, Marie de Gournay* (Paris, 1910), p. 55–77, for text of *Egalité des Hommes et des Femmes;* quoted in Mary Sumner

Benson, *Women in Eighteenth Century America: A Study of Opinion and Social Usage* (New York: Columbia University Press, 1935), p. 15.

2. Cotton Mather, "Diary," *Massachusetts Historical Society Collections*, ser. 7, 7–8 (1911–12), 2: 325.
3. John Bunyan, *The Pilgrim's Progress* (London, 1792), pp. 364–365.
4. Cotton Mather, *Ornaments for the Daughters of Zion* (Cambridge, 1691), pp. 5–7. The book had an extended period of usefulness. George Whitefield, the revivalist preacher, read it in 1740 and, recommending it to all women, sent it to Benjamin Franklin for printing.
5. Mather, *Ornaments*, p. 5. His reference is most likely to Anne Bradstreet, although he did not mention the gifted poet by name.
6. Thomas Foxcraft, A Sermon . . . after the Funeral of Mrs. Elizabeth Foxcraft (1721), p. iii; quoted in Benson, p. 106. Sewall, "Letter to John Winthrop in Winthrop Papers," *Mass. Hist. Soc. Colls.*, ser. 6, (5) 6: 403 (emphasis added). In *Talitha Cumi* [Young Woman arise] *or An Invitation to Women to look after their Inheritance in the Heavenly Mansions*, Sewall refuted the idea, sometimes propounded in England, that women had no place in heaven. He cited Matthew 22: 30 that there was neither marrying nor giving in marriage in heaven. Three women would certainly rise again: Eve, the mother of all living; Sarah, the mother of the faithful; and Mary, the mother of our Lord. If these three were to rise again, Sewall believed that all women would.
7. Thomas Prince, *A Sermon Occasioned by the Death of Mrs. Deborah Prince* (Boston, 1744), pp. 21–23. Her writings were published at the time of her funeral sermon. Benjamin Colman, *Reliquiae Turellae, et Lachrymae Paternae* (Boston, 1735), pp. 78–79.
8. Mather, *Ornaments*, pp. 44–45; "Diary," 1: 108, note. In a Boston church of 300–400 communicants, only 100 were men; I Timothy 2: 11; Corinthians 14: 34; Titus 2: 5.
9. Colman, pp. 67, 79; *Ornaments*, pp. 3–4.
10. Mary Astell, *An Essay in Defense of the Female Sex*, 4th ed. (London, 1730), pp. 136–39; quoted in Benson, p. 30. Daniel Defoe, *The Earlier Life and the Chief Earlier Works of Daniel Defoe*, ed. Henry Morley (London, 1899), pp. 144–45.
11. *Tatler* (1710), no. 248, p. 400. *Spectator* (1710), no. 310, p. 77. For other articles concerned with helping women, see *Spectator*, nos. 4, 10, 15, 66, 606; and *Tatler*, no. 200.
12. William Wollaston, *The Religion of Nature Delineated* (London, 1726), p. 159. For an evaluation of the influence of the *Spectator* on Benjamin Franklin's writing, see George Horner, "Franklin's Dogood Papers re-examined," *North Carolina University Studies in Philology* 37 (1940): 501–23.
13. Benjamin Franklin, *Reflections on Courtship and Marriage: In Two Letters to a Friend* (Philadelphia, 1750), pp. 23; 4; 15.
14. John Gregory, *A Father's Legacy to his Daughter* (London, 1788), pp. 31, 11.
15. Jean Jacques Rousseau, *Emilius and Sophia: or, A New System of Education*, trans. A Citizen of Geneva (London, 1783), 3: 177–78; 233.
16. Enos Hitchcock, *Memoirs of the Bloomsgrove Family . . . containing sentiments*

on a *Mode of Domestic Education, Suited to . . . the United States*, 2 vols. (Boston, 1790), 2: 15–17; 44–46; quoted in Benson, p. 159.

17. Mary Wollstonecraft, *A Vindication of the Rights of Woman* (New York: W. W. Norton & Co., 1967), pp. 53; 72, 224; 213, 219; 4. For her criticism of Rousseau, see pp. 58, 60, 66, 88–89, 128–48.
18. Charles Brockden Brown, *Alcuin: A Dialogue* (New York: Grossman Publishers, 1971), pp. 13–14; 29.
19. Benson, pp. 176–177.
20. Ezra Stiles, *The Literary Diary of Ezra Stiles*, ed. F. B. Dexter, 3 vols. (New York, 1901), 3: 315, 2: 584, 557; 2: 490, 3: 15.
21. Clinton Rossiter, *Seedtime of the New Republic: The Origins of the American Tradition of Political Liberty* (New York, Harcourt Brace Jovanovich, Inc. 1953), pp. 362; 225–26.
22. Ibid. For feminist activity in Europe during this period, see Jane Abray, "Feminism in the French Revolution," *American Historical Review* 80 (Feb. 1975): 43–62.
23. *The Lawes Resolutions of Womens Rights; or The Lawes Provision for Women* (London, 1632), pp. 124–25. Rossiter, p. 158.
24. Salem Town Records, quoted in Edith Abbott, *Women in Industry* (New York: D. Appleton & Co., 1913), p. 32.
25. Province Laws, 1: 213; quoted in Abbott, p. 33 (emphasis added).
26. Quoted in Abbott, p. 33. Arthur W. Calhoun, *A Social History of the American Family from Colonial Times to the Present* (Cleveland, The Arthur Clark Co., 1917), 2: 105–07. Abigail Foote, Diary (1775); quoted in Alice Morse Earle, *Home Life in Colonial Days* (New York: Macmillan Co., 1917), p. 253.
27. Elisabeth Dexter, *Colonial Women of Affairs: Women in Business and the Professions in America Before 1776* (Boston: Houghton Mifflin Co., 1931), p. 182. Carl Bridenbaugh, *Cities in Revolt* (London and New York: Oxford University Press, 1955), p. 140. Elisabeth Dexter, *Career Women of America 1776–1840* (New Hampshire: Marshall Jones Co., 1950), p. 19. For examples of women's lives on the frontier, see Dee Brown, *The Gentle Tamers: Women of the Old Wild West* (New York: G. P. Putnam's Sons, 1968), pp. 11–67.
28. Dexter, *Colonial Women*, p. 49.
29. Bridenbaugh, *Revolt*, p. 358. *Boston Evening Post*, 26 Feb. 1759. *American Mercury*, 27 June 1728. *New York Gazette*, 28 Aug. 1766; quoted in Dexter, *Colonial Women*, p. 21.
30. Michel-Guillaume Jean de Crèvecoeur, *Letters from an American Farmer* (Philadelphia, 1793), pp. 135–59. Dexter, *Colonial Women*, p. 33.
31. *New York Journal*, 21 Jan. 1733: Carl Bridenbaugh, *Cities in the Wilderness* (London and New York: Oxford University Press, 1939), p. 343. For activities of southern women see Julia Cherry Spruill, *Women's Life and Work in the Southern Colonies* (New York: W. W. Norton & Co., 1972), pp. 232–314).
32. Bridenbaugh, *Revolt*, p. 176. Dexter, *Colonial Women*, p. 105. *New York Journal*, 14 Sept. 1747.
33. Dexter, *Colonial Women*, p. 171.
34. Dexter, *Colonial Women*, p. 109. *Pennsylvania Gazette*, 23 May 1754, 29 Aug.

1754, 21 Mar. 1748: Zadeck Tompson, *History of Vermont* (Vermont, 1853), 3: 110; quoted in Dexter, *Colonial Women,* p. 185.

35. Lawrence Cremin, *American Education: The Colonial Experience 1607–1783* (New York: Harper & Row, 1970), p. 129. Nancy Shippen, *Her Journal Book* (Philadelphia, 1935), p. 14.
36. Bridenbaugh, *Revolt,* pp. 176–77. Dexter, *Colonial Women,* p. 93. Emily Vanderpoel, *Chronicles of a Pioneer School from 1792–1833* (Cambridge, Mass., University Press, 1903).
37. Rossiter, p. 158.
38. Dexter, *Colonial Women,* p. 190.

CHAPTER 2

1. Walt Whitman, "Pioneers! O Pioneers," in *American Poetry and Prose,* ed. Norman Foerster, 2 vols. (Boston: Houghton Mifflin Co., 1957), 2: 903–06.
2. Charles Joseph Faulkner, "The Policy of the State with Respect to her Slave Population" (Paper read before the Virginia House of Delegates, Richmond, 20 Jan. 1832); quoted in Henry Nash Smith, *Virgin Land* (New York: Random House, 1950), p. 152.
3. John Adams, *The Adams-Jefferson Letters* (Chapel Hill: University of North Carolina Press, 1959), 2: 358; quoted in William R. Taylor, *Cavalier and Yankee* (New York: George Braziller, 1961), p. 2.
4. Glyndon Van Deusen, *The Jacksonian Era* (New York: Harper & Row, 1959), p. 10. Alexis de Tocqueville, *Democracy in America,* ed. Philip Bradley (New York: Alfred A. Knopf, 1945), 1: 22.
5. Robert Remini, *Martin Van Buren and the Making of the Democratic Party* (New York: Columbia University Press, 1951), p. 11.
6. *Life and Letters of Joseph Story,* ed. William W. Story (Boston, 1851), 1: 563, quoted in Van Deusen, p. 31. *The Diary of Philip Hone,* ed. Allan Nevins (New York: Arno Press Rep., 1976), p. 142.
7. Whitney Cross, *The Burned-over District: The Social and Intellectual History of Enthusiastic Religion in Western New York 1800–1850* (New York: Harper & Row, 1965), p. 13.
8. Charles Finney, quoted in Paul Goodman and Frank Otto Gatell, *U.S.A.: An American Record* (New York: Holt, Rinehart & Winston, 1972), p. 191.
9. Goodman and Gatell, p. 151. *Western Recorder* 8 (10 May 1831): 75. Charles G. Finney, *Lectures to Professing Christians* (New York, 1832), p. 106; quoted in Cross, p. 202. The number of prominent ministers who turned to *belles lettres* as a means of self-expression and control is evidence of the dramatic shift in the relationship between the minister and his culture in the period from the Second Great Awakening to the Civil War. For further development of this idea see Ann Douglas, "Heaven Our Home: Consolation Literature in the Northern United States, 1830–1860," *American Quarterly* 26 (December 1974): 498. Examples of literary efforts of the clergy during the antebellum era will be found in chaps. 2–4.

10. *Recollections of Samuel Beck,* ed. H. E. Scudder (Philadelphia, 1877), pp. 276–77; quoted in Douglas Miller, *Jacksonian Aristocracy, Class and Democracy in New York 1830–1860* (London and New York: Oxford University Press, 1967), p. 9. John Godfred Saxe, "Railroad Chorus," in Frank Luther, *Americans and Their Songs* (New York: Harper & Bros., 1942), p. 57.
11. Paul Gates, *The Farmer's Age: Agriculture, 1815–1860* (New York, 1960), p. 160. Michael A. Lebowitz, "The Jacksonians: Paradox Lost," in *Towards a New Past: Dissenting Essays in American History,* ed. Barton F. Bernstein (New York: Random House, 1968), p. 72.
12. Walter Hugins, *Jacksonian Democracy and the Working Class* (Stanford, California, Stanford University Press, 1960), p. 53. Lebowitz, p. 75.
13. Van Deusen, p. 7. Richard C. Wade, "An Agenda for Urban History," in *American History, Retrospect and Prospect,* ed. George A. Billias and Gerald N. Grob (New York: The Free Press, 1971), p. 391.
14. Richard C. Wade, "Urbanization," in *The Comparative Approach to American History,* ed. C. Vann Woodward (New York: Basic Books, 1968), p. 190.
15. Bridenbaugh, *Revolt,* p. 133. Also see Sam B. Warner, Jr., *The Private City* (Philadelphia: University of Pennsylvania Press, 1968), pp. 3–21.
16. Remini, p. 5. Chilton Williamson, *American Suffrage;* quoted in Miller, p. 12. Miller, p. 14.
17. John Pintard, *"Letters from John Pintard to his Daughter Eliza Noel Pintard Davidson, 1816–1833," New York Historical Society Collections* 70–83 (1937–40), 3: 184. *Hone,* p. 9.
18. Samuel Woodworth, "The Meeting of the Waters of Hudson and Erie," in Lester Levy, *Grace Notes in American History: Popular Sheet Music from 1820–1900* (Oklahoma: Oklahoma University Press, 1967), p. 58. Levi Beardsley, *Reminiscences* (New York, 1852), p. 219.
19. Robert Ernst, *Immigrant Life in New York 1825–1863* (New York: Ira J. Friedman, Inc., 1949), p. 151.
20. For an analysis of the effect of the printing revolution on antiabolitionists see Leonard L. Richards, *Gentlemen of Property and Standing* (London and New York: Oxford University Press, 1970), pp. 71–73, 106–67.
21. Tocqueville, 1, pp. 289–90, note.
22. Quoted in Miller, p. 45.
23. *Hone,* p. 241.
24. *The Diary of George Templeton Strong,* ed. Allan Nevins and Milton Halsey Thomas (New York: Octagon, 1974), 1: 63. Captain Frederick Marryat, *Diary in America with Remarks on its Institutions* (New York, 1839), pp. 16–20.
25. Miller, p. 88. Ernst, p. 129. Miller, p. 96. Quoted in Ray Allen Billington, *The Protestant Crusade, 1800–1860* (New York: Quadrangle, 1964), p. 200.
26. Charles Dickens, *American Notes for General Circulation* (London, 1892), pp. 114, 117–18, 123–31, 137.
27. Pintard, 3: 51–52.
28. *Strong,* 1: 94.
29. Thomas L. Nichols, *Forty Years American Life 1821–1861* (New York: Stackpole Sons, 1937), p. 195. Tocqueville, 2: 190, "Only an Emigrant," in Levy, p. 57.

30. Grund, *Aristocracy in America* (R. Bentley: London, 1839), 1: 10. Also see pp. 52, 170.
31. Tocqueville, 2: 201. Thomas Hamilton, *Men and Manners in America* (London, 1833), pp. 389–90.
32. Tocqueville, 1: 230.
33. Mr. Hedderwick, *Glasgow Chronicle* (24 May 1823); quoted in Bayard Still, *Mirror for Gotham* (New York: New York University Press, 1956), pp. 80, 78. *Strong*, 2: 24.
34. "Recollection of New-York," *Iris* (1844), p. 38.
35. *Hone*, p. 54. Still, p. 138.
36. Charles N. Glaab and A. Theodore Brown, *A History of Urban America* (New York: The Macmillan Company, 1967), p. 95. *Strong*, 2: 320. *Hone*, p. 451.
37. Glaab and Brown, p. 96. Still, p. 137. *Strong*, 2: 56–57, 99.
38. Lydia Maria Child, *Letters* (Boston, 1882), pp. 94, 193.
39. Ibid., p. 94.
40. Georg Semmel, "The Metropolis and Mental Life," in *Classic Essays on the Culture of Cities*, ed. Richard Sennett (New York: Appleton-Century Crofts, 1969), p. 58. Samuel B. Halliday, *The Lost and Found or Life Among the Poor* (New York: Blakeman & Mason, 1859), p. 182. Rev. John Todd, *The Moral Influence, Dangers, and Duties Connected With Great Cities* (Northampton, Mass., 1841), pp. 18–20.
41. Richard Rapson, "The American Child as Seen by British Travelers 1845–1935," *American Quarterly* 17 (1965): 520–34. For a discussion of children's adaptability to the wilderness in colonial America, see Bernard Bailyn, *Education in the Forming of American Society* (New York: Random House, 1960).
42. *Monthly Religious Magazine* (1860); quoted in Calhoun, 3: 187.
43. *Ladies' Magazine* (1830), pp. 441.
44. Timothy Dwight, *Things As They Are: Or Notes of a Traveller through Some of the Middle Northern States* (New York, 1834), p. 31. A. Thomason [Andrew Bell], *Men and Things in America* (London, 1835), p. 20; quoted in Still, p. 81. Fredrika Bremer, *The Homes of the New World: Impressions of America*, trans. Mary Howitt (New York, 1853), 2: 107.
45. Lydia Maria Child, *Letters from New York* (New York: C. S. Francis and Co., 1845), p. 286. Stephen Thernstrom and Peter Knights, "Men in Motion: Some Data and Speculations About Urban Population Mobility in Nineteenth Century America," *Journal of Interdisciplinary History* 1 (Autumn 1970–Spring 1971): 10, 23.
46. Jesse Hopkins, *The Patriot's Manual* (New York: William Williams, 1828), p. 136.
47. James Kirk Paulding, *The Backwoodsman: A Poem* (Philadelphia, 1818), pp. 80–81.
48. Alfred Street, "A Forest Walk," *Gift of Sentiment* (New York, 1953), p. 27; Quoted in Smith, p. 159.
49. Timothy Flint, *Western Monthly Review* 1 (July 1827), 169–70; quoted in Smith, p. 159.
50. "The Marble Faun," *Works of Nathaniel Hawthorne* (Boston, 1882), 6: 346–47; also see Nathaniel Hawthorne, "The Artist of the Beautiful," in Foerster, 1:

640–41, 644. "My Kinsman, Major Molineux," in Foerster, 1: 609, 614–18. It is important to note that prourban literature also existed, although it was scant indeed. Walt Whitman described Boston as "joyous, receptive . . . magnificiently tolerant." See Walt Whitman, *Specimen Days* (New York: New American Library, 1961), pp. 242, 250.

51. Nathaniel Hawthorne, "The Celestial Railroad," in Foerster, 1: 674–80.
52. Morton and Lucia White, *The Intellectual Versus the City* (New York: Mentor, 1964), pp. 46–49.
53. Edgar Allan Poe, "The City in the Sea," in Foerster, 272–73.
54. Child, *Letters,* p. 68. Poe, "Man of the Crowd," in *The Complete Tales and Poems of Edgar Allan Poe* (New York: Random House, 1938), pp. 478–81.
55. "The Murder of Marie Rogêt," in *Complete Tales,* p. 169.
56. David B. Davis, *Homicide in American Fiction, 1798–1860* (Ithaca, N.Y.: Cornell University Press, 1957), pp. 262–63.
57. Edward Zane Carroll Judson [Ned Buntline] *The Mysteries and Miseries of New York* (New York, 1848), p. 55.
58. Newton Mallory Curtis, *The Matricide's Daughter* (New York, n.d.), p. 106.
59. Ibid., p. 81.

CHAPTER 3

1. John Neal, "Woman," *Boston Book* (1836), p. 244. Rev. J. F. Stearns, *Female Influence and the True Christian Mode of its Exercise, A Discourse delivered in the First Presbyterian Church in Newburyport* (July 1837), p. 23.
2. Tocqueville, 2: 99. Grund, *Aristocracy* 1: 120; 203, 148.
3. Mrs. A. J. Graves, *Girlhood and Womanhood* (Boston: T. H. Carter & Co., 1844), p. 103. Grund, 1: 45. Thorstein Veblen, *The Theory of the Leisure Class: An Economic Study of Institutions* (New York: Viking Press, 1945), pp. 168; 36.
4. Child, *Letters,* p. 40. *Strong,* 2: 262. Quoted in Still, p. 142.
5. W. S. Tryon, ed., *My Native Land* (Chicago: University of Chicago Press, 1952), p. 54; quoted in Still, p. 134. Quoted in Still, p. 142.
6. William N. Bobo, *Glimpses of New York by a South Carolinian* (Charleston, 1852), p. 145. Adam G. de Gurowski, *America and Europe* (New York, 1857), pp. 371–72.
7. Abbott, p. 218. Grund, *Aristocracy* 1: 150.
8. Abbott, pp. 250–51. Dexter, *Career Women,* p. 214.
9. Todd, pp. 18–20.
10. Crèvecoeur, pp. 46–48. *Southern Literary Messenger* 2 (March 1836): 277. Quoted in H. N. Smith, *Virgin Land,* pp. 241–242.
11. Graves, p. 179–80. Mary Grant, "Home," *Forget-me-not* (1848), p. 270. *Godey's Lady's Book* (1840), p. 80. *Amulet* (1846), pp. 281–82. "My Birth Place," *Ladies' Diadem* (1853), p. 99.
12. Grant, "Home," p. 270. "The Cottage Girl's Return Home," *Ladies' Magazine* (1830), pp. 104–105. "Home of Youth," *Ladies' Magazine* (1829), p. 229. *Ladies'*

Magazine (1829), p. 22. Catharine Sedgwick, "Love of Nature," *American Literary Emporium* (1848), p. 28. *American Literary Emporium* (1848), p. 183.

13. Sedgwick, "Love of Nature," p. 28.
14. Horace Bushnell, *The American National Preacher* (1840), p. 107. William B. Taylor, Esq., "Home," *Ladies' Garland* (1839), p. 243. Donald Grant Mitchell, *Reveries of a Bachelor: Or a Book of the Heart* (New York, 1850), p. 59.
15. Ladies' Repository (1845), p. 54. Timothy Shay Arthur, "Confessions of a Platonic Lover," *Baltimore Book* (1839), p. 107.
16. Nathaniel W. Chittenden, *Influence of Woman Upon the Destinies of a People* (New York, 1837), p. 16.
17. *Ladies' Magazine* (1830), p. 441. James Fenimore Cooper, *The Crater; or Vulcan's Peak* (New York: Stringer & Townsend, 1855), 2: 89. Charles Meigs, *Lecture on Some of the Distinctive Characteristics of the Female* (Philadelphia, 1847), pp. 10–15.
18. *Ladies' Literary Cabinet* (1822), p. 141. William Eliot, Jr., *Lectures of Young Women* (Boston, 1853), pp. 55–56. Stearns, p. 23.
19. G. S. Hillard, *A First Class Reader* (Boston: Hickling, Swan and Brown, 1856), p. 485. Miss A. Hall, *The Literary Reader for Academies and High Schools* (Boston, John P. Jewelt & Co., 1850), p. 352.
20. "The Social Position and Culture due to Woman," *Two Addresses Before the Maternal Association* (New York: John Gray, 1846), p. 23.
21. *Hints and Sketches* (New York: John S. Taylor, 1839), p. 28 (emphasis added).
22. *Ladies' Repository* (1842), p. 110.
23. Tocqueville, 2: 212.
24. *Forget-me-not* (1848), p. 105. William B. Taylor, Esq., "Female Influence," *Ladies' Garland* (1839), p. 187.
25. Jesse Peck, *The True Woman: Or, Life and Happiness at Home and Abroad* (New York: Carlton & Porter, 1857), p. 343.
26. Rev. Hubbard Winslow, *A Discourse delivered in The Bowdoin Street Church* (Boston: Weeks, Jordan & Co., 1837), p. 8.
27. *Ladies' Repository* (1842), p. 146. Sherlock, "Woman," *Forget-me-not* (1828), p. 46. *Ladies' Garland* (1837), p. 16.
28. Stearns, p. 14. Virginia Cary, *Letters on Female Character* (Virginia, 1828), p. 43. Meigs, p. 9. Elizabeth Sandford, *Woman in her Social and Domestic Character* (Boston: Otis, Broaders & Co., 1842), p. 13.
29. Bushnell, p. 120, *Strong*, 1: 179. James Fenimore Cooper, *The Ways of the Hour* (New York: J. Fagan, 1850), p. 204. *Ladies' Magazine* (1820), p. 559.
30. *Christian Wreath* (1847), p. 268. "Social Position and Culture," p. 27. Washington Irving, "The Broken Heart," *Ladies' Literary Companion* (1820–21), p. 12.
31. Grund, *Aristocracy*, 1: 202.

CHAPTER 4

1. Stearns, pp. 15–16.
2. Chandler Gilman, M.D., *Introductory Address to the Students in Medicine of the*

College of Physicians and Surgeons of the University of the State of New York (New York, 1840), pp. 15–17.

3. George Burnap, *The Sphere and Duties of Woman* (Philadelphia: John Murray, 1848), pp. 172, 68. Ray Palmer, D.D., *An Address on the Education of Woman Delivered at the Anniversary of the Pittsfield Young Ladies' Institute* (Albany: Gray, Sprague & Co., 1852), p. 10. Charles Butler, *The American Lady* (Philadelphia: Hogan & Thompson, 1836), p. 27.
4. Joseph Richardson, *The American Reader*, 2d ed. (Boston: Lincoln and Edmonds, 1813), pp. 20–23. Quoted in Ruth Miller Elson, *Guardians of Tradition: American Schoolbooks of the Nineteenth Century* (Nebraska: University of Nebraska Press, 1964), p. 304. *Rhymes for the Nursery* (Boston, 1837); quoted in David Grimsted, ed., *Notions of the Americans 1820–1860* (New York: George Braziller, 1970), p. 235.
5. George Gordon, "The Return," *Amethyst* (1831), p. 166. "Poor Mary-Anne," *Boston Musical Miscellany* (Boston: J. T. Buckingham, 1811), p. 78. Lewis J. Cist, "Death of the Beautiful," *Godey's Lady's Book* (1845), p. 222. *Boston Musical*, p. 78. T. S. Arthur, *The Maiden: A Story for My Young Countrywomen* (Philadelphia: Henry F. Anners, 1848), p. 32.
6. Grund, *Aristocracy* 1: 87; 99. Horace Bushnell, *Women's Suffrage: The Reform Against Nature* (New York: C. Scribner & Co., 1869), pp. 109, 159. *Strong*, 2: 129.
7. Stearns, p. 22. *The World Enlightened, Improved and Harmonized by Woman!* (Philadelphia: John H. Gihon & Co., 1840), p. 8.
8. Chittenden, p. 21. "Piety in Woman," *Ladies' Garland* (1839), p. 228. Meigs, pp. 10–15. Stearns, p. 11. "Female Piety," *Ladies' Literary Cabinet* (1820), p. 156. "Religion in Women," *Ladies' Garland* (1837), p. 225, Sandford, p. 35.
9. Stearns, p. 9. Gardiner Spring, *The Excellence and Influence of the Female Character* (New York: F. & R. Lockwood, 1825), p. 29. Idem, "Influence of the Female Character," *Ladies' Garland* (1837), p. 122.
10. Richardson, p. 21. "Charming Nancy," *Boston Musical Miscellany*, p. 119.
11. *Female Monitor; or the Whole Duty of Woman. By a Lady, Revised, Corrected and Improved*, 2d ed., New York: n.d., p. 25. Thomas Branagan, *The Excellency of the Female Character Vindicated* (Philadelphia: J. Rakestrow, 1808), p. 75. Pintard 2: 17; Marryat, pp. 244–47. Barbara Welter, "The Cult of True Womanhood, 1820–1860," *American Quarterly* 18 (1966): 151–74, identifies piety, purity, submissiveness, and domesticity as the essential traits for antebellum women.
12. J. Green, "The Pride of the Village," *Musical Carcanet: A Choice Collection of the Most Admired Popular Songs* (New York: Collens & Hannay, 1832), 52; *Female Monitor*, p. 25. Chittenden, p. 17.
13. Helen E. Roberts, "Marriage, Redundancy or Sin," in *Suffer and Be Still*, ed. Martha Vicinus (Bloomington: Indiana University Press, 1972), pp. 63–64.
14. Roberts, pp. 70–72.
15. For a different interpretation see ibid., pp. 68–69.
16. William Acton, *The Functions and Disorders of the Reproductive Organs in Youth, in Adult Age, and in Advanced Life: Considered in their Social and Psychological Relations* (Philadelphia, 1865), p. 133; quoted in Carl Degler, "What

Ought To Be and What Was: Women's Sexuality in the Nineteenth Century," *American Historical Review* 79 (Dec. 1974): 1467; 1478.

17. *Advocate* (1835), p. 5.
18. Josiah Gilbert Holland, *Letters to the Jones* (New York: Charles Scribner, 1863), p. 211. J. A. Segur, *Influence, Rights and Appeal of Women* (Albany, 1842), p. 97. Samuel Patterson, "*Female Piety, Ladies' Garland* (1849), p. 36.
19. Tocqueville, 2: 201. "Advice to Unmarried Ladies," *Ladies' Companion* (1836), p. 101. Washington Irving, "The Wife," *Ladies' Garland* (1837), p. 53 (emphasis added). T. S. Arthur, "Confessions," p. 102.
20. T. S. Arthur, "Bear and Forbear," *American Keepsake* (1851), p. 264. "The Mission of Woman," *Christian Wreath* (1847), pp. 267–68. Rensselaer Bentley, *The American Instructor* (Hudson, N.Y., 1824), p. 162.
21. *Strong,* 1: 206. *Ladies' Repository* (1842), p. 17. *Ladies' Companion* (1836), p. 296; Charles Pierce, *The Portsmouth Miscellany: Or, Lady's Library of Improvement* (Portsmouth, N.H., 1804), p. 67. *The Child's Spelling Book* (Conn.: John Babcock, 1798), p. 100.
22. J. G. Palfred, "A Good Daughter," *Boston Book* (1836), p. 191. Noah Webster, *An American Selection of Lessons in Reading and Speaking* (Conn.: Hudson and Goodwin, 1789), 66. *The New Pleasing Instructure: Or, Young Lady's Guide to Virtue and Happiness* (Boston: Thomas & Andrews, 1799), p. 125. "Vilikin and His Dinah," in Sigmund Spaeth, *Read 'Em and Weep* (New York: Arco Publishing Co., 1959), p. 53.
23. Spring, *Excellence*, p. 26. William Henry Fry, "Romance," in *A Program of Early and Mid-Nineteenth Century American Songs,* ed. John T. Howard (New York: J. Fischer & Bros., 1931), p. 29. Butler, pp. viii, 22.
24. Burnap, p. 64. Charles Burdett, *Blonde and Brunette* (New York: D. Appleton & Co., 1858), pp. 178–79. *Ladies' Companion* (1836), p. 230. Harriet Beecher Stowe, *The Minister's Wooing* (New York: Delby and Jackson, 1859), 567. Burdett, p. 179.
25. Gilman, p. 19. *Ladies' Literary Cabinet* (1822), p. 5. "The Son Unguided, his Mother's Shame," *Two Addresses before the Maternal Association* (New York: John Gray, 1846), p. 6. Spring, *Excellence,* p. 5.
26. T. S. Arthur, *Married and Single: Or, Marriage and Celibacy Contrasted, in a Series of Domestic Pictures* (New York: Harper & Bros., 1845), p. 12. Burnap, p. 108. Roberts, p. 48.
27. Arthur, *Maiden,* p. 154, Samuel Woodworth, *The Deed of Gift,* in *Yankee Doodle-Do: A Collection of Songs of the Early American Stage,* comp. Vernon Greville (New York: Payson and Clarle, 1927), p. 10. "The Bride's Farewell," *Ladies' Pearl and Literary Gleaner* (1840), p. 13. *Godey's Lady's Book* (1843), p. 140.
28. "The Old Maid's Lament," in *Songs of Other Days,* ed. Fanny Snow Knowlton (Boston: Oliver Ditson Co., 1922), p. 75. "My Grandma's Advice," Knowlton, p. 92. Burdett, *Blonde,* p. 179.
29. "An Old Maid," *Ladies' Magazine* (1830), p. 290. Burdett, *Blonde,* p. 179 (emphasis added).
30. Tocqueville, 2: 201. Anton Philip Heinrich, "The Musical Bachelor," in Howard,

p. 1. Quoted in Abner Alden, *The Reader*, 4th ed. (Boston: Thomas & Andrew, 1814), p. 184.

31. See N.Y.S. *Assembly Documents* (28 Apr. 1845), #237, p. 1; *N.Y.S. Assembly Journal*, 69th sess. (1846), p. 135; N.Y.S. *Assembly Documents* (18 Feb. 1841), #143, p. 1; N.Y.S. *Senate Documents* (9 Mar. 1836), #68, p. 1; N.Y.S. *Assembly Documents* (26 May 1836), #328, p. 1. N.Y.S. *Assembly Documents* (13 Feb. 1850), #73, p.1.
32. *Public Ledger and Daily Transcript of Philadelphia*, quoted in Calhoun, 2: 8.
33. *Ladies' Magazine* (1828), pp. 202; 203.
34. *Ladies' Magazine* (1828), p. 203. *Ladies' Magazine* (1831), p. 511. Robert Dale Owen, *Situations* (New York: published at the office of the Free Enquirer, 1830), 14. Grund, *Aristocracy* 1: 89.

CHAPTER 5

1. Caroline Dall, *College, Market and Court or Woman's Relation to Education* (Boston, 1867), pp. 172–73. Arthur M. Schlesinger, *New Viewpoints in American History* (New York: Macmillan Co., 1922), p. 134.
2. Matthew Carey, *A Plea for the Poor No. II* (Philadelphia, 1831), p. 5. The acceptance of only one standard for all women induced poor females, at great personal sacrifice, to emulate the fashionable woman-belle ideal. Anne Royall reported: "I have known young ladies (those who have no dependence but their industry) . . . sit up till 12 o'clock at night to complete a suit of clothes, the proceeds of which was to purchase a fine cap, or a plume of feathers to deck herself for church. Hundreds of those females thus maintain themselves in a style of splendor" (*Sketches of Life, History and Manners in the United States* [New Haven, 1826], 261). Bushnell, *Women's Suffrage*, p. 85.
3. Still, p. 90. Walt Whitman, *Aurora*, quoted in Still, p. 91. Calhoun, 2: 239.
4. Harriet Martineau, *Society in America* (Paris, 1842), 2: 169. Grund, *Aristocracy* 1: 136. Ernst, p. 66.
5. Pintard, 2, 373. Quoted in Miller, p. 178.
6. Child, *Letters*, pp. 280–81. *Ladies' Repository* (1841), quoted in Calhoun, 2: 225. "Mrs. Chaloner's Visit," *Gift* (1839), p. 297. Maria McIntosh, *Two Lives* (New York: D. Appleton & Co., 1846), p. 293.
7. Quoted in Calhoun, 2: 277; 231–34; 237.
8. Jane G. Swisshelm, *Letters to Country Girls* (New York: J. C. Riker, 1853), p. 130. Branagan, p. 83. "Young Ladies at Home," *Golden Keepsake* (1851), p. 184; Peck, p. 47.
9. Grund, *Aristocracy* 1: 146. *Ladies' Magazine* (1830), pp. 182–84; 314. "Would-be-Genteel," *Jewel* (1837), p. 24.
10. Tocqueville, 2: 201. Martineau, 2: 158–59.
11. Meigs, p. 29. Cooper, *Ways*, p. 43. *Strong*, 1: 284; 2: 184.
12. Stearns, pp. 17–23; 24. *Ladies' Garland* (1839), p. 199.
13. *Gift of Friendship* (1847), p. 200. Miller, pp. 20–21. *Maternal Association*, "The Social Position and Culture due to Woman," (1846), p. 22.

14. J. W. Corson, M.D., "Woman in the Chamber of Sickness," *Ladies' Repository* (1842), p. 187.
15. *Ladies' Magazine* (1830), p. 31.
16. Abner Alden, *The Speaker* (Boston: Thomas & Andrew, 1810), 2: 230. *Female Monitor*, p. 21. Sandford, p. 91. Burnap, p. 91. Alden, *Reader*, p. 101.
17. *Ladies' Companion* (1836), p. 81. Sarah J. Hale, *Keeping House and Housekeeping* (New York, 1845), p. 39. For an account of one woman's unsuccessful battle for custody, see Shippen, *Her Journal Book*. Samuel Putnam, *Introduction to the Analytical Reader*, 2d ed. (Boston: Perkins and Marvin, 1830), 1: 44.
18. *Ladies' Companion* (1836), pp. 91; 32, 60. Samuel Bayard Woodward, *Hints for the Young, In Relation to the Health of Body and Mind* (Boston, 1856), pp. 7–23. See also George R. Calhoun, *Report of the Consulting Surgeon on Spermatorrhea, or Seminal Weakness, Impotence, the Vice of Onanism, Masturbation or Self-Abuse, and Other Diseases of the Sexual Organs* (Philadelphia, 1853); Samuel Gregory, *Facts and Important Information for Young Women on the Subject of Masturbation* (Boston, 1857); *A Treatise on the Diseases Produced by Onanism*, trans. from French with notes and an appendix by an American Physician (New York, 1832).
19. *Ladies' Literary Cabinet* (1822), p. 70.
20. "The Clever Woman," in Sigmund Spaeth, *Weep Some More, My Lady* (New York: Doubleday, Page & Co., 1927), p. 52. T. S. Matteson, *The Novel Reader*, *Winter Wreath* (1853).
21. Butler, pp. 167, 156–58, 156, *Ladies' Companion* (1836), p. 70.
22. Grund, *Aristocracy* 2: 55; 1: 88. *Maternal Association*, "The Social Position and Culture Due to Woman," (1846), p. 30. *Ladies' Magazine* (1828), p. 197, (Baltimore, 1859), pp. 1–50.
23. *Arthurs' Home Magazine*. vii, p. 123, quoted in Calhoun, 2: 222; Graves, quoted in Calhoun, 2: 133.
24. Quoted in Calhoun, 2: 133. Grund, *Aristocracy* 2: 105.
25. "The Friendship of Woman," *Ladies' Magazine* (1829), p. 569. Edward Zane Carrol Judson [Ned Buntline], *The G'hals of New York* (New York, n.d.), p. 147. "The Journal of Esther Burr," *New England Quarterly* (1930), 3: 301.
26. *Ladies' Magazine* (1831), p. 158.
27. *Ladies' Literary Cabinet* (1819), p. 85. *Woman's Worth or, Hints to Raise the Female Character* (New York: D. Appleton & Co., 1848), p. 148. Alden, *Speaker*, 3: 229. Patrick Henry, "Advice of a Father to his Only Daughter," *Ladies' Garland* (1839). "Be Not Angry," in *Musical Carcanet* (New York: Collins & Hannay, 1832), p. 89. *Ladies' Companion* (1836), p. 209.
28. Holland, p. 265. *Ladies' Literary Cabinet* (1819), p. 46 (emphasis added). Tocqueville, 2: 212. Ralph, "Domestic Happiness," *Ladies' Literary Cabinet* (1820), p. 108. Burnap, pp. 79, 187. *The World Enlightened*, p. 11.
29. "She Hath Done What She Could," or, The Duty and Responsibility of Woman, *A Sermon, preached in the Chapel of St. Mary's School*. By the Rector, and printed for the pupils (Raleigh, 1847), p. 1.

CHAPTER 6

1. *Advocate* (1858), p. 23.
2. Quoted in *Hone*, p. 145. *The American Diaries of Richard Cobden*, ed. Elizabeth H. Cavely (Princeton: Greenwood, 1952), p. 29. *Water-Cure Journal* (1847), p. 151. James Fenimore Cooper, *Gleanings in Europe*, ed. Robert E. Spiller (New York: Kraus Repr., 1930), 2: 92–97; Nathaniel Hawthorne, "Our Old Home," in Works, 7: 66–68, 390–91.
3. Joel Hawes, D.D., A Looking-glass for Ladies, *An Address delivered at the Eighth Anniversary of the Mount Holyoke Female Seminary* (Boston: Wm. D. Ticknor & Co., 1845), p. 8. Quoted in Dinah Maria Craik, *A Woman's Thoughts About Women* (Columbus, Ohio: Follett, Foster & Co., 1858), intro. Quoted in Amy L. Reed, "Female Delicacy in the Sixties," *Century* (1915), pp. 855–64.
4. S. W. Benedict, *Woman, She Was, Is, and Should Be* (New York, 1849), p. 63. George Burnap, "Health of American Women," *Ladies' Wreath* (1849–50), p. 186.
5. Catharine Beecher, *Duty of American Women to their Country* (New York: Harper & Bros., 1845), p. 158.
6. Catharine Beecher, *Letters to the People on Health and Happiness* (New York, 1855), pp. 121–33.
7. Edward Dixon, *Woman and Her Diseases from Cradle to Grave* (New York, 1857), pp. 134–40.
8. Burnap, "Health," pp. 185–86. Beecher, *Letters*, pp. 165–75.
9. William P. Dewes, *A Treatise on the Diseases of Females* (Philadelphia, 1843), pp. 17; 14.
10. *Water-Cure Journal* (1845), pp. 37; 44.
11. Quoted in Harvey Graham, *Eternal Eve: The History of Gynecology and Obstetrics* (New York: London [New York] Hutchinson, 1960, [1951]), p. 495.
12. Kathryn Kish Sklar, "All Hail Pure Cold Water," *American Heritage* (Dec. 1974), p. 67.
13. Ann D. Wood, "The Fashionable Diseases: Woman's Complaints and Their Treatment in Nineteenth Century America," *Journal of Interdisciplinary History* 4 (1973): 25–52. P. Smith, *Daughters*, p. 132.
14. "Insanity: From Combe's Work on Mental Derangement," *Ladies' Magazine* (1835), pp. 461–63. W. A. Alcott, "Female Attendance on the Sick," *Ladies' Magazine* (1834), p. 302. Martineau, 2: 183.
15. Beecher, *Letters*, p. 121.
16. *Diary of Sarah Connell Ayer* (Portland, Maine: Lefavor-Tower Co., 1910), pp. 43; 37.
17. Elizabeth Prentiss, *The Life and Letters of Elizabeth Prentiss* (New York: Anson D. F. Randolph & Co., 1882), pp. 65–73.
18. "Extracts from the Diary of Mrs. Ann Warder," *Pennsylvania Magazine of History and Biography* (1893) 17: 452. Journals of Sarah Stearns, 1813–18, vol. 1, Mss coll., Schlesinger Library, A-14. *The Writings of Nancy Maria Hyde* (Norwich, Conn.: R. Hubbard, 1816), p. 65. *Memoirs of the Late Mrs. Susan Hun-*

tington of Boston (Boston: Crocker and Brewster, 1826), p. 31. "Diary of Mrs. Laura Clark, June 21–Oct. 26, 1818," *The Firelands Pioneer*, n.s. (1920), p. 2312.

19. Melva (pseud.), *Home Whispers to Husbands and Wives* (New York: American Female Guardian Society, 1859), p. 29. *Water-Cure Journal* (1847), p. 60.
20. H. B. Stowe to Calvin Stowe, 1847, Mss. coll., Schlesinger Library.
21. Ibid.
22. Edward T. James, ed., *Notable American Women 1607–1950* (Cambridge, Mass.: Harvard University Press, Belknap Press, 1971), 3: 393–402.
23. O. Spurgeon English, M.D., and Gerald H. J. Pearson, M.D., *Emotional Problems of Living* (New York: W. W. Norton & Co., 1963), pp. 508–12. For a discussion of anxiety see Maurice Stein, Arthur J. Vidich, and David Manning White, eds., *Identity and Anxiety: Survival of the Person in Mass Society* (New York: The Free Press, 1960).
24. H. B. Stowe to C. Stowe, 27 May 1849, Mss coll., Schlesinger Library.
25. *Journal and Letters of Hannah Backhouse* (London, 1858), p. 14. Prentiss, p. 114.
26. Elizabeth Prentiss, letter, 24 Apr. 1843 in Prentiss, p. 71. *Backhouse*, p. 4.
27. Prentiss, p. 114. H. B. Stowe to C. Stowe, 27 May 1849. *Backhouse*, p. 11.
28. *Backhouse*, p. 11.
29. Ibid., pp. 14; 2; 13, 33.
30. Catharine Sedgwick to Mrs. Watson, 20 Apr. 1810; Sedgwick *Life and Letters*, p. 87.
31. Hyde, p. 216.
32. Ibid., p. 78. *Memoir of Miss Hannah Adams*, Written by herself with additional notices by a friend (Boston: Gray & Bowen, 1832), pp. 34–35.
33. *Backhouse*, pp. 5–6.
34. Huntington, pp. 182–83; 318.
35. Sarah Ayer, letter, 1811; in Ayer p. 376. *Backhouse*, p. 4. See, for example, Catharine Sedgwick to Mrs. Channing, 25 Sept. 1821; in Sedgwick, *Life and Letters*, p. 121.
36. *Backhouse*, p. 13. Ayer, pp. 374–75.
37. Prentiss, p. 70.
38. Susan Huntington, letter, 30 Aug. 1811; *Memoirs* p. 55 letter, May 1818, p. 167.
39. Journals of S. Stearns, 1 May 1814. Prentiss, p. 100.
40. Shippen, p. 149. Ellen Parker, "Diary," *New Hampshire Hist. Soc. Colls.* 11 (1915): 130–62. *The Journal of Mary Peacock*, Life a Century Ago as seen in Buffalo and Chautaugua County by a 17 year old girl (Buffalo, 1938), pp. 50–75, Backhouse, p. 8.
41. Catharine Beecher to Mrs. Cogswell, 1837, Mss coll., Schlesinger Library. Prentiss, p. 272. Ayer, pp. Appendex; 37–72.
42. In those diaries written by married women between 1800 and 1860 husbands are rarely mentioned. In not one of the journals examined did the husband emerge as a supportive companion to his wife.
43. Quoted in Frederick Lewis Pattee, *The Feminine Fifties* (New York: D. Appleton-Century Co., 1940), p. 110. *Ladies' Literary Cabinet* (1819), p. 49. *Ladies' Magazine* (1828), p. 33.

44. Mrs. Farrar, *Young Ladies' Friend* (Boston, 1837), p. 135. Catharine Sedgwick, *Life and Letters*, Dewey, ed. (New York: Harper & Bros., 1871), pp. 153; 249.
45. *The Three Sisters* (London: W. Clowes & Sons, 1856), pp. 8–9.
46. Caroline Chesebro, *The Children of Light: A Theme for the Time* (New York: Redfield, 1853), pp. 156–210; 31.
47. Catharine Sedgwick, *Married or Single?* (New York: Harper & Bros., 1858), 1: 160.
48. Anna, "Truth in Fiction," *Evergreen* (1850). Chesebro, p. 29.
49. Mary Howitt, "Single Sisters," *Keepsake* (1845), p. 62. "Ada Lester's Story," *Ladies' Wreath* (1858), pp. 123–38. Julia Delafaye-Brehier, "Two Sisters," *Ladies' Scrap Book* (1845), p. 58."Some Passages in the Life of an Old Maid," *Garland* (1830), p. 85.
50. "Poor Will Newbery," *Amulet* (1846), p. 178. "A Life Without Love," *Ladies' Wreath* (1858), p. 153. Sedgwick, *Married*, 1: 204.
51. Harriet Beecher Stowe, "The Tea Rose," *Flora's Gems* (1846), pp. 44–45. *Ladies' Casket* (1848), p. 106. "Blanch Raymond," *Rose* (1845), pp. 164–69.
52. Catharine Sedgwick, *Live and Let Live* (New York: Harper & Bros., 1837), p. 79. Maria McIntosh, *The Lofty and the Lowly* (New York: D. Appleton & Co., 1853), 2: 24. *Three Sisters*, p. 20.
53. *Three Sisters*, pp. 16–17.
54. Harriet Beecher Stowe, "Cousin William," *Gift* (1839), p. 211. Graves, p.v., "Choosing How to Die," *Ladies' Casket* (1848), p. 26.
55. *Three Sisters*, p. 6. Eliza Farnham, *Eliza Woodson* (New York: A. J. Davis & Co., 1864), p. 53.
56. Mrs. S. S. B. K. Wood, *Ferdinand and Elmira* (Baltimore, 1809), p. 189. Fanny Fern [Sarah Parton], *Ruth Hall: A Domestic Tale: or The Present Time* (New York: Mason Bros., 1855), p. 21.
57. Eliza Leslie, "The Mysterious Picture," *Affection's Gift* (1832), pp. 208–21.
58. Ibid.
59. Fern, p. 36. McIntosh, *The Lofty*, 1: 71. Caroline Warren, *The Gamesters: Or Ruins of Innocence* (Boston: J. Shaw, 1828), p. 287.
60. Caroline Hentz, *Ernest Linwood* (Philadelphia, 1869), p. 327. Stowe, *Minister's Wooing*, p. 106. Amalie Winter, "A Simple Tale of Love," *Amaranth* (1848), p. 136.
61. Stowe, *Minister's Wooing*, p. 70.
62. Lydia Jane Pierson, "The Wash-Woman's Story," *Ladies' Garland* (1849), p. 75. Emma C. Einbury, "Elsie Grey," *American Juvenile Keepsake* (1834), p. 31. Warren, pp. 277–80.
63. Mrs. M. A. Felter, "Straws of Destiny," *Forget-me-not* (1850), p. 17.
64. Mary Hawthorne Reyburn, "Alice Howard," *Baltimore Book* (1839), pp. 33–34. Maria Williams, "Julia Nelson," *Amethyst* (1831), p. 264.
65. Warren, pp. 280–81. An authoress, *Rose* (1844), p. 42.
66. Mrs. D. Clarke, "Grace Brown—A Sketch for Mothers and Daughters," *Forget-me-not* (1850), p. 25. Helena Wells, *Constanta Neville* (London, 1800), 1: 172. S. S. B. K. Wood, *Amelia: Or the Influence of Virtue* (Portsmouth, N.H., 1802), p. 14.

67. Camila Toulmin, "The Painter's Revealing," *Amaranth* (1848), p. 88. Chesebro, p. 227. Also see "The Shoemaker's Daughter," *Amaranth* (1854), p. 128; "The Young Devotee," *Coral* (184?), p. 106.
68. B. H. S., "The Troubler of his Own House," *Ladies' Casket* (1848), p. 99. "My Borrowing Neighbor," *American Keepsake* (1851), p. 130. Sedgwick, *Married,* 1: 153.
69. Mrs. Lydia Jane Pierson, "The Wife's Promise," *Ladies' Garland* (1839), p. 196.
70. Maria, "Sketch from Real Life," *Forget-me-not* (1826), p. 335. Eliza Walker, "Widow's Daughter," *Amaranth* (1847), p. 279. Einbury, p. 31.
71. Einbury, p. 85. Eliza McNulty, *Forget-me-not* (1846), p. 245.
72. "Cousin Lucy," *Amaranth* (1854), p. 248.
73. Mrs. Shelley, "The Parvenue," *Amaranth* (1848), p. 266.
74. Mrs. C. Gilman, "The March of Mind," *Gift* (1847), p. 199. Sedgwick, *Married,* 1: 89. Also see Mrs. Emiline Smith, "The Murdered Traveller," *Forget-me-not* (1850), p. 65; Mrs. S. E. Hall, "The Daily Governess," *Keepsake* (1845), p. 57.
75. Augusta Evans, *Beulah* (New York: Derby and Jackson, 1860), p. 170.
76. Stowe, *Minister's Wooing,* p. 4. Susan Warner, *The Wide, Wide World* (New York: G. P. Putnam & Co., 1853), 2: 152. Mrs. C. Hale, "Mary Grey," *Rose* (1842), p. 12. Susan Warner, *Queechy* (New York: George P. Putnam, 1852).

CHAPTER 7

1. Tocqueville, I 106–10.
2. Charles Foster, *An Errand of Mercy: The Evangelical United Front 1790–1837* (Chapel Hill: University of North Carolina Press, 1960), p. 138. Mohl, *Poverty in New York 1783–1825* (London and New York: Oxford University Press, 1971), pp. 135; 170. Clifford Griffin, *Their Brother's Keeper* (New Jersey, 1960), p. 10, Melder, p. 234.
3. Timothy L. Smith, *Revivalism and Social Reform* (New York: Harper & Row, 1957), pp. 12; 148–204. Carroll Smith Rosenberg, *Religion and the Rise of the American City: The New York City Mission Movement 1812–1870* (Ithaca, N.Y.: Cornell University Press, 1971), pp. 8.
4. Mohl, p. 149. Society for the Relief of Poor Widows with Small Children (SRPW), Constitution and By-Laws (1803), p. 5.
5. Mohl, pp. 148–50. SRPW Annual Report (1816).
6. SRPW, By-Laws (1803); *By-laws and Regulations of the SRPW* (New York: J. Seymour, 1811). Regulations of the New York Asylum for Lying-in Women, quoted in Henry Cammann and Hugh Camp, *The Charities of New York, Brooklyn, and Staten Island* (New York: Hurd and Houghton, 1868), p. 409.
7. T. L. Smith, *Revivalism,* pp. 135–78. Rosenberg, pp. 277–80.
8. Quoted in Foster, p. 94. William Jay, *A Letter to the Right Reverend Bishop Hobart Occasioned by the Strictures on Bible Societies Contained in his late Charge to The Convention of N.Y.* (New York: John P. Haven, 1823), p. 74; also see William Jay, *A Letter to the Right Rev. Bishop Hobart in Reply to the Pamphlet Addressed By Him to the Author, under the signature of corrector* (New York: John P. Haven, 1823). Winslow, p. 14.

9. "Answer to a letter from the Secretary of a Female Cent Society," *Panoplist* 12 (1816): 256–60. Rev. J. K. Brownson, "Address to the Young Ladies of the Oakland Female Seminary," *Ladies' Repository* 5 (1845): 162.
10. Moses Stuart, *Sermon Delivered by the Request of the Female Charitable Society in Salem at the Anniversary* (1815), p. 19.
11. Samuel Worcester, *A Discourse Delivered in the Tabernacle in Salem Before the Salem Female Charitable Society at their Annual Meeting* (27 Sept. 1809), p. 7.
12. Matthew La Rue Perrine, *Women Have a Work to do in the House of God* (New York, 1817), pp. 4–20.
13. Rosenberg, p. 54.
14. Female Missionary Society for the Poor of the City of New York and its Vicinity, Annual Report (1821), pp. 5–9.
15. Rosenberg, p. 4.
16. *Advocate of Moral Reform* (1835), pp. 72; 35.
17. *Advocate* (1835), p. 1. Reprinted from the *New England Spectator*, *Advocate* (1835), pp. 4; 66, (1837) 340.
18. *Advocate* (1837), p. 340. See Rosenberg, p. 277.
19. *Advocate* (1840), p. 54.
20. In 1847 periodical changed name to *Advocate & Family Guardian* (1859), p. 264. SRPW, Address of the First Directress (19 Nov. 1811). Association for the Relief of Respectable, Aged, Indigent Females, Annual Report (1828), p. 5.
21. *Advocate* (1858), p. 28.
22. *Ladies' Wreath* (1848–49), pp. 111; 168. Orphan Asylum in the City of New York, (1820), p. 109.
23. *Advocate* (1858), 218.
24. Association for the Relief of Respectable, Aged, Indigent Females, Annual Report (1848), p. 1. *Advocate* (1866), p. 317; (1856), p. 83.
25. Sedgwick; *Life and Letters*, p. 265. Mrs. Sarah Martyn, "New York in the Olden Time," *Ladies' Wreath* (1847–48), p. 285.
26. New York Female Benevolent Society, Annual Report (1834), p. 2; Plea for the Orphan, Delivered on the Anniversary of the Female Charitable Society of Newburyport, May 21, 1822, p. 25.
27. Williams, p. 25. Joanna Mathews, *A Short History of the Orphan Asylum Society in the City of New York* (New York: Anson D. F. Randolph and Co., 1893), p. 25. Penitent Females' Refuge in the City of Boston, Third Annual Report (1821), p. 15. New York Female Benevolent Society, Annual Report (1840), p. 6. James W. Thompson, Sermon Delivered by the Request of the Female Charitable Society in Salem (1832). Irving Francher, *A History of the Troy Orphan Asylum* (New York: Whitehurst Printing & Binding Co., 1933), p. 33.
28. Isabella Graham, *The Power of Faith exemplified in The Life and Writings of Mrs. Isabella Graham of New York* (New York, 1816), pp. 467–69.
29. Joanna Bethune, *Life of Mrs. Isabella Graham* (New York: John S. Taylor, 1839), preface. *One Hundred Years of Work with Girls in Boston*, Issued by the Boston Society for the Care of Girls, formerly The Boston Female Asylum (1919), pp. 1–19. Also see *An Account of the Rise and Progress and Present State of the Boston Female Asylum together with the Act of Incorporation also, the Bye-laws and Rules and Regulations adopted by the Board of Managers* (1810).

30. *One Hundred Years*, pp. 1–19.
31. Abiel Abbot, A Discourse Delivered Before the Members of the Portsmouth Female Asylum on The Lord's Day, Aug. 9, 1807. Also see Francher, Williams, pp. 2–10. Elijah Parish, A Sermon preached before the Members of the Female Charitable Society of Newburyport on the 5th Anniversary (1808); Female Charitable Society of Newburyport, Act of Incorporation (1808); William Bently, A Discourse delivered in the East Meeting-House in Salem, Sept. 2, 1807 at the Annual Meeting of the Salem Female Charitable Society. Mathews, p. 25.
32. Bethune, p. 61. *Orphan Asylum in the City of New York: Origin and History* (New York: Bonnell, Silver & Co., 1896), p. 6.
33. New York Female Society for the Aid of Foreign Missions. *Constitution* (1814), preamble. Brooklyn Female Bible Society, Fifth Annual Report (1826), p. 5. Association for the Relief of Respectable, Aged, Indigent Females, Annual Report (1831), p. 11. Penitent Females, Annual Report (1831), p. 11. Penitent Females' Refuge in the City of Boston, Annual Report (1825), p. 24.
34. Female Charitable Society of Newburyport, Act of Incorporation. Penitent Females' Refuge in the City of Boston, Appeal to the Public (1839). Mathews, p. 17. Female Missionary Society for the Poor of the City of New York and its Vicinity, Annual Report (1820–21), p. 4.
35. Ayer, 303; 233. New York Female Union Society for Promotion of Sabbath Schools, Annual Report (1822), p. 1.
36. See SRPW, By-laws and Regulations, New York 1811–1813. Orphan Asylum in the City of New York, Annual Report (1810).
37. SRPW, By-laws and Regulations, N.Y. 1811–1813.
38. Female Bethel Association of New York, Constitution & By-laws (1836).
39. Cammann and Camp, p. 519.
40. *Commercial Advertiser*, 19 Nov. 1814, 2 Dec. 1814, 27 Jan. 1825, 19 Jan. 1824. New York *Evening Post*, 18 Feb. 1817, 26 Jan. 1825. SRPW, Minute Books, 1797–1932, entry for 15 Nov. 1821. James Hardie, *Description of New York* (New York, 1827), p. 284. Society for Employing the Poor of Boston, Annual Report (1820). Ladies' Depository of New York, Twenty-second Annual Report (1855). Society for the Promotion of Industry, Annual Report (1816). Seamen's Aid Society, Annual Report (1835).
41. Ayer, p. 237. Huntington, pp. 113–260.
42. Huntington, p. 123. This observation is based on a comparison of the lists of officers and members of more than one hundred female voluntary societies over a sixty-year period.
43. Bethune, p. 52, SRPW, Report of the Board of Directors (Apr. 1800), p. 14. Cammann and Camp, p. 250.
44. Graham, p. 469. *Orphan Asylum: Origin and History*, I p. 332.
45. Seamen's Aid Society, Annual Reports (1851), p. 1 (1838), p. 4.
46. Mathews, p. 29. Seamen's Aid Society, Annual Report (1851), p. 1.
47. Cammann & Camp, p. 248. Seamen's Aid Society, Annual Reports (1836), pp. 5–8 (1839), pp. 9–11.
48. Seamen's Aid Society, Annual Report (1836), p. 8.
49. Graham, p. 467. Bethune, p. 52.

50. Orphan Asylum in the City of New York, Annual Reports (1813), p. 1; Seamen's Aid Society, Annual Report (1836), p. 3. SRPW, Address of the First Directress (1811).
51. Timothy Alden, *A Discourse Delivered before the Members of the Portsmouth Female Asylum* (1804), p. 10. Pintard, 1, 93, 105, 100.
52. New York Female Benevolent Society, *Seventh Annual Report* (1841), p. 13. Bethune, p. 53. Orphan Asylum in the City of New York, *Annual Report* (1819), p. 104. Bethune, p. 55.
53. Association for the Relief of Respectable, Aged, Indigent Females, Annual Report (1819). 5 SRPW, Annual Report (1815), pp. 24–25.
54. The volunteers generally refrained from discussing the plight of impoverished males. Seamen's Aid Society, Annual Report (1838), p. 7.
55. Ibid. (1836), p. 10.
56. Ibid. (1837), pp. 13–16.
57. Society for Employing the Poor of Boston, Constitution and By-laws and an extract from the Report of the Managers For the First Three Months (1820), p. 1. Female Assistance Society, Annual Report (1835/36), pp. 4–8.
58. Seamen's Aid Society, Annual Reports (1836), p. 9; (1837), p. 7; (1836), p. 18.
59. *Association for the Relief of Respectable, Aged, Indigent Females, Annual Report* (1826), p. 7.

CHAPTER 8

1. *Advocate* (1848), p. 338.
2. Judson, *Mysteries*, p. 106; app. Also see George Lippard, *New York: Its Upper Ten and Lower Million* (Cincinnati, 1853); *Sanitary Condition of the City: Report of the Council of Hygiene and Public Health of the Citizens' Association of New York* (New York: Arno Press and the New York Times, 1970), pp. 10, 37, 138.
3. *Memoir and Select Remains of the Late Rev. John R. McDowall* (New York: Leavitt Lord & Co., 1838). *Magdalen Report*, reprinted in *McDowall's Journal* (1834), 2: 33–39.
4. *Hone*, p. 45. *Commercial Advertiser*, 24 Aug. 1831; reprinted in J. R. McDowall, *Magdalen Facts* (New York, 1832), p. 71. Quoted in *McDowall's Journal* (1834), 2: 39.
5. *Memoir and Select Remains*. Cammann and Camp, pp. 370–71.
6. Cammann and Camp, pp. 369–71. Inwood House, N.Y., *Missionary Labors Through a Series of Years Among Fallen Women by the New York Magdalen Benevolent Society* (New York, 1870). New York Female Benevolent Society, First Annual Report (1834), p. 2; First Report of the Executive Committee (1830), p. 25. Inwood House, *Missionary Labors*, p. 70.
7. New York Female Benevolent Society, Seventh Annual Report (1839); 7 First Report of the Executive Committee (1830), p. 25. Annual Report (1834), p. 11. Also see Inwood House, *Missionary Labors*.
8. New York Female Benevolent Society, Annual Report (1838), pp. 6–8.
9. *McDowall's Journal* 1: 36. Rev. Ralph Wardlaw, *Lectures on Magdalenism* (New

York: J. S. Redfield Clinton Hall, 1843); pp. 46, 77–78. Charles Christian, *A Brief Treatise on the Police of the City of New York* (New York, 1812), p. 16.

10. New York Female Benevolent Society, First Annual Report (1834), pp. 20–24; Seventeenth Annual Report (1850), p. 10. *Advocate* (1835), p. 64.
11. *Advocate* (1835), pp. 64; 31 (emphasis added).
12. Ibid., pp. 72; 84.
13. Ibid., (1835), p. 7. Also see ibid. (1835), pp. 2; 85; (1846), p. 18; (1837), p. 256.
14. Quoted in H. R. Howard, *The Lives of Helen Jewett and Richard P. Robinson* (New York, n.d.), p. 121.
15. *Hone*, p. 213.
16. New York *Sun*, quoted in *Advocate* (1836), p. 87.
17. *Advocate* (1836), p. 87.
18. Ibid. (1835), p. 65.
19. Ibid. (1853), p. 62; (1837), p. 348; (1835), p. 67; (1837), pp. 221; 348.
20. Ibid. (1835), p. 96; (1838), pp. 100; 107. Also see ibid. (1836), p. 9.
21. *Commercial Advertiser* (8 Aug. 1836). New York *Sun* (23 Aug. 1845), p. 2. *Commercial Advertiser* (8 Aug. 1836). New York *Evening Post* (2 Oct. 1845).
22. *Advocate* (1835), p. 63; (1837), p. 326; (1836), p. 100; (1835), pp. 1–2.
23. "The Province of Woman," *Advocate* (1837), p. 333.
24. Ibid.
25. *Advocate* (1838), p. 83.
26. Ibid. (1837), p. 333.
27. Ibid. (1835), p. 59; (1837), pp. 213; 371, (1838), p. 100. Also see ibid. (1836), p. 9.
28. Ibid. (1838), p. 100; (1836), pp. 60; 64. Also see ibid. (1836), p. 38; (1835), p. 67.
29. Ibid. (1838), pp. 19; 145; (1835), p. 35.
30. Ibid. (1835), p. 2; (1836), pp. 9; 116; (1838), p. 100.
31. Ibid. (1838), p. 82; (1836), pp. 25; 65; 149; (1845), p. 87.
32. Ibid. (1837), p. 228; (1836), p. 9; (1840), p. 82; (1835), p. 64.
33. New York Female Moral Reform Society, Fourth Annual Report, reprinted in *Advocate* (1838), pp. 80; 3 (emphasis added).
34. *Advocate* (1841), p. 168; (1838), p. 40.
35. Ibid. (1842), p. 172; (1844), pp. 29; 166; (1845), p. 62.
36. Ibid. (1836), pp. 4; 16; (1838), p. 5; (1840), p. 82; (1839), p. 555; (1840), p. 81.
37. Ibid. (1843), p. 87; (1845), p. 167; (1844), p. 87.
38. Ibid. (1838), p. 87; (1840), p. 99; (1844), p. 87; (1835), p. 66.
39. Ibid. (1846), pp. 38, 183; (1840), p. 32; (1838), p. 183; (1837), p. 207. For additional letters expressing the sense of community see ibid. (1841), p. 92; (1836), p. 25; (1837), p. 190; (1836), p. 163; (1838), p. 36; (1841), p. 5; (1843), p. 47.
40. Ibid. (1840), p. 23; (1837), p. 364–65.
41. Ibid. (1837), p. 265.
42. Ibid. (1837), pp. 328–31.
43. Ibid. (1837), p. 325–28.
44. Ibid. (1838), pp. 3–5.
45. Ibid. Carroll Smith Rosenberg, "Beauty, the Beast and the Militant Woman: A Case Study in Sex Roles and Social Stress in Jacksonian America," *American Quarterly* 23 (Oct. 1971): 582–83, discusses the Grimké letter. She asserts that

after its publication, "the *Advocate* never again published the work of an overt feminist. . . . In rejecting Sarah Grimké's feminist manifesto, the Society's members implicitly agreed to accept the role traditionally assigned woman: the self-sacrificing, supportive, determinedly chaste wife and the mother who limited her 'sphere' to domesticity and religion." Rosenberg's analysis, however, has serious flaws. Particularly after 1840 the *Advocate* repeatedly published the works of overt feminists, including articles by such noted women as Lydia Maria Child and Jane G. Swisshelm. In addition, as will be demonstrated in chapters 9 and 11, the *Advocate* continuously and explicitly refuted the traditional role assigned to antebellum women and urged a feminist critique of society.

46. *Advocate* (1838), p. 55.
47. Ibid. (1845), p. 40; (1840), p. 106.
48. Ibid. (1838), p. 87.

CHAPTER 9

1. *Advocate* (1840), pp. 82, 5; (1848), p. 92.
2. Ibid. (1840), pp. 146; 50. New York *Tribune*, quoted in *Advocate* (1843), p. 60.
3. *Advocate* (1846), p. 154.
4. *Ibid.*
5. Helen Brown [American Female Guardian Society], *Our Golden Jubilee: A Retrospect 1834–1884* (New York, 1884), p. 14. *Walks of Usefulness or Reminiscences of Mrs. Margaret Prior* (New York: American Female Moral Reform Society, 1844), pp. 14, 72. Sarah Bennett, *Woman's Work Among the Lowly*, Memorial volume of the first forty years of the American Female Guardian Society, 1877), p. 139. Idem, *Wrought Gold: A Model Life for Christian Workers* (New York: American Female Guardian Society, 1874), pp. 119, 27.
6. Bennett, *Wrought Gold*, p. 42.
7. *Advocate* (1838), p. 28 (emphasis added).
8. *Advocate* (1838), p. 51.
9. Ibid. (1842), p. 10; (1840), p. 153.
10. Ibid. (1845), p. 19; (1845), p. 21. See also ibid. (1847), p. 153; (1838), p. 79.
11. Ibid. (1845), pp. 33–34; p. 108.
12. Ibid. (1845), p. 109; (1836), p. 171.
13. Ibid. (1843), p. 24; (1836), pp. 171; 136. Also see ibid. (1840), p. 25.
14. Ibid. (1844), p. 165.
15. Ibid. (1844), pp. 29; 151; 86; 7.
16. American Female Moral Reform Society, Annual Report (1846), p. 81. *Advocate* (1844), p. 7, (1845), p. 109. For other articles decrying the condition of female laborers see *Advocate* (1840), p. 58; (1846), p. 90; (1845), p. 175; American Female Guardian Society, Annual Report (1848), p. 85; *Advocate* (1845), pp. 109; 82.
17. *Advocate* (1846), p. 119.
18. Ibid., (1842), p. 106; (1846), p. 50.
19. Ibid. (1843), p. 86; (1848), p. 23.
20. Ibid. (1845), p. 82.

21. Ibid. (1846), pp. 49–50.
22. Ibid. (1841), p. 69; (1838), p. 117.
23. Ibid. (1845), p. 41.
24. Ibid. (1837), p. 325; (1838), p. 121; (1845), pp. 121; 130.
25. Ibid. (1838), p. 121; (1846), p. 49.
26. Ibid. (1845), p. 169.
27. Ibid. (1842), p. 108; (1841), pp. 40; 71.
28. Ibid. (1846), p. 49.
29. Ibid. (1838), p. 93.
30. Ibid. (1844), pp. 41; 115. Also see ibid. (1840), pp. 46; 83; (1846), pp. 36; 13.
31. Ibid. (1838), pp. 93–94; 61.
32. Ibid. (1841), p. 176.
33. Ibid. (1840), pp. 46; 83.
34. Ibid. (1844), p. 149. New York *Tribune,* reprinted in *Advocate* (1844), p. 28. Philadelphia *Public Ledger,* reprinted in *Advocate* (1844), p. 58. For other expressions of support see *Extracts from the Report of the Select Committee of the Ohio Legislature,* in *Advocate* (1842), p. 15; N.Y.S. *Senate Documents* (3 Mar. 1847), #68, pp. 1–12.
35. *Advocate* (1840), pp. 34–35; (1841), p. 189.
36. Ibid. (1845), p. 53; (1841), p. 189; (1847), p. 100; (1848), p. 45. For legislative debate on The Act to Punish Seduction as a Crime see N.Y.S. *Assembly Documents* (23 Mar. 1842), #134, pp. 1–13; (9 Feb. 1844), #363, pp. 1–5; (10 Mar. 1842), #159, pp. 1–18; (23 Apr. 1840), #333, pp. 1–5; (23 Jan. 1845), #23, pp. 1–5; and N.Y.S. *Senate Documents* (13 Mar. 1847), #68, pp. 1–17.
37. *Advocate* (1848), pp. 79; 67.
38. Ibid. (1841), p. 105.
39. Ibid. (1840), p. 63; (1845), p. 64. Margaret Dye, *Wrecks and Rescues* (New York: American Female Guardian Society, 1859), p. 208.
40. Flora Northrup, *The Record of a Century* (New York: American Female Guardian Society, 1934), pp. 208; 24. *Advocate* (1840), p. 103.
41. *Advocate* (1845), p. 62; (1841), p. 106; (1845), p. 156; (1846), p. 158. Dye, p. 119.
42. Sedgwick, *Life and Letters*, p. 292.
43. Female Department of the New York Prison Association, First Annual Report (1845), intro.; Second Annual Report (1846), p. 58.
44. Ibid., Second Annual Report (1846), pp. 58–59, 127. C. M. Kirkland, *The Helping Hand: Comprising an Account of The Home for The Discharged Female Convict and an Appeal in Behalf of that Institution* (New York: Charles Scribner, 1853), p. 37.
45. Kirkland, p. 31.
46. Female Department of the New York Prison Association, Second Annual Report (1846), p. 126; Fourth Annual Report (1848–49), pp. 12, 2.
47. Kirkland, p. 59. Female Department of the New York Prison Association, Fifth Annual Report (1850), pp. 8–11.
48. Female Department of the New York Prison Association, Fourth Annual Report (1849), pp. 4–6. Kirkland, p. 39. Mary Ann Johnson, assistant matron, Mount Pleasant Female Prison, letter (10 July 1844), reprinted in Female Department of

the New York Prison Association, Second Annual Report (1846), pp. 59–60; Ninth Annual Report (1854), pp. 5–10.

49. Female Department of the New York Prison Association, Fifth Annual Report (1850), p. 7; Sixth Annual Report (1851), p. 52.
50. Female Department of the New York Prison Association, First Annual Report (1845), intro.; Ninth Annual Report (1854), p. 4; Eighth Annual Report (1853), p. 4.
51. The discussion of deviance is based on Emile Durkheim, *The Division of Labor in Society,* trans. George Simpson (New York: The Free Press, 1964), pp. 70–110.
52. Female Department of the New York Prison Association, Eighth Annual Report (1853), p. 4; Fifth Annual Report (1850), p. 6.
53. Kirkland, pp. 83–87. Child, *Letters*, p. 207.
54. New York Female Benevolent Society, First Annual Report (1834), pp. 20–23 (emphasis added). *Advocate* (1844), p. 115; (1845), p. 65. *Advocate* (1838), p. 164; (1843), p. 127. Female Department of the New York Prison Association Sixth Annual Report (emphasis added) p. 6.
55. *Advocate* (1844), p. 70. Female Department of the New York Prison Association, Fifth Annual Report (1850), p. 6. *Advocate* (1843), p. 69. Female Department of the New York Prison Association, Second Annual Report (1846), p. 129.
56. Female Department of the New York Prison Association, Seventh Annual Report (1852), p. 4.
57. Kirkland, p. 51. Female Department of the New York Prison Association, Seventh Annual Report (1852), p. 4.

CHAPTER 10

1. Riverdale Children's Association (formerly Association for the Benefit of the Colored Orphan), 1836–1956: 120th Anniversary (New York), pp. 1–2. Association for the Benefit of the Colored Orphan, Eighteenth Annual Report (1854), p. 11. Cammann and Camp, pp. 295–391.
2. Association for the Benefit of the Colored Orphan, Fifth Avenue Report (1841), p. 6; Cammann & Camp, p. 395
3. William P. Letchworth, *Homes of Homeless Children: A Report on Orphan Asylums and Other Institutions for the Care of Children,* Transmitted to the Legislature with the Annual Report of the Board of the New York State Board of Charity, January 14, 1876, pp. 328, 325. Cammann and Camp, p. 273. Orphan's Home and Asylum of the Protestant Episcopal Church, First Annual Report (1851), p. 1; Third Annual Report (1854), p. 6. See, for example, orphanages listed in Letchworth.
4. Cammann and Camp, pp. 503; 241.
5. Cammann and Camp, pp. 377, 525. Graham Home for Old Ladies, Brooklyn (Brooklyn's Home for the Relief of Respectable, Aged, Indigent Females), Second Annual Report (1852), pp. 1–10. St. Luke's Home for Indigent Christian Females, First Annual Report (1852), pp. 1–8.
6. Cammann and Camp, p. 303. Bremer, 2: 601.

7. An Act to Incorporate the New York Ladies' Home Missionary Society of the Methodist Episcopal Church (New York, 1856). Cammann and Camp, p. 351. *The Old Brewery and the New Mission House at the Five Points* (New York, 1854).
8. Letchworth, p. 302. *Old Brewery,* pp. 161; 192, 170–72.
9. *Old Brewery,* pp. 50; 300.
10. Quoted in *Old Brewery,* p. 64.
11. New York Female Assistance Society, Twenty-third Annual Report (1836/37), p. 9. SRPW, Annual Report (1844), p. 6.
12. SRPW, Annual Report (1854), p. 4. Seamen's Aid Society, Fourth Annual Report (1837), p. 5.
13. Seamen's Aid Society, Fourth Annual Report (1837), pp. 17–18.
14. Ibid.
15. Ibid., p. 19 (emphasis added).
16. *Ladies' Depository,* Twenty-Second Annual Report (1855), p. 6. H. Brown, *Golden Jubilee,* p. 22. Report of the House of Industry and Home for the Friendless, presented May 1948 (New York), p. 1. *Advocate* (1846), p. 70. Northrup, p. 30.
17. Report of the House of Industry, p. 1. Northrup, p. 30.
18. Bennett, *Woman's Work,* pp. 77; 153. H. Brown, *Golden Jubilee,* p. 68.
19. Bennett, *Woman's Work. Advocate* (1842), p. 8. Sedgwick, *Life and Letters,* p. 322.
20. Mariners' Family Industrial Society of the Port of New York, Fourteenth Annual Report (1858), p. 4. Woman's Benevolent Society of the Calvary Church, Annual Report (1850/51), pp. 10–15. New York House and School of Industry, Thirteenth Annual Report (1864), p. 6. Ladies' Helping Hand Association, N.Y., Fourth Annual Report (1869), p. 8. Working Women's Protective Union, Fifth Annual Report (1868), p. 16. Alice Henry, *Women and the Labor Movement* (New York: Arno Press and the New York Times, 1971), p. 48.
21. H. Brown, *Golden Jubilee,* p. 42. Eventually industrial schools were founded also for boys.
22. For description of industrial schools throughout New York State see Letchworth, pp. 350–425. German Industrial School, Annual Report (1855), p. 22. Letchworth, p. 379. Wilson Industrial School for Girls, Fourth Annual Report (1857), pp. 4–6; Seventh Annual Report (1860), p. 2.
23. Wilson Industrial School for Girls, Fourth Annual Report (1857), p. 2.
24. Brooklyn Industrial School Association and Home for Destitute Children, An Outline History (1898), pp. 1–10. Cammann and Camp, p. 562.
25. *Advocate* (1854), p. 40. For an earlier attempt at day care, see Society for the Relief of Half Orphan and Destitute Children, Seventh Annual Report (1842), pp. 4–5; Letchworth, p. 354.
26. Nursery for the Children of Poor Women, Act of Incorporation (New York: 1854).
27. Nursery and Children's Hospital, Twenty-second Annual Report (1876), p. 8; Fourth Annual Report (1858).
28. Woman's Hospital Association, First Anniversary Meeting (1856), p. 15. Woman's Hospital Association, Annual Report (1856), p. 20. Thomas Addis Emmet, M.D.,

Reminiscences of the Founders of the Woman's Hospital Association (New York, 1899), p. 6.

29. Woman's Hospital Association, Annual Report (1856), p. 21. Elizabeth Blackwell, *Pioneer Work in Opening the Medical Profession to Women* (New York, 1895), p. 162. Emmet, p. 3. Woman's Hospital Association, Annual Report (1856), p. 21. Emmet, p. 10.
30. *Woman's Hospital Association, First Anniversary Meeting* (1856), p. 15.
31. Cammann and Camp, p. 80.
32. Blackwell, p. 158. New York Infirmary for Women and Children, Act of Incorporation, reprinted in Cammann and Camp, p. 79. New York Infirmary, Sixty-fifth Annual Report (1920), p. 5. New York Dispensary for Poor Women and Children, First Annual Report (1855), reprinted in Blackwell, p. 234. New York Infirmary, Fifth Annual Report (1858), p. 6.
33. Dispensary for Poor Women, First Annual Report (1855), p. 234. New York Infirmary, Fifth Annual Report (1858), p. 6.
34. New York Infirmary Sixth Annual Report (1859), p. 6, Blackwell, p. 183. New York Dispensary, First Annual Report (1855), p. 234.
35. New York Infirmary, Annual Report (1859), p. 9, Blackwell, p. 162.
36. New York Infirmary, Sixth Annual Report (1859), p. 9.
37. A Brief History of the Woman's Medical College of the New York Infirmary for Women and Children (n.d.), p. 1. New York Medical College and Hospital for Women, Second Annual Announcement and Constitution (New York, 1864), p. 9.
38. New York Infirmary, Seventh Annual Report (1860), p. 6. James, 1: 164. See list of graduates in Woman's Medical College of New York Infirmary, Annual Catalogue and Announcement, S. Angel (1872), p. 12.
39. New York Infirmary, Fourth Annual Report (1857), pp. 8–9.

CHAPTER 11

1. *Advocate* (1857), p. 4.
2. Ibid. (1854), p. 33.
3. Ibid. (1858), p. 207; (1855), p. 166; (1856), p. 124.
4. Ibid. (1857), p. 180 (emphasis added).
5. *Ladies' Wreath* (1846), p. 186. Eliza Farnham, *Woman and Her Era* (New York: A. J. Davis Co., 1864), 2: 288 (emphasis added).
6. *Advocate* (1854), p. 34. Melva, p. 189.
7. *Advocate* (1854), p. 130. *Ladies' Wreath* (1847), p. 105. Catharine Sedgwick, *The Linwoods* (New York: Harper & Bros., 1835), 2: 285. Idem, *Married*, preface (emphasis added).
8. *Advocate* (1858), p. 155; (1854), p. 186; (1858), p. 207. Sedgwick, *Live and Let Live*, p. 182. *Ladies' Wreath* (1846), p. 232. *Golden Keepsake* (1851), p. 230.
9. *Advocate* (1854), p. 33; (1855), p. 93; (1852), p. 3.
10. Ibid. (1852), p. 3; (1851), p. 3.
11. Ibid. (1851), p. 23. Also see ibid (1854), p. 33.
12. Swisshelm, *Letters to Country Girls*, pp. 47, 54, 73–75. Also see Arthur J. Lar-

sen, ed., *Crusader and Feminist: Letters of Jane Grey Swisshelm 1858–1864* (Saint Paul: Minnesota Historical Society, 1934).

13. Farnham, *Woman*, 2: 350–51 (emphasis added).
14. *Advocate* (1854), p. 127; (1851), p. 77; (1856), p. 57. *Ladies' Wreath*, p. 233. Melva, pp. 14, 216; 167.
15. Kraditor, *Up from the Pedestal*, p. 14. *Ladies' Wreath* (1846), pp. 106; 108.
16. *Ladies' Wreath* (1846), p. 105. Also see *Golden Keepsake* (1851), p. 73.
17. *Ladies' Wreath* (1846), p. 19–22.
18. *Golden Keepsake* (1851), pp. 73; 24. *Ladies' Wreath* (1846), p. 22.
19. *Advocate* (1857), p. 53.
20. *Advocate* (1855), p. 37.
21. Ibid. (1854), p. 45; (1852), p. 77. Also see *Advocate* (1852), p. 66; (1855), p. 8; (1854), p. 33; (1852), pp. 135, 149.
22. Swisshelm, *Letters to Country Girls*, p. 75.
23. Caroline M. Kirkland, *A Book for the Home Circle* (New York: Charles Scribner, 1853), pp. 76–81.
24. *Advocate* (1854), p. 34; (1858), p. 103.
25. Ibid. (1858), p. 102.
26. Ibid. (1855), pp. 59; 186.
27. Ibid. (1857), p. 4; (1857), p. 4.
28. Ibid. (1855), p. 169; (1851), p. 23; (1857), p. 4.
29. Swisshelm, *Letters to Country Girls*, p. 81.
30. *Advocate* (1857), p. 63; (1856), pp. 131; 130; (1851), p. 186.
31. Ibid. (1859), p. 264; (1850), p. 2.
32. *Ladies' Wreath* (1858), p. 81. *Advocate* (1857), p. 217.
33. This demand that history be revised to reflect woman's attainments has only recently been revived by contemporary feminists. Farnham, *Woman*, 2: 320.
34. *Ladies' Wreath* (1846), p. 8.
35. *Golden Keepsake* (1851), p. 83. *Ladies' Wreath* (1846), p. 83.
36. *Advocate* (1860), p. 6; (1858), p. 218.
37. Ibid. (1858), p. 218; (1852), p. 26.
38. Ibid. (1852), pp. 24–27.
39. Ibid.
40. Ibid. (emphasis added to #6). *Ladies' Wreath* (1846), p. 28. *Golden Keepsake* (1851), p. 2.
41. *Advocate* (1854), p. 45; (1855), p. 69. Ibid (1852), pp. 62–63; 117; Also see: *Advocate* (1859), p. 143; (1860), p. 126.
42. Ibid. (1858), p. 102.
43. Farnham, *Woman*, 2: 322.

SUMMARY

1. *Advocate* (1860), p. 70.

Bibliography

Primary Sources

MONOGRAPHS

Allestree, Richard. *The Ladies' Calling*. Oxford, 1677.

———. *Some Reflections on Marriage*. 4th ed. London, 1730.

Beecher, Catharine. *Duty of American Women to their Country*. New York: Harper & Bros., 1845.

———. *Essay on Slavery and Abolitionism—with Reference to the Duty of American Females*. Philadelphia: Henry Perkins, 1837.

———. *The Evils Suffered by American Women and American Children*. New York: Harper & Bros., 1846.

———. *Letters to the People on Health and Happiness*. New York, 1855.

Birney, Catherine. *The Grimké Sisters: Sarah and Angelina Grimké: The first American Women Advocates of Abolition and Woman's Rights*. Boston: Lee & Shepard, 1885.

Bushnell, Horace. *The American National Preacher*. 1840.

———. *Women's Suffrage: The Reform Against Nature*. New York: C. Scribner & Co., 1869.

Carey, Matthew. *Appeal to the Wealthy of the Land Ladies as well as Gentlemen on the Character, Conduct, Situation and Prospects of Those whose sole Dependence for Subsistence is on the Labour of their hands*. Philadelphia: 1833.

———. *Miscellaneous Essays*. Philadelphia: Carey & Hart, 1838.

Child, F. M. *The History of Condition of Women in various Ages and Nations*. 2 vols. New York: C. S. Francis & Co., 1849.

Child, Lydia M. *Isaac T. Hopper*. Boston: John P. Jewett & Co., 1853.

Craik, Dinah Maria. *A Woman's Thoughts About Women*. Columbus, Ohio: Follett, Foster & Co., 1858.

Dall, Caroline. *College, Market and Court or Woman's Relation to Education*. Boston, 1867.

[Defoe, Daniel]. *The Earlier Life and the Chief Earlier Works of Daniel Defoe*. Edited by Henry Morley, London, 1899.

Dewes, William P. *A Treatise on the Diseases of Females*. Philadelphia, 1843.

Dirix, M. E. *Woman's Complete Guide to Health*. New York, 1869.

Dixon, Edward. *Woman and Her Diseases from Cradle to Grave*. New York, 1857.

Farnham, Eliza W. *Woman and Her Era*. 2 vols. New York: A. J. Davis & Co., 1864.

Fuller, Margaret. *Woman in the Nineteenth Century*. Boston: John P. Jewett & Co., 1855.

Gregory, Samuel. *Facts and Important Information for Young Women on the Subject of Masturbation*. Boston, 1857.

Howard, H. R. *The Lives of Helen Jewett and Richard P. Robinson*. By the Editor of the New York National Police Gazette. New York, n.d.

Mather, Cotton. *Ornaments for the Daughters of Zion or the Character and Happiness of a Virtuous Woman*. Cambridge, Mass., 1691.

McDowall, J. R. *Charges Preferred Against the N.-Y. F.B.S. and the Auditing Committee in 1835 and 1836*. New York, 1836.

———. *Magdalen Facts*. New York, 1832.

———. *McDowall's Defence*. New York, 1836.

McIntosh, Maria. *Woman in America Her work and Her Reward*. New York: D. Appleton and Co., 1850.

Memoir and Select Remains of the Late Rev. John R. McDowall. The martyr of the Seventh Commandment in the Nineteenth Century. New York: Leavitt Lord & Co., 1838.

Mott, Lucretia. *Discourse on Woman*. Philadelphia: T. B. Peterson, 1850.

Owen, Robert Dale. *Situations*. New York, 1830.

Penny, Virginia. *Employments of Women*. Boston: Walker, Wise & Co., 1863.

Rousseau, Jean Jacques. *Emilius and Sophia: Or, A New System of Education*. Translated by A Citizen of Geneva. London, 1783.

Sanger, William. *History of Prostitution—Its Extent, Causes and Effects*

Throughout the World. Being an official report to the Board of Almshouse Governors of the City of New York. New York: Harper & Bros., 1858.

Stanton, Elizabeth Cady; Anthony, Susan B.; and Gage, Matilda Joslyn, eds. *History of Woman Suffrage.* Vol. 1, *1848–1861*. Rochester, N.Y.: Charles Munn, 1889.

Wardlaw, Ralph, Rev. *Lectures on Magdalenism.* New York: J. S. Redfield, Clinton Hall, 1843.

Wollaston, William. *The Religion of Nature Delineated.* London, 1726.

Wollstonecraft, Mary. *A Vindication of the Rights of Woman.* New York: W. W. Norton & Co., 1967.

Woodward, Samuel Bayard. *Hints for the Young, In Relation to the Health of Body and Mind.* Boston, 1856.

PERIODICALS, GIFT BOOKS, AND LITERARY ANNUALS

Advocate of Moral Reform. 1835–60. Renamed *Advocate and Family Guardian*, 1847.

Affection's Gift: Or a Holiday Present. New York: J. C. Riker, 1832.

The Album of Love. New York: Leavitt & Allin, 1853.

The Amaranth: Or Token of Remembrance. Boston, 1847, 1848, 1854.

American Juvenile Keepsake. New York, 1834–1839.

American Keepsake. New York, 1851.

American Literary Emporium or Friendship's Gift. New York: C. H. Camp, 1848.

The Amethyst. Baltimore: N. C. Brooks, 1831.

The Amulet. Boston, 1846.

Atlantic Souvenir Christmas and New Year's Offering. Philadelphia: H. C. Carey & I. Lea, 1826–29.

Baltimore Book. Baltimore, 1839.

A Book for the Home Circle. New York: Charles Scribner, 1853.

Book of the Months: A Gift for the Young. Boston: William Crosby & Co., 1839.

Boston Book: Being Specimens of Metropolitan Literature Occasional and Periodical. Boston: Light & Horton, 1836, 1837.

Boudoir Annual. Boston: Phillips and Sampson, 1846.

The Casket or, Flowers of Literature, Wit and Sentiment. Boston, 1824, 1829.

The Christian Offering or Churchman's Annual. New York: Sherman & Trevett, Protestant Episcopal Press, 1839.

Christian Wreath, Religion, Morality, Literature. Philadelphia, 1847.

Christmas Blossoms, and New Year's Wreath. Boston: Philips & Sampson, 1847, 1849.

The Coral: A Gift for all Seasons. New York: Cornish Lamport & Co., 1838; 184?

The Dahlia: Or Memorial of Affection. New York: James P. Geffing, 1842.

Daughter's own Book: Or Practical Hints from a Father to his daughter. Boston: Lilly, Wait, Colman & Holden, 1833.

The Evergreen: Or Gems of Literature for 1850. New York: J. C. Burdick, 1850.

Family Circle and Parlor Annual. New York: Daniel Newell, 1840, 1841, 1842.

Flora's Gem: Or the Bouquet for all Seasons. New York, 1846.

Forget-me-not. New York: Nafis & Cornish, 1846, 1848–50.

Forget me not. Philadelphia, 1826, 1828.

The Fountain. Philadelphia, 1847.

The Garland. New York: Josiah Drake, 1830.

Gem of the Season. New York: Leavitt, Trow & Co., 1846.

The Gift: A Christmas and New Year's Present. Philadelphia: E. L. Carey & A. Hart, 1836, 1839, 1840, 1847.

Gift of Friendship: A Token of Remembrance for 1847. Philadelphia, 1847.

Gift of Sentiment. New York: 1853.

Godey's Lady's Book. 1840–70.

Golden Keepsake: Or Ladies' Wreath, a Gift for all seasons. New York: J. M. Fletcher & Co., 1851–53.

Hyacinth. New York, 1831.

The Iris or Annual Visitor for 1844. New York: Robert P. Bixby & Co., 1844.

The Jewel: Or Token of Friendship. New York: Bancroft & Holley, 1837.

The Keepsake: A Christmas, New Years, and Birthday Present for 1845. New York: D. Appleton & Co., 1845.

Lady's Cabinet Album. New York: Peabody & Co., 1834, 1835, 1839, 1846.

Ladies' Casket: A Gift of Friendship for the Young. New York, 1848.

Ladies' Companion: A Monthly Magazine of Literature and the Arts. New York, 1836–38.

The Ladies' Garland: Devoted to Literature, Amusement and Instruction. Philadelphia, 1837–39, 1841, 1848–49.

Ladies' Indispensable Assistant, being a companion for the Sister, Mother & Wife. New York: F. J. Dow & Co., 1850.

Ladies' Literary Cabinet. New York: Broderick & Retter, 1819–22.

Ladies' Magazine. 1828–32.

The Ladies' Pearl and Literary Gleaner. 1840–42.

Ladies' Repository and Gatherings of the West. Cincinnati, 1842, 1843.

Ladies' Scrap Book. Hartford, 1820, 1845.

Ladies' Wreath. 1846–58.

Liberty Bell. By Friends of Freedom. Boston, 1839.

McDowall's Journal. 2 vols. 1834.

The Panoplist. Vol. 12. 1816.

Remember Me: A Religious and Literary Miscellany, Intended as a Christmas and New Year's Present. Philadelphia, 1829.

The Rose: Or Affection's Gift. New York: D. Appleton & Co., 1842–45.

The Spectator. In 12 vols. Philadelphia: James Crissy, 1838.

The Tatler. Complete in 1 vol. Philadelphia: J. J. Woodward, 1831.

The Water-Cure Journal. 1845–48.

TRAVELERS' ACCOUNTS, GUIDEBOOKS

Beardsley, Levi. *Reminiscences*. New York, 1852.

Bernard, John. *Retrospections of America 1797–1811*. Edited by Mrs. Bayle Bernard. New York, 1887.

Bobo, William N. *Glimpses of New York by a South Carolinian (who had nothing else to do)*. Charleston, 1852.

Bremer, Fredrika. *The Homes of the New World: Impressions of America*. Translated by Mary Howitt. 2 vols. New York, 1853.

Cavely, Elizabeth H., ed. *The American Diaries of Richard Cobden*. Princeton: Princeton Univ. Press, 1952.

Christian, Charles. *A Brief Treatise on the Police of the City of New York*. New York, 1812.

Cooper, James Fenimore. *America and the Americans*. London, 1836.

Crèvecoeur, Michel-Guillaume Jean de. *Letters from an American Farmer*. Philadelphia, 1793.

Dickens, Charles. *American Notes for General Circulation*. London, 1892.

Dwight, Timothy. *Things As They Are: Or Notes of a Traveller through Some of the Middle Northern States*. New York, 1834.

Grund, Francis J. *The Americans in their Social, Moral and Political Relations*. 2 vols. London: R. Bentley, 1837.

———. *Aristocracy in America*. 2 vols. London, 1839.

Gurowski, Adam G. de. *America and Europe*. New York, 1857.

Hamilton, Thomas. *Men and Manners in America*. London, 1833.

Hardie, James. *Description of New York*. New York, 1827.

Kemble, Frances A. *Journal*. 2 vols. Philadelphia, 1835.

Lambert, John. *Travels through Canada, and the United States of North America in the Years 1806, 1807 and 1808*. London, 1814.

Mackay, Alexander. *The Western World.* Vol. 1. London, 1850.

Martineau, Harriet. *Society in America.* 2 vols. Paris, 1842.

Miller's New York as it is: Or Stranger's Guide-Book to the Cities of New York, Brooklyn and Adjacent places. New York: J. Miller, 1866.

Nichols, Thomas L. *Forty Years of American Life 1821–1861.* New York, 1937.

Royall, Anne. *Sketches of Life, History and Manners in the United States.* New Haven, 1826.

Sanitary Condition of the City: Report of the Council of Hygiene and Public Health of the Citizens Association of New York. New York: Arno Press and the New York Times, 1970.

Tocqueville, Alexis de. *Democracy in America.* Edited by Philip Bradley. New York, 1945.

Wyse, Frances. *America: Its Realities and Resources.* London, 1846.

SERMONS

Abbot, Abiel, A.M. A Discourse Delivered Before the Members of the Portsmouth Female Asylum on The Lord's Day, Aug. 9, 1807.

Aiden, Timothy. A Discourse Delivered before the Members of the Portsmouth Female Asylum. 1804.

Bentley, William. A Discourse delivered in the East Meeting-House in Salem, Sept. 2, 1807 at the Annual Meeting of the Salem Female Charitable Society.

Colman, Benjamin. Reliquiae Turellae, et Lachrymae Paternae. Boston, 1735.

Edwards, Justin. Joy in Heaven over the Penitent—a Sermon—Delivered in Park Street Church—Before the Penitent Females' Refuge Society—Dec. 18, 1825—by Justin Edwards—Pastor of the South Church in Andover. Andover, 1826.

Jay, William. *A Letter to the Right Reverend Bishop Hobart Occasioned by The Strictures on Bible Societies Contained in his late Charge to The Convention of N.Y.* New York: John P. Haven, 1823.

———. *A Letter to the Right Rev. Bishop Hobart in Reply to the Pamphlet Addressed By Him to the Author, under the signature of corrector.* New York: John P. Haven, 1823.

———. *A Reply to a letter addressed to the Right Rev. Bishop Hobart.* By William Jay in a Letter to that gentleman. New York: T. & J. Swords, 1823.

———. *A Reply to a Letter to The Right Rev. Bishop Hobart occasioned by the Strictures on Bible Societies, contained in his late address to the Convention of N-Y.* New York: T. & J. Swords, 1823.

Lathrop, John, D.D. A Discourse delivered before the Members of the Boston Female Asylum Sept. 21, 1804 Being their Fourth Anniversary.

Miller, Samuel. A Sermon preached March 13, 1808 for the Benefit of the City of New York for the Relief of Poor Widows with Small Children.

Milnor, James. The Widow & Her Mites: A Sermon, preached in St. George's Church, in the City of N-Y on Sunday Evening, the 7th of Nov. 1819. By the Rev. James Milnor, D.D. For the Benefit of the N.Y.C. Dispensary 1819.

Morse, Jedidiah. A Sermon Preached in Brattle-Street Church, Boston. Sept. 25, 1807. Before the Managers of the Boston Female Asylum, on their Seventh Anniversary.

Nott, Elephalet. A Discourse delivered in the Presbyterian Church in the city of Albany before the Ladies' Society for the Relief of Distressed Women & children. March 18, 1804.

Onderdonk, Benjamin T. A Plea for the Religious Charity Schools. A Sermon, preached in Trinity Church, and St. Paul's and St. John's Chapels N.Y. for the Benefit of the N.Y. Episcopal Charity School. 1825.

Parish, Elijah. A Sermon preached before the members of the Female Charitable Society of Newburyport. 1808.

A Pastoral Address to Young Women, by the Rector of St. Timothy's Church Philadelphia. 1843.

Peabody, Andrew. A Sermon preached Before the Society for the Relief of Aged Females at Newburyport, Mass. 1840.

Perrine, Matthew La Rue. Women Have a Work to do in the House of God. New York, 1817.

Prince, Rev. John. A Discourse Delivered Before the Salem Female Charitable Society. Sept. 17, 1806.

Prince, Thomas. A Sermon Occasioned by the Death of Mrs. Deborah Prince. Boston, 1744.

"She Hath Done What She Could," or The Duty & Responsibility of Woman. A Sermon, preached in the Chapel of St. Mary's School, By the Rector, and printed for the pupils. Raleigh, 1847.

Spring, Gardiner. *The Excellence and Influence of the Female Character.* A Sermon, preached in the Presbyterian Church in Murray-Street at the Request of the N-Y Female Missionary Society. New York: F. & R. Lockwood, 1825.

———. A Sermon Preached April 21, 1811 for the Benefit of a Society of Ladies Instituted for the Relief of Poor Widows with Small Children. New York.

Stafford, W. A New Missionary Field. A Report to the Female Missionary Society for the Poor of the City of N-Y. March, 1817.

Stearns, J. F. Female Influence and the True Christian Mode of its Exercise. A Discourse delivered in the First Presbyterian Church in Newburyport. July 30, 1837.

Stuart, Moses. Sermon Delivered by Request of the Female Charitable Society. In Salem at the Anniversary (1815).

Sunderland, Rev. Byron. *Discourse to Young Ladies.* Delivered the 22 day of Jan. 1857. Washington: Cornelius Wendall, 1857.

Thompson, James W. Sermon. Delivered by the Request of the Female Charitable Society in Salem. 1832.

Tuttle, Isaac Henry. The Church's Ministrative Care. A Sermon preached in St. Luke's Church, N.Y.C. St. Luke's Day, 1851 in Behalf of The Object then proposed and commenced, viz. St. Luke's Home for Destitute Christian Females.

Williams, S. P. Plea for the Orphan Delivered on the Anniversary of the Female Charitable Society of Newburyport, May 21, 1822.

Winslow, Rev. Hubbard. *A Discourse delivered in The Bowdoin Street Church July 9, 1837.* Boston: Weeks, Jordan & Co., 1837.

Worcester, Samuel. A Discourse Delivered in the Tabernacle in Salem Before the Salem Female Charitable Society at their Annual meeting Sept. 27, 1809.

Yates, Andrew. "Charity the Evidence of Piety." A Sermon Delivered in the North Presbyterian Church in Hartford. Sept. 13, 1812 at the request of the Female Beneficent Society.

POPULAR SONGS

The Basket or Musical Pocket Companion: A Collection of the most popular songs, duets, marches, dances, etc. New York: James F. Hewitt, 1832.

Boston Musical Miscellany. Boston: J. T. Buckingham, 1811.

Fatout, Paul. "The Melodies of the Ladies' Books." *Musical Quarterly* 31 (Oct. 1945): 464–77.

Greville, Vernon, comp. *Yankee Doodle-Do: A Collection of Songs of the Early American Stage.* New York: Payson and Clarke, 1927.

Howard, John T., ed. *A Program of Early and Mid-Nineteenth Century American Songs.* New York: J. Fischer & Bros., 1931.

Knowlton, Fanny Snow, ed. *Songs of Other Days.* Boston: Oliver Ditson Co., 1922.

Levy, Lester. *Grace Notes in American History: Popular Sheet Music from 1820–1900.* Oklahoma: Oklahoma University Press, 1967.

Luther, Frank. *Americans and Their Songs.* New York: Harper & Bros., 1942.

Musical Bouquet: An Institute Choir for the School Room and Social Circle. New York: Ivison and Phinney, 1856.

Musical Carcanet: A Choice Collection of the Most Admired Popular Songs. New York: Collins & Hannay, 1832.

Spaeth, Sigmund. *Read 'Em and Weep.* New York: Arco Publishing Co., 1959.

———. *Weep Some More, My Lady.* New York: Doubleday, Page & Co., 1927.

The Washingtonian Harp: a Collection of Original Songs. New York: Saxton and Miles, 1843.

BOOKS OF INSTRUCTION

Abell, Mrs. F. G. *Woman in Her Various Relations; containing Practical Rules for American Females.* New York: Holdridge, 1851.

Alcott, William A. *Letters to a Sister: Or Woman's Mission.* Buffalo: George H. Derby & Co., 1850.

Benedict, S. W. *Woman, She Was, Is and Should Be.* New York, 1849.

Branagan, Thomas. *The Excellency of the Female Character Vindicated: Being an investigation Relative to the Cause and Effects of The Encroachments of Men Upon the Rights of Women.* Philadelphia: J. Rakestraw, 1808.

Burnap, George. *The Sphere and Duties of Woman: A Course of Lectures.* Philadelphia: John Murray, 1848.

Butler, Charles. *The American Lady.* Philadelphia: Hogan & Thompson, 1836.

Cary, Mrs. Virginia. *Letters on Female Character, addressed to a Young Lady on the death of her mother.* Richmond, Va., 1828.

Chapin, E. H. *Duties of Young Women.* Boston: Putnam & Brothers, 1856.

Chittenden, Nathaniel W. *Influence of Woman Upon the Destinies of a People: Being an oration of Salutatory Addresses—delivered at the annual Commencement of Columbia College.* Oct. 3, 1837. New York, 1837.

Cobbold, Rev. Richard. A. M. *A Character of Woman, in a Lecture delivered at the Hanover Square Rooms.* April 13, 1848 for the Benefit of the Governesses Benevolent Institution. London, 1848.

Daughter's own Book: Or Practical Hints from a Father to his Daughter. Boston: Lilly, Wait, Colman, and Holden, 1833.

Dodsley, Robert. *The Whole Duty of Woman.* Philadelphia: Edward Earles, 1817.

Eddy, Daniel Clark. *A Young Woman's friend.* Boston: Wentworth & Co., 1857.

Gilman, Chandler, M.D. *Introductory Address to the Students in Medicine of the College of Physicians and Surgeons of the University of the State of New York.* New York, 1840.

Gregory, Dr. John. *A Father's Legacy to His Daughter.* London, 1788.

Eliot, William, Jr. *Lectures of Young Women.* Boston, 1853.

The Female Monitor: Or, The Whole Duty of Woman. By a Lady, Revised, Corrected, and Improved. 2d ed. New York, n.d.

Fénelon, François de. *L'Education des Filles.* Translated by Kate Lupton. Boston, 1891.

Hawes, Joel, D.D. *A Looking-glass for Ladies.* An Address delivered at the Eighth Anniversary of the Mount Holyoke Female Seminary. Boston: Wm. D. Ticknor & Co., 1845.

Hints and Sketches, by an American Mother. New York: John S. Taylor, 1839.

Hitchcock, Enos. *Memoirs of the Bloomsgrove Family . . . containing Sentiments on a Mode of Domestic Education, Suited to . . . the United States.* 2 vols. Boston, 1790.

Holland, Josiah Gilbert. *Letters to the Jones.* New York: Charles Scribner, 1863.

Hopkins, Jesse. *The Patriot's Manual.* New York: William Williams, 1828.

Meigs, Charles, M.D. *Lectures on Some of the Distinctive Characteristics of the Female delivered before the Class of the Jefferson Medical College.* January 5, 1847. Philadelphia, 1847.

Mitchell, Donald Grant ["Ik Marvel"]. *Reveries of a Bachelor: Or a Book of the Heart.* New York, 1850.

Palmer, Ray, D.D. *An Address on the Education of Woman. Delivered at the Anniversary of the Pittsfield Young Ladies' Institute.* Albany: Gray, Sprague & Co., 1852.

Peck, Jesse T. *The True Woman: Or, Life and Happiness at Home and Abroad.* New York: Carlton & Porter, 1857.

Rush, Benjamin. *Thoughts Upon Female Education.* Philadelphia, 1789.

Sandford, Elizabeth. *Woman in her Social and Domestic Character.* Boston: Otis, Broaders & Co., 1842.

Segur, J. A. *Influence, Rights and Appeal of Women.* Albany, 1842.

Swisshelm, Jane G. *Letters to Country Girls.* New York: J. C. Riker, 1853.

Todd, Rev. John. *The Moral Influence, Dangers, and Duties, Connected with Great Cities.* Northampton, Mass., 1841.

Wallis, S. Teackel. *Leisure: Its Moral and Political Economy.* Baltimore, 1839.

West, Mrs. Jane. *Letters to a Young Lady in which the Duties and Characteristics of Women are Considered: Chiefly with a Reference to Prevailing Opinions.* New York, 1806.

Woman's Worth or, Hints to Raise the Female Character. New York: D. Appleton & Co., 1848.

The World Enlightened, Improved and Harmonized by Woman! A Lecture delivered in the city of New York before the Young Ladies' Society for Mutual Improvement, by a Lady of Philadelphia. Philadelphia: John H. Gihon & Co., 1840.

Young, Hon. Samuel. *Suggestions on the Best Mode of Promoting Civilization and Improvement: Or The Influence of Woman on the Social Shade.* A Lecture delivered before the Young Men's Association for Mutual Improvement in the City of Albany. January 24, 1837. Albany, 1837.

SCHOOLBOOKS

Alden, Abner. *An Introduction to Spelling and Reading in Two Volumes.* Boston: Ezra Lincoln, 1819.

———. *The Reader.* 4th ed. Boston: Thomas & Andrew, 1814.

———. *The Speaker.* 3 vols. Boston: Thomas & Andrew, 1810.

Alexander, Caleb. *The Young Gentlemen and Ladies' Instructure.* Boston: E. Larkin & W. P. L. Blake, 1797.

Bentley, Rensselaer. *The American Instructor.* Hudson, N.Y., 1824.

Bingham, Caleb. *The Columbian Orator.* 8th ed. Boston: Manning & Loring, 1807.

The Child's Spelling Book. Connecticut: John Babcock, 1798.

Elson, Ruth Miller. *Guardians of Tradition: American Schoolbooks of the Nineteenth Century.* Nebraska: University of Nebraska Press, 1964.

Miscellanies, Moral and Instructive in Prose and Verse. Philadelphia: Joseph James, 1787.

The New Pleasing Instructure: Or, Young Lady's Guide to Virtue and Happiness. Boston: Thomas & Andrews, 1799.

Pierce, Charles. *The Portsmouth Miscellany: Or, Lady's Library of Improvement.* Portsmouth, N.H., 1804.

Putnam, Samuel. *Introduction to the Analytical Reader.* Vol. 1. 2d ed. Boston: Perkins and Marvin, 1830.

Richardson, Joseph. *The American Reader.* 2d ed. Boston: Lincoln & Edmonds, 1813.

Webster, Noah. *An American Selection of Lessons in Reading and Speaking.* Connecticut: Hudson and Goodwin, 1789.

REPORTS OF URBAN FEMALE VOLUNTARY ASSOCIATIONS

An Account of the Boston Female Asylum, With the Act of Incorporation. 1833.

An Account of the Rise and Progress and Present State of the Boston Female Asylum together with the Act of Incorporation also, the Bye-laws and Rules and Regulations adopted by the Board of Managers. 1810.

American Female Guardian Society and Home. Annual Report, no. 25 (for the year ending May 1859).

American Female Guardian Society and Home for the Friendless. Annual Reports, nos. 13–22, 26 (1846/47–1855/56, 1859/1860).

American Moral Reform Society. Annual report presented by the executive committee, no. 3 (1837/38).

American Tract Society. Principles & Facts. New York, 1854.

——— Proceedings of a Public deliberative Meeting of the American Tract Society held in the Broadway Tabernacles, New York, Oct. 25, 26, 27, 1842.

Andrews, Charles. *History of the New York African Free School.* New York, 1830.

Appeal to the public in behalf of The Penitent Females Refuge in the City of Boston. 1839.

Association for the Benefit of the Colored Orphan. Annual Reports, nos. 5–27 (1841–63).

Association for the Relief of Respectable, Aged, Indigent Females in New York. Annual Reports, 1814–63.

Barnard, W. F. *Forty Years at Five Points.* New York, 1893.

Bennett, Sarah. *Woman's Work Among the Lowly.* Memorial volume of the first forty years of the American Female Guardian Society and Home for the Friendless. New York: AFGS, 1877.

——— *Wrought Gold.* New York: AFGS, 1874.

Bethesda Society of Boston. Annual reports, 1821–94.

Blackwell, Elizabeth. *Pioneer Work in Opening the Medical Profession to Women.* New York, 1895.

Boston Children's Friend Society. Circular, Act of Incorporation. Organized Dec. 1833, Incorporated 1834 Report. 1837.

Boston Female Anti-Slavery Society. Annual reports, 1835, 1837, 1839, 1844.

A Brief History of the Woman's Medical College of the New York Infirmary for Women and Children. New York, N.d.

Brooklyn Female Bible Society. Annual Reports, 1826–28.

Brooklyn Industrial School Association and Home for Destitute Children. An Outline History. 1898.

[Brown, Helen]. American Female Guardian Society. *Our Golden Jubilee: A Retrospect from 1834–1884.* New York, 1884.

Cammann, Henry, and Camp, Hugh. *The Charities of New York, Brooklyn, and Staten Island.* New York: Hurd and Houghton, 1868.

Children's Friend Society, the Industrial School of Albany. Annual Reports, nos. 1–2 (1857–58).

[Dye, Margaret]. *Wrecks and Rescues.* By an Early Member of the Board of Managers of the American Female Guardian Society. New York: AFGS, 1859.

Emmet, Thomas Addis, M.D. *Reminiscences of the Founders of the Woman's Hospital Association.* New York, 1899.

Female Bethel Association of New York. Constitution & By laws. 1836.

Female Bible and Religious Tract Society of Kings County. Constitution and Report and First Annual Report. New York, 1816.

Female Charitable Society of Newburyport. Act of Incorporation. 1808.

Female Missionary Society for the Poor of the City of New York and its Vicinity. Annual Reports, nos. 2, 5 (1818, 1820–21).

Female Samaritan Society of Boston. Annual Report, 1817.

Five Points Mission. Annual Reports, 1851/52–1896/97.

Graham Home for Old Ladies, Brooklyn (Brooklyn's Home for the Relief of Respectable, Aged, Indigent Females). Annual reports, 1852, 1858–60.

Industrial School Association for German Girls. Annual Reports, nos. 3, 10, 13 (1855/56, 1862/63, 1865/68).

Inwood House, New York Female Benevolent Society. Annual Reports, nos. 1–30 (1834–63).

Inwood House, N.Y. *Missionary Labors Through a Series of Years Among Fallen Women*, New York, 1870.

Kirkland, C. M. *The Helping Hand: Comprising an Account of the Home for The Discharged Female Convict and an Appeal in Behalf of that Institution.* New York: Charles Scribner, 1853.

Ladies' Anti-Slavery Society. *Liberty Chimes.* Providence, 1845.

Ladies' Christian Union—New York. Annual Reports, nos. 4–18 (1860/61–75/76).

Ladies' Depository of New York. Annual reports, nos. 22, 30, 36–54 (1855, 1863, 1869–87).

Ladies' Helping Hand Association, N.Y. Annual reports, nos. 4–23 (1869–88).

Letchworth, William P. *Homes of Homeless Children: A Report on Orphan Asylums and Other Institutions for the Care of children. Transmitted to the Legislature with the annual report of the Board of N.Y. State Board of Charity.* January 14, 1876.

Magdalen Society. Constitution & bye-laws. New York, 1812.

Magdalen Society of Philadelphia. Annual Report, 1860.

Mariners' Family Asylum of the Port of New York. Annual Report, no. 14 (1858).

Mariners' Family Industrial Society of the Port of New York. Memorial & Petition. 1854.

——— Report. Dec. 1843.

Mathews, Joanna. *A Short History of the Orphan Asylum Society in the City of New York*. New York: Anson D. F. Randolph and Co., 1893.

Melva [pseud.]. *Home Whispers to Husband and Wives*. New York: American Female Guardian Society, 1859.

New York Dorcas Society. Annual Reports, 1838–40.

New York Female Assistance Society for the Relief and Religious Instruction of the Sick Poor. Annual Reports, 1835–96.

New York Female Auxiliary Bible Society. Annual Reports, 1817/18–60.

New York Female Benevolent Society. Third Annual Report, 1836.

New York Female Bethel Union. Third Annual Report, May 1838.

New York Female Moral Reform Society. Annual Reports, 1840–46.

——— Constitution & Circular. 1834.

New York Female Society for the Aid of Foreign Missions. Constitution. 1814.

New York Female Union Society for Promotion of Sabbath Schools. Annual Reports, 1818–26.

New York House and School of Industry. Annual Reports, nos. 13, 15 (1864, 1866).

New York Infirmary for Women and Children. Annual Reports, 1857–60, 1920.

——— By-laws. 1855.

New York Magdalen Society. Address in Behalf of the New York Magdalen Asylum, 1831.

——— First Annual Report of the Executive Committee. January 1, 1830.

New York Medical College and Hospital for Women. Annual Announcement and Constitution. 1864.

——— Eighth Annual Report: 1870–71.

New York Society for the Relief of the Widows and Orphans of Medical Men. Report. 1849.

New York Women's Bible Society. Annual reports, 1854, 1857, 1860.

[Northrup, Flora]. *The Record of a Century 1834–1934*. New York: AFGS, 1934.

Nursery and Children's Hospital. Annual Reports, nos. 4, 22 (1858, 1876).

Nursery and Child's Hospital of New York. Annual Reports, 1854, 1863/64, 1866.

Nursery for the Children of Poor Women. Act of Incorporation. New York, 1854.

Nursery for the Children of Poor Women in the City of New York. Charter 1854. *Constitution, By-Laws and Regulations.* New York: Billin & Brothers, 1855.

Old Brewery and the New Mission House at the Five Points. By Ladies of the Mission. New York: Stringer & Townsend, 1854.

One Hundred Years of Work with Girls in Boston. Issued by the Boston Society for the Care of Girls, formerly The Boston Female Aslyum. 1919.

Orphan Asylum in the City of New York. Annual Reports, nos. 5–66 (1810–76).

Orphan Asylum in the City of New York: Origin and History 1806–1896. 2 vols. New York: Bonnell, Silver & Co., 1896.

Orphan's Home and Asylum of the Protestant Episcopal Church in New York. Annual Reports, nos. 1–15 (1851–66).

Penitent Females Refuge in the City of Boston. Appeal to the Public. 1839.

Petition of Mrs. Caroline M. Thompson of Mass. to the Honorable Legislature of New York in aid of the Woman's Hospital. Albany, 1857.

Philadelphia Female Anti-Slavery Society. Annual Reports, nos. 4–25 (1837–58).

Phlopedos [pseud.]. *A Few Remarks about Sick Children in New York and the Necessity of a Hospital for them.* New York: William C. Bryant & Co., 1852.

Pierce, Bradford K. *A Half Century with Juvenile Delinquents: Or, The New York House of Refuge and its Times.* New York: D. Appleton & Co., 1869.

Plan of the Society for the Promotion of Industry with the First Annual Report of Managers. New York, 1816.

Prison Association of New York. Annual Reports, nos. 1–4 (1844–47).

Report of the House of Industry and Home for the Friendless. Presented May 1848. New York.

Riverdale Children's Association. 1836–1956: 120th Anniversary. New York.

St. Luke's Home for Indigent Christian Females. Annual Reports, 1852, 1854, 1856–58, 1860.

Seamen's Aid Society. Annual Report of the Managers, nos. 3–9 (1836–42).

"The Social Position and Culture Due to Woman." *Address before the Maternal Association* [of the Amity Street Baptist Church]. New York: John Gray, 1846.

Society for Employing the Poor of Boston. Constitution and By-laws and an extract of the Report of the Managers For the First Three Months. 1820.

Society for the Encouragement of Faithful Domestic Servants in New York. Annual Reports, 1826, 1836.

Society for the Promotion of Industry. Annual Report, 1816.

Society for the Relief of Half Orphan and Destitute Children. Annual reports, nos. 7, 16, 23, 25 (1842, 1852, 1859, 1861).

Society for the Relief of Poor Widows with Small Children. Address of the First Directress. 1811.

———. By-laws and Regulations. New York, 1811–13.

———. Constitution and By-Laws. 1803.

———. Minute Books, 1797–1932.

———. Report of the Board of Directors, April, 1800.

Society of the Reformation of Juvenile Delinquents. Annual Reports of the Managers of the Society in the City of New York, nos. 1–35 (1825–60).

"The Son Unguided, his Mother's Shame," *Address before the Maternal Association* of the Amity-Street Baptist Church. New York: John Gray, 1845.

Wilson Industrial School for Girls. Annual Reports, nos. 4, 6, 7, 9 (1857–1862).

Woman's Benevolent Society of the Calvary Church. Annual Reports, 1850/51, 1852/53.

Woman's Hospital Association. First Annual Report. Presented by the Executive Committee at the Anniversary Meeting, Feb. 9, 1856. New York.

Woman's Medical College. Final Catalogue: 1864–1899. New York, 1899.

Woman's Medical College of the New York Infirmary. Annual Catalogue and Announcement. 1872.

Women's Prison Association and Home. Annual Reports, S. Angel nos. 1–31 (1845–75).

A *Working Woman of Boston*. The Aristocrats and Trade Union Advocate, a colloquial Poem respectfully dedicated to the Members of the Boston Trades Union of Vicinity. Boston: Leonard W. Kimball, 1834.

Working Woman's Protective Union. A report of its Condition and the results secured after 31 years of activity. New York, 1900.

——— Annual reports, nos. 5, 7, 9 (1867, 1869, 1871).

NEWSPAPERS

American Mercury. 1728.

Boston Evening Post. 1759.

Commercial Advertiser. 19 Nov. 1814, 2 Dec. 1814, 19 Jan. 1824, 27 Jan. 1825, 8 Aug. 1836.

New York *Evening Post*. 18 Feb. 1817, 26 Jan. 1825, 2 Oct. 1845.

New York Journal. 1733.

New York *Sun*. 23 Aug. 1845.

PUBLIC DOCUMENTS

The Charter of the City of New York with notes thereon. Also A treatise on the powers and duties of the mayor, aldermen & assistant aldermen. New York: McSpedon & Baker, 1851.

Documents of the Board of Aldermen & Board of Assistants. 1831/32–1833/34.

Hamilton Alexander. *Hamilton's Report on the Subject of Manufactures, Made in his Capacity of Secretary of the Treasury on the 5th of December, 1791*. Philadelphia: W. Brown, 1827.

Laws of the State of New York. 26th sess. 13 Apr. 1803.

Manual of the Corporation of the City of New York 1841/42, 1845/46, 1847/1866.

Minutes of the Common Council of the City of New York: 1781–1831. New York: M. B. Brown Printing & Binding Co., 1917.

New York State. *Assembly Documents.* 1836, 1840–50.

New York State *Assembly Journal.* 1840–48.

New York State: *Senate Documents.* 1830–36, 1840–50.

New York State *Senate Journal.* 1846–48.

Proceedings of the joint meeting of the Boards of Aldermen & Assistant Aldermen. 1831/36–1840/42.

DIARIES, MEMOIRS, LETTERS—MALE

Adams, Charles, ed. *Works of John Adams, Second President of the United States.* Boston, 1850–56.

Edwards, Jonathan. *Works.* New York, 1829.

Franklin, Benjamin. *Reflections on Courtship and Marriage: In Two Letters to a Friend.* Philadelphia, 1750.

Mather, Cotton. "Diary," *Massachusetts Historical Society Collections,* ser. 7, vols. 7–8 (1911–12).

Nevins, Allan (ed.). *The Diary of Philip Hone.* New York, Arno Press Repr 1976.

Pintard, John. "Letters from John Pintard to his Daughter Eliza Noel Pintard Davidson, 1816–1833," *New York Historical Society Collections* 70–83 (1937–40).

Sewall, Samuel. "Letter to John Winthrop in the Winthrop Papers, *Massachusetts History Society Collections,* ser. 6, vol. 6 (5). (Ser. 6 v).

Stiles, Ezra. *The Literary Diary of Ezra Stiles.* Edited by F. B. Dexter. 3 vols. New York, 1901.

[Strong, George T.]. *The Diary of George Templeton Strong.* Edited by Allan Nevins and Milton Halsey Thomas. 2 vols. New York, Octagon 1974.

NOVELS—MALE

Arthur, T. S. *The Lady at Home: Or Happiness in the Household.* Philadelphia: Chestnut Street, 1853.

———. *The Maiden: A Story for My Young Countrywomen.* Philadelphia: Henry F. Anners, 1848.

———. *Married and Single: Or, Marriage and Celibacy Contrasted, in a Series of Domestic Pictures.* New York: Harper & Bros., 1845.

Brown, Charles Brockden. *Alcuin: A Dialogue.* New York: Grossman Publishers, 1971.

Bunyan, John. *The Pilgrim's Progress.* London, 1792.

Burdett, Charles. *Blonde and Brunette or The Gothamate Arcady.* New York: D. Appleton & Co., 1858.

———. *The Elliot Family: Or the Trials of New-York Seamstresses.* New York: Baker & Scribner, 1850.

Cooper, James F. *The Crater; or Vulcan's Peak: A Tale of the Pacific.* New York: Stringer & Townsend, 1855.

———. *The Heidenmauer: Or the Benedictines.* 2 vols. Philadelphia: Carey, Lea & Blanchard, 1836.

———. *The Ways of the Hour.* New York: J. Fagan, 1850.

Curtis, Newton Mallory. *The Matricide's Daughter.* New York, n.d.

———. *The Star of the Fallen.* New York, n.d.

———. *The Victim's Revenge.* New York, n.d.

Halliday, Samuel B. *The Lost and Found or Life Among the Poor.* New York: Blakeman & Mason, 1859.

Hawthorne, Nathaniel. *Works of Nathaniel Hawthorne.* Vols. 5–6. Boston, 1882.

Judson, Edward Zane Carrol [Ned Buntline]. *The G'hals of New York.* New York, n.d.

———. *The Mysteries and Miseries of New York.* New York, 1848.

Lippard, George. *New York: Its Upper Ten and Lower Million.* Cincinnati, 1853.

The Match Girl. Boston: E. O. Libby & Co., 1859.

Mathews, Cornelius. *Chantielier: A Thanksgiving Story of the Peabody Family.* New York: J. S. Redfield, 1850.

Neal, John. *Keep Cool.* 2 vols. Baltimore: Joseph Cushing, 1817.

Paulding, James Kirk. *The Backwoodsman: A Poem.* Philadelphia, 1818.

Poe, Edgar Allan. *The Complete Tales and Poems of Edgar Allan Poe.* New York: Random House, 1938.

Richardson, Samuel. *Pamela: Or Virtue Rewarded.* 4 vols. Stratford-upon-Avon, 1929.

Spiller, Robert E., ed. James Fenimore Cooper *Gleanings in Europe.* New York, 1930.

Watterston, George. *Glencarn or The Disappointments of Youth.* 2 vols. Alexandria, Va., 1810.

Whitman, Walt. *Specimen Days.* New York: New American Library, 1961.

DIARIES, MEMOIRS, LETTERS—FEMALE

Adams, Hannah. *Memoir of Miss Hannah Adams.* Written by herself with additional notices by a friend. Boston: Gray & Bowen, 1832.

Ayer, Sarah. *Diary of Sarah Connell Ayer.* Portland, Maine: Lefavor-Tower Co., 1910.

Beecher, Catharine. 25 letters to Louise Wait, 1819–25. Mss coll., Schlesinger Library.

Bethune, Joanna. *Life of Mrs. Isabella Graham by her daughter.* New York: John S. Taylor, 1839.

Burgess, Hannah Rebecca (Crowell). Diary, 5 Aug.–5 Dec. 1852, 25 Feb.–8 Jun. 1854. Mss coll. Schlesinger Library, A–58.

Callender, Eunice. Diaries, 1808–24. Mss coll., Schlesinger Library, A–C15.

Child, Lydia Maria. *Letters.* Boston, 1882.

———. *Letters from New York.* New York: C. S. Francis and Co., 1845.

Clarke, Caroline Richards. *Diary of Caroline Cowles Richards 1852–1872.* New York: Canandaigua, 1908.

Cooper, Susan Fenimore. *Rural Hours.* New York: G. P. Putnam, 1850.

Dall, Sarah K. H. Letters, 1852–58. Mss coll., Schlesinger Library.

Davidson, Mary Ann Ferrin. "An Autobiography and a Reminiscence." *Annals of Iowa,* ser. 3, 37 (Summer 1963–Spring 1965).

Davis, Mary Gardiner. Letter, journal, and scrapbook. Mss coll., Schlesinger Library, A–70.

"Diary and Letters of Caira Robbins 1794–1881," *Lexington Historical Society Proceedings* (1905–10), no. 4, pp. 61–81.

"Diary of Mary Orne Tucker 1802," *Essex Institute Historical Collection* (1941), no. 77, pp. 306–38.

Diary of M.I.M. 1854. Mss coll., Schlesinger Library, A–D 539.

"Diary of Mrs. Laura Clark, June 21–Oct. 26, 1818." *The Firelands Pioneer,* n. s. (1920), pp. 2308–26.

Dwight, Elizabeth. Cabot Papers, correspondence of mother, 1844–52. Mss coll., Schlesinger Library, A–99 V 5–8.

Dwight, Margaret Van Horn. *A Journey to Ohio in 1810.* Yale Historical Manuscripts. New Haven: Yale University Press, 1912.

Graham, Isabella. *The Power of Faith Exemplified in The Life and Writings of Mrs. Isabella Graham of New York.* New York, 1816.

Hallowell, Anna, ed. *James and Lucretia Mott: Life and Letters.* Boston: Houghton Mifflin Co., 1896.

Harker, Mary Haines. "Diary (May–Dec. 1853)," *Virginia Quarterly Review* 11 (1935): 61–81.

Harper, Ida, ed. *The Life and Work of Susan B. Anthony.* Vol. 1. Indianapolis: Hollenbeck Press, 1908.

The Holyoke Diaries 1709–1856. Salem, Mass., 1911.

Huntington, Susan. *Memoirs of the Late Mrs. Susan Huntington of Boston.* Boston: Crocker and Brewster, 1826.

Hyde, Nancy. *The Writings of Nancy Maria Hyde of Norwich, Conn.* Norwich, Conn.: R. Hubbard, 1816.

Journal and Letters of Hannah C. Backhouse. London, 1858.

"The Journal of Esther Burr." *New England Quarterly* (1930), no. 3, pp. 297–315.

Larsen, Arthur J., ed. *Crusader and Feminist: Letters of Jane Grey Swisshelm 1858–1864.* St. Paul: Minnesota Historical Society, 1934.

"Letters of Mrs. Higginson 1827," *Cambridge Historical Society Publications* (1906), no. 2, pp. 20–32.

"Lydia Smith's Journal, 1805–1806," *Mass. Historical Society Proceedings* (1914–15), no. 47, pp. 508–35.

"Mrs. Mary Dewell's Journal from Philadelphia to Kentucky 1787–1788," *Pa. Mag. History* (1904), no. 28, pp. 182–98.

Parker, Inez Eugenia Adams. "Early Recollections of Oregon Pioneer Life," *Oregon Pioneer Association Transactions,* 56 Annual Reunion (1928): 38–53.

Peacock, Mary. *The Journal of Mary Peacock.* Life a century ago as seen in Buffalo and Chautaugua County by a 17-year-old-girl in Boarding School and elsewhere. Buffalo, 1938.

Porter, Anne Eliza. Diaries of a young woman in Bedford, 1845–86. Mss coll., Schlesinger Library, M–29.

Prentiss, Elizabeth. *The Life and Letters of Elizabeth Prentiss.* New York: Anson D. F. Randolph & Co., 1882.

Prior, Margaret. *Walks of Usefulness or Reminiscences of Mrs. Margaret Prior.* New York: American Female Moral Reform Society, 1844.

Reeves, Mrs. Edward H. A trip to Oregon in 1851. Mss coll., Schlesinger Library, A R 332.

Sedgwick, Catharine. *Life and Letters.* Edited by Dewey. New York: Harper & Bros., 1871.

Shippen, Nancy. *Her Journal Book.* Philadelphia, J. B. Lippincott Co., 1935.

Stanton, Elizabeth Cady. *Eighty Years and More: Reminiscences 1815–1897.* N.p., 1898.

Stearns, Sarah Ripley. Journals, 1813–18. 3 vols. Mss coll., Schlesinger Library, A–14.

Stowe, Harriet Beecher. Letters, 1847–77. Mss coll., Schlesinger Library.

Tryphena Ely White's Journal 1805–1905. Being a record, written one hundred years ago, of the daily life of a young lady of Puritan heritage. Published by her granddaughter, Kellogg Port Kent. New York, 1904.

Vanderpoel, Emily. *Chronicles of a Pioneer School 1792–1833.* Cambridge, Mass., University Press, 1903.

———. *More Chronicles of a Pioneer School from 1792–1833.* Cambridge, Mass., University Press, 1920.

Walker, Mary Jane. School journal, 12 Apr. 1848–22 Feb. 1849. Mss coll., Schlesinger Library, A–w 18.

[Warder, Mrs. Ann]. "Extracts from the Diary of Mrs. Ann Warder" (1786). *Pennsylvania Magazine of History and Biography* 17 (1893).

Watson, Sarah. Private journal, 1833–1836, 1835. Mss coll., Schlesinger Library, A–85.

Wells, Daniel. "Diary of Miss Rebecca Dickinson 1787–1807." In *A History of Hatfield, Massachusetts.* 1910.

NOVELS—FEMALE

Botsford, Margaret. *Adelaide.* Philadelphia, 1816.

Chesebro, Caroline. *The Children of Light: A Theme for the Time.* New York: Redfield, 1853.

Child, Lydia Marie. *Hobomok.* Boston, 1824.

Evans, Augusta. *Beulah.* New York: Derby and Jackson, 1860.

———. *Resignation.* 2 vols. Boston: John B. Russell, 1825.

Farnham, Eliza. *Eliza Woodson or, The Early Days of one of the Workers.* A Story of American Life. New York: A. J. Davis & Co., 1864.

Fern, Fanny [Sarah Parton]. *Ruth Hall: A Domestic Tale Or the Present Time.* New York: Mason Bros., 1855.

The Fortunate Discovery: Or, the History of Henry Villars. By a Young Lady of the State of New York. New York: Samuel Campbell, 1798.

Graves, Mrs. A. J. *Girlhood and Womanhood: Or, Sketches of My Schoolmates.* Boston: T. H. Carter & Co., 1844.

Hentz, Caroline. *Ernest Linwood.* Philadelphia: T. B. Peterson & Bros., 1869.

Hentz, C. L. *Eoline.* Philadelphia, 1869.

———. *Marcus Warland.* Philadelphia, 1852.

Holmes, Mary. *Meadow Brook.* New York: Charleton Publisher, 1881.

Holmes, M. J. *Tempest and Sunshine.* New York, 1855.

McIntosh, Maria. *Charms and Counter Charms.* New York: D. Appleton, 1849.

———. *The Lofty and the Lowly.* 2 vols. New York: D. Appleton & Co., 1853.

———. *Two Lives.* New York: D. Appleton & Co., 1846.

Sedgwick, Catharine. *Hope Leslie: Or, Early Times.* 2 vols. New York: Harper & Bros., 1862.

———. *The Linwoods.* 2 vols. New York: Harper & Bros., 1835.

———. *Live and Let Live: Or Domestic Service Illustrated.* New York: Harper & Bros., 1837.

———. *Married or Single?* 2 vols. New York: Harper & Bros., 1858.

Sigourney, Lydia. *The Intemperate and the Reformer.* Boston, 1843.

Smith, Elizabeth Oakes. *Riches Without Wings.* Boston, 1838.

Southworth, E. D. E. N. *The Curse of Clifton.* Philadelphia, 1852.

———. *The Deserted Wife.* Philadelphia, 1855.

———. *The Discarded Daughter.* Philadelphia, 1852.

Stowe, Harriet Beecher. *The Minister's Wooing.* New York: Delby and Jackson, 1859.

The Three Sisters: A Sketch from Life. A Contribution Towards the Establishment of An Hospital For Women & Children in N.Y. London:. W. Clowes & Sons, 1856.

Warner, Susan. *Queechy.* 2 vols. New York: George P. Putnam, 1852.

———. *The Wide, Wide World.* 2 vols. New York: G. P. Putnam & Co., 1853.

Warren, Caroline. *The Gamesters: Or Ruins of Innocence.* An original novel. Boston: J. Shaw, 1828.

White, Fanny. *The Life and Death of, being a complete and interesting history of the career of that notorious lady.* New York, 1860.

Secondary Sources

BOOKS

Abbott, Edith. *Women in Industry: A Study in American Economic History.* New York: D. Appleton & Co., 1913.

Bailyn, Bernard. *Education in the Forming of American Society.* New York: Random House, 1960.

Benson, Mary Sumner. *Women in Eighteenth Century America: A Study of Opinion and Social Usage.* New York: Columbia University Press, 1935.

Bernard, Jacqueline. *The Children You Gave Us: A History of 150 Years of Service to Children, Jewish Child Care Association of N.Y.* New York: Bloch Publishing Company, 1973.

Bernstein, Barton F., ed. *Towards a New Past.* New York: Random House, 1968.

Billington, Ray Allen. *The Protestant Crusade 1800–1860.* New York: Quadrangle, 1964.

Bleyer, William Grosvenor. *Main Currents in the History of American Journalism.* Cambridge, Mass.: The Riverside Press, 1927.

Booth, Salley Smith. *The Women of '76.* New York: Hastings House, 1973.

Bridenbaugh, Carl. *Cities in Revolt: Urban Life in America 1743–1776.* London and New York: Oxford University Press, 1955.

———. *Cities in the Wilderness: The First Century of Urban Life in America 1625–1742.* London and New York: Oxford University Press, 1939.

Brown, Herbert Ross. *The Sentimental Novel in America.* North Carolina: Duke University Press, 1940.

Calhoun, Arthur W. *A Social History of the American Family from Colonial Times to the Present.* Vol. 2, *From Independence through the Civil War.* Cleveland, 1918.

Chambers, Peggy. *A Doctor Alone: A Biography of Elizabeth Blackwell, the first woman doctor 1821–1910.* London, 1956.

Cremin, Lawrence. *The American Common School.* New York, Teachers College, Columbia University Press, 1951.

———. *American Education: The Colonial Experience 1607–1783.* New York: Harper & Row, 1970.

Cross, Whitney. *The Burned-over District: The Social and Intellectual History of Enthusiastic Religion in Western New York 1800–1850.* New York: Harper & Row, 1965.

Davis, David B. *Homicide in American Fiction, 1789–1860: A Study in Social Values.* Ithaca, N.Y.: Cornell University Press, 1957.

Dexter, Elisabeth Anthony. *Career Women of America 1776–1840.* New Hampshire: Marshall Jones Co., 1950.

———. *Colonial Women of Affairs: Women in Business and the Professions in America Before 1776.* Boston: Houghton Mifflin Co., 1931.

Durkheim, Emile. *The Division of Labor in Society.* Translated by George Simpson. New York: The Free Press, 1964.

Earle, Alice Morse. *Home Life in Colonial Days.* New York: Macmillan Co., 1917.

English, O. Spurgeon, M.D., and Pearson, Gerald H. J., M.D. *Emotional Problems of Living*. New York: W. W. Norton & Co., 1963.

Ernst, Robert. *Immigrant Life in New York 1825–1863*. New York: Ira J. Freidman, Inc., 1949.

Fancher, Irving. *A History of the Troy Orphan Asylum*. Troy, N.Y.: Whitehurst Printing & Binding Co., 1933.

Foerster, Norman, ed. *American Poetry and Prose*. 2 vols. Boston: Houghton Mifflin Co., 1957.

Foster, Charles. *An Errand of Mercy: The Evangelical United Front 1790–1837*. Chapel Hill: University of North Carolina Press, 1960.

Gates, Paul. *The Farmer's Age: Agriculture, 1815–1860*. New York, 1960.

Glaab, Charles N., and Brown, A. Theodore. *A History of Urban America*. New York: Macmillan Co., 1967.

Goodman, Paul, and Gatell, Frank Otto. *U.S.A.: An American Record*. New York: Holt, Rinehart & Winston, 1972.

Graham, Harvey. *Eternal Eve: The History of Gynecology and Obstetrics*. New York, London [N.Y.]: Hutchinson, 1951.

Griffin, Clifford. *Their Brother's Keeper*. New Jersey: New Brunswick, Rutgers University Press, 1960.

Grimsted, David, ed. *Notions of the Americans 1820–1860*. New York: George Braziller, 1970.

Handlin, Oscar, ed. *This Was America*. Cambridge, Mass.: Harvard University Press, 1949.

Harrar, James A., M.D. *The Story of the Lying-in Hospital of the City of N.Y. Published by The Society of the Lying-in Hospital*, 1938.

Henry, Alice. *Women and the Labor Movement*. New York: Arno Press and the *New York Times*, 1971.

Hugins, Walter. *Jacksonian Democracy and the Working Class*. California, Stanford University Press, 1960.

Kouwenhoven, John A. *The Columbia Historical Portrait of New York*. New York: Doubleday & Co., 1953.

Kraditor, Aileen. *The Ideas of the Woman Suffrage Movement 1890–1920*. New York: Columbia University Press, 1965.

———. *Means and Ends in American Abolitionism: Garrison & His Critics on Strategy & Tactics 1834–1850*. New York: Pantheon Books, 1967.

———. *Up From the Pedestal: Selected Writings in the History of American Feminism*. Chicago: Quadrangle Books, 1968.

Livingood, W. W. *Our Textbooks Yesterday and Today*. New York: American Institute of Graphic Arts, 1953.

Miller, Douglas. *Jacksonian Aristocracy, Class and Democracy in New York 1830–1860*. London and New York: Oxford University Press, 1967.

Meyers, Marvin. *The Jacksonian Persuasion: Politics and Belief.* California: Stanford University Press, 1960.

Mohl, Raymond. *Poverty in New York 1783–1825.* London and New York: Oxford University Press, 1971.

Nietz, John A. *Old Textbooks.* Pittsburgh: University of Pittsburgh Press, 1961.

O'Neill, William L. *Everyone Was Brave.* Chicago: Quadrangle Books, 1969.

Pattee, Frederick Lewis. *The Feminine Fifties.* New York: D. Appleton-Century Co., 1940.

Pickett, Robert S. *House of Refuge: Origins of Juvenile Reform in the New York State, 1815–1857.* Syracuse: Syracuse University Press, 1969.

Remini, Robert. *Martin Van Buren and the Making of the Democratic Party.* New York: Columbia University Press, 1951.

Richards, Leonard L. *Gentlemen of Property and Standing.* London and New York: Oxford University Press, 1970.

Rosenberg, Carroll Smith. *Religion and the Rise of the American City: The New York City Mission Movement 1812–1870.* Ithaca, N.Y.: Cornell University Press, 1971.

Rossiter, Clinton. *Seedtime of the New Republic: The Origins of the American Tradition of Political Liberty.* New York: Harcourt Brace Jovanovich, 1953.

Schlesinger, Arthur M. *New Viewpoints in American History.* New York: Macmillan Co., 1922.

Sennett, Richard, ed. *Classic Essays on the Culture of Cities.* New York: Appleton-Century-Crofts, 1969.

Smith, Henry Nash. *Virgin Land: The American West as Symbol and Myth.* New York: Random House, 1950.

Smith, Page. *Daughters of the Promised Land.* Boston: Little, Brown & Co., 1970.

Smith, Timothy L. *Revivalism and Social Reform: American Protestantism on the Eve of the Civil War.* New York: Harper & Row, 1957.

Spruill, Julia Cherry. *Women's Life and Work in the Southern Colonies.* New York: W. W. Norton and Co., 1972.

Stein, Maurice; Vidich, Arthur J.; and White, David Manning, eds. *Identity and Anxiety: Survival of the Person in Mass Society.* New York: The Free Press, 1960.

Still, Bayard. *Mirror for Gotham: New York as seen by contemporaries from Dutch days to the present.* New York: New York University Press, 1956.

Taylor, George B. *The Transportation Revolution 1815–1860.* New York, 1951.

Taylor, William R. *Cavalier and Yankee.* New York: George Braziller, 1961.

Thompson, Ralph. *American Literary Annuals and Gift Books 1825–1865.* New York: Archon Books, 1936.

Tyler, Alice Felt. *Freedom's Ferment.* New York: Harper & Bros., 1962.

Van Deusen, Glyndon. *The Jacksonian Era.* New York: Harper & Row, 1959.

Veblen, Thorstein. *The Theory of the Leisure Class: An Economic Study of Institutions.* New York: Viking Press, 1945.

Vicinus, Martha, ed. *Suffer and Be Still: Women in the Victorian Age.* Bloomington: Indiana University Press, 1972.

Warner, Sam B., Jr. *The Private City.* Philadelphia: University of Pennsylvania Press, 1968.

Warren, Roland F. *Perspectives on the American Community: A Book of Readings.* Chicago: Rand, McNally & Co., 1966.

White, Morton and Lucia. *The Intellectual Versus the City: From Thomas Jefferson to Frank Lloyd Wright.* New York: Mentor, 1964.

Wilson, Dorothy Clarke. *Lone Woman: The Story of Elizabeth Blackwell, The First Woman Doctor.* Boston: Little, Brown & Co., 1970.

Woodward, C. Vann, ed. *The Comparative Approach to American History.* New York: Basic Books, 1968.

Young, Clifford M. *Women's Prisons Past and Present: State Commission of Correction.* Albany: The Summary Press, Elmira Reformatory, 1932.

ARTICLES

Davis, David B. "Paranoia and American Politics: Some Themes of Counter-Subversion; An Analysis of Anti-Masonic, Anti-Catholic and Anti-Mormon Literature." *Mississippi Valley Historical Review* (Sept. 1960), no. 47, pp. 205–24.

Degler, Carl. "What Ought To Be and What Was: Women's Sexuality in the Nineteenth Century." *American Historical Review* 79 (Dec. 1974): 1467–90.

Douglas, Ann. "Heaven Our Home: Consolation Literature in the Northern United States, 1830–1860." *American Quarterly* 26 (Dec. 1974): 495–516.

Ekirch, Arthur, Jr. "Thomas Eddy and the Beginnings of Prison Reform in New York." *New York History* (1943), no. 24, pp. 376–91.

Freedman, Estelle B. "The New Woman: Changing Views of Women in the 1920s." *Journal of American History* (September 1974), no. 61, pp. 374–93.

Horner, George. "Franklin's Dogood Papers Re-examined." *North Carolina University Studies in Philology* 37 (1940): 501–23.

Kelly, Gordon R. "Literature and the Historian." *American Quarterly* 26, no. 2 (May 1974): 141–60.

Kittredge, William. "School Books: Past, Present & Future." *Publisher's Weekly* (1935), pp. 129, 977–80, 1438–40.

Lerner, Gerda. "Women's Rights and American Feminism." *American Scholar* 40 (Spring 1971): 235–48.

Rapson, Richard. "The American Child as Seen by British Travelers 1845–1935." *American Quarterly* 17 (1965): 520–34.

Reed, Amy L. "Female Delicacy in the Sixties." *Century* (1915), pp. 855–64.

Rosenberg, Carroll Smith. "Beauty and the Beast and the Militant Woman: A Case Study in Sex Roles and Social Stress in Jacksonian America." *American Quarterly* 23, no. 4 (Oct. 1971): 562–84.

Skar, Kathryn Kish. "All Hail Pure Water." *American Heritage* (Dec. 1974), pp. 64–70.

Thernstrom, Stephen, and Knights, Peter. "Men in Motion: Some Data and Speculations About Urban Population Mobility in Nineteenth Century America." *Journal of Interdisciplinary History* 1 (Autumn 1970–Spring 1971): 7–37.

Wade, Richard C. "An Agenda for Urban History." In *American History, Retrospect and Prospect*, edited by George A. Billias and Gerald N. Grob, pp. 367–98. New York: The Free Press, 1971.

———. "Urbanization." In *The Comparative Approach to American History*, edited by C. Vann Woodward. New York: Basic Books, 1968.

Wells, Kate G. "Women in Organizations." *Atlantic* (1880), no. 6, pp. 360–67.

Welter, Barbara. "The Cult of True Womanhood, 1820–1860." *American Quarterly* 18 (1966): 151–74.

Wohl, R. Richard. "The 'Country Boy' Myth and Its Place in American Urban Culture: The Nineteenth Century Contribution." *Perspectives in American History* (1969), no. 3, pp. 77–159.

Wood, Ann D. "The Fashionable Diseases: Woman's Complaints and Their Treatment in Nineteenth Century America." *Journal of Interdisciplinary History* 4 (1973), pp. 25–52.

Index